# ILLUSION OF ORDER

BERNARD E. HARCOURT

# Illusion of Order

## The False Promise of Broken Windows Policing

HARVARD UNIVERSITY PRESS

Cambridge, Massachusetts, and London, England

2001

*Library of Congress Cataloging-in-Publication Data*

Harcourt, Bernard E., 1963–
Illusion of order : the false promise of broken windows policing / Bernard E. Harcourt.
p. cm.
ISBN 0-674-00472-8
1. Crime.   2. Law enforcement.   3. Criminal justice, Administration of.
4. Police administration.   I. Title.
HV6025 .H297 2001
364—dc21       2001016809

For Mia Ruyter and our children,
Isadora and Léonard

# Contents

# Acknowledgments

I am deeply grateful to Seyla Benhabib, Duncan Kennedy, and Richard Tuck for providing me with guidance and encouragement at every turn. I am also indebted to Toni Massaro, Frank Michelman, Martha Minow, Ted Schneyer, and Carol Steiker for reading, commenting, and provoking me through so many different versions of this manuscript. Special thanks to David Garland, who read the final draft of the book and provided me with detailed criticisms and suggestions, and to Gary King, Michael Tomz, and the Data Center staff in the Government Department at Harvard University for comments and assistance on the quantitative analysis. I am also especially grateful to Dan Kahan and Tracey Meares for reading and commenting on earlier portions, and for being such graceful debaters and generous critics. I thank as well George Kelling and James Q. Wilson for reading earlier portions and sharing their reactions.

I also thank the many colleagues and friends who have read and commented on various portions of the manuscript, including especially Bruce Ackerman, Barbara Atwood, Tom Christiano, Suzie Dovi, Thomas Ertman, Jeffrey Fagan, Joel Feinberg, David Golove, Michael Gottfredson, Travis Hirschi, Bonnie Honig, Jim Jacobs, David Kennedy, David Macarthur, Chris Maloney, Calvin Morrill, Stephen Morse, Cary Nederman, Dorothy Roberts, Richard Rorty, Tanina Rostain, Michael Sandel, Stephen Schulhofer, Susan Silbey, David Siu, Loïc Wacquant, Lloyd Weinreb, and Robert Williams. I am grateful for outstanding research assistance to Craig LaChance, Tim Jafek, and Jenna

Karadbil, and for exceptional librarian assistance to Maureen Garmon. I also am grateful to Michael Aronson at Harvard University Press for guidance at critical junctures. I thank Susan Silbey at the *Law and Society Review* and the editors at the *Michigan Law Review* and the *Journal of Criminal Law and Criminology* for allowing me to draw in part on work previously published in their journals.

I have always felt deeply indebted, and extremely grateful, to my professors at Princeton University—Sheldon Wolin, Rudiger Bittner, and Bernard Yack—who inspired me to study political and social theory, and to return to the study of social thought after several years in legal practice. I am equally indebted to Seyla Benhabib, who facilitated the return in so many ways.

Renée and Caroline Harcourt gave me constant support, love, and encouragement—and comments and proofreading assistance—for which I am, as always, infinitely grateful. I dedicate this book with love and apologies to Mia Ruyter—my partner and life companion, and my best and most humorous critic—and our children, Isadora and Léonard.

# CHAPTER 1

# Punishment and Criminal Justice at the Turn of Century

In July 1994, New York City mayor Rudolph Giuliani and police commissioner William Bratton began implementing an order-maintenance policing strategy emphasizing proactive and aggressive enforcement of misdemeanor laws against quality-of-life offenses such as graffiti writing, loitering, public urination, public drinking, aggressive panhandling, turnstile jumping, and prostitution. The policy, which became known as "the quality-of-life initiative," was premised on the writings and research of James Q. Wilson, George L. Kelling, and Wesley G. Skogan. In *Police Strategy No. 5: Reclaiming the Public Spaces of New York*, Giuliani and Bratton set forth the conceptual framework for their new policing initiative:

> More than ten years ago, James Q. Wilson and George L. Kelling, authors of the ground breaking article, " [Broken Windows:] The Police and Neighborhood Safety" in the March, 1982 issue of *The Atlantic Monthly*, postulated the "broken windows" thesis that unaddressed disorder is a sign that no one cares and invites both further disorder and more serious crime. By examining the Wilson-Kelling hypothesis in more than 40 cities, Wesley Skogan has found that disorder is indeed the first step in what he terms "the downward spiral of urban decay." (1994e:6)

In June 1992 the Chicago city council enacted an anti-gang loitering ordinance prohibiting citizens from standing together in any public place "with no apparent purpose," if a police officer reasonably believed that one or more of them were gang members. Failure to obey a police officer's order to disperse was punishable by a fine of up to $500, by incarceration of up to six months, by community service of up to 120 hours, or by any combination of the three (Chicago Municipal Code §8–4–015 [added June 17, 1992]). The city council held hearings prior to enacting the ordinance and incorporated its findings in a preamble which set forth the underlying logic of the ordinance. "In many neighborhoods throughout the City, the burgeoning presence of street gang members in public places has intimidated many law abiding citizens." The council explained, "Members of criminal street gangs avoid arrest by committing no offense punishable under existing laws when they know the police are present, while maintaining control over identifiable areas by continued loitering." As a result, the council found, "aggressive action is necessary to preserve the city's streets and other public places so that the public may use such places without fear" (*Morales* 1997:58).

The Chicago Police Department vigorously enforced the anti-gang loitering ordinance, resulting in the issuance of over 89,000 orders to disperse and the arrest of over 42,000 people during the period 1993–1995 (*Morales* 1999:49). In New York City, the quality-of-life initiative produced between 40,000 and 85,000 additional adult misdemeanor arrests per year during the period 1994–1998, and an even greater number of stops and frisks during a period of sharply declining crime rates (New York State, Division of Criminal Justice Services 2000).

These and other similar police strategies constitute a new order-maintenance approach to criminal justice that emerged in the 1980s and 1990s. It is an approach that focuses on increased police-citizen contact as a way to create and maintain order in our urban streets and to decrease serious crime. The approach is reflected in police precincts and city halls across the country in the renewed emphasis on *order-maintenance policing*, a subset of the larger concept of community policing that emphasizes proactive enforcement of misdemeanor laws and zero tolerance for minor offenses.

In criminology and police studies, this approach is embodied in the broken windows theory, one of the leading criminal justice theories today. The theory can be traced back to James Q. Wilson and George L. Kelling's article, "Broken Windows," and it provides that minor forms of disorder, such as graffiti, litter, panhandling, and prostitution, if left unattended, will result in neighborhood decline and increased serious criminal activity (1982:31). In the legal academy, the approach is reflected in a new and dynamic school of thought—social norm theory—which has become one of the leading contemporary movements in legal theory. Under the rubric of "the New Chicago School," this movement focuses attention on the way law and social norms interact, and on how the interaction regulates human behavior. Its proponents argue that policing techniques such as anti-gang loitering ordinances, youth curfews, and order-maintenance policing are effective because they change the social meaning of practices such as gang membership and juvenile gun possession. They contend that, by changing social meaning, these techniques may reduce criminal behavior and encourage obedience to law (Kahan 1997b:2479; Kahan and Meares 1998b:821; Lessig 1998:669–670). In political science, sociology, and public administration, researchers refer as well to the disorder-crime nexus, or, more generally, to the link between disorder and crime (Skogan 1990:73–77; Sampson and Raudenbush 1999:604–605), as well as to proactive or aggressive policing (Wilson and Boland 1978 and 1981; Jacob and Rich 1981; Decker and Kohfeld 1985).

The order-maintenance approach has received remarkably favorable attention in the popular press, in scholarly journals, in public policy circles, and in academia. The media refer to the "now famous" "Broken Windows" essay as "the bible of policing" and "the blueprint for community policing" (Jones 1997; DiIulio 1996; Cullen 1997). Jeffrey Rosen writes in the *New Republic* that "[b]roken windows has helped reduce crime in cities across the nation" (2000:24). Michael Massing, in the *New York Review of Books*, claims that "the Broken Windows model has had undeniable successes" (1998:36). "There is little dispute that the theory works," says the *American Bar Association Journal* (Barnes 1998). It has sparked "a revolution in American policing," according to the *Christian Science Monitor,* in an article headlined "One Man's Theory Is Cutting Crime in Urban Streets" (Nifong 1997). A similar headline in the *New York Times* reads: "James Q. Wilson Has Insights, Like Those on Cutting Crime, That Tend to Prove Out" (Bernstein 1998). *U.S. News and World Report,* in a cover story on crime, declares that "[c]learly, smarter policing was spectacularly decisive in some cities like New York" (Witkin 1998:33).

Wesley Skogan, a political scientist at Northwestern University, conducted an empirical study of the broken windows theory and concludes that "'[b]roken windows' do need to be repaired quickly" (1990:75). George Kelling, co-author of "Broken Windows" and of a more recent book titled *Fixing Broken Windows*, contends that Skogan "established the causal links between disorder and serious crime—empirically verifying the 'Broken Windows' hypotheses" (Kelling and Coles 1996:24). Dan Kahan at Yale Law School reports that order-maintenance policing "has been used with startlingly successful results in New York City" (1997b:2488; 1997a:372), and adds that "[t]he work of criminologist Wesley Skogan supplies empirical support for the 'broken windows' hypothesis" (1997a:369; 1997b:2488 n.62). Other legal academics rely heavily on the broken windows theory and, in varying degrees, support order-maintenance policing (Ellickson 1996:1171–73, 1177–79, 1182; Livingston 1997:581–591). As Columbia law professor Debra Livingston suggests, the "Broken Windows" essay has been "'widely cited,' has become 'one of the most influential articles on policing,' and has helped to create what some have termed a 'consensus' in community and problem-oriented policing circles that the neglect of quality-of-life problems was a deficiency of urban policing in the period into the 1980s" (1997:584).

## Criminal Justice at the Turn of Century

The order-maintenance approach has become one of the leading theories in the criminal justice arena and has helped shape one of the two most important turn-of-century trends in criminal justice in America, namely, the proliferation of order-maintenance policing strategies. The other dramatic trend has been the exponential rise in incarceration since the 1970s. Whereas, in 1970, there were fewer than 200,000 citizens in federal and state prisons nationwide, by 1996 the number had increased to over 1.1 million, with another 500,000-plus citizens held in local jails (*Statistical Abstract* 1998:228–229; Dolinko 1999:1720). At the time of this writing about 2 million men and women are incarcerated in prisons and jails in this country. This "incarceration mania" (Caplow and Simon 1998) has received, for some time now, much critical attention in the media (Rocawich 1987; Lacayo 1989; Langan 1991; Smolowe 1994; "Crime in America" 1996; Wray 1998). Excellent scholarship has been written addressing the surge in incarceration in this country and what has come to be known as the penal-industrial complex (Zimring and Hawkins 1995; Tonry 1996 and 1999; Beckett 1997; Wacquant 1998 and 1999; Garland 2001). What has received far less attention and scrutiny is the crackdown on disorderly conduct and the aggressive enforcement of misdemeanor laws and ordinances—the order-maintenance approach to criminal justice. With a few notable exceptions (Fagan, Zimring, and Kim 1998; Roberts 1999; Wacquant 1999; Sampson and Raudenbush 1999), the broken windows theory and order-maintenance policing continue to receive extremely favorable reviews in policy circles, academia, and the press.

Ironically the continued popularity of order-maintenance policing is due, in large part, to the dramatic rise in incarceration. Broken windows policing presents itself as the only viable alternative to three-strikes and mandatory minimum sentencing laws. Order-maintenance proponents affirmatively promote youth curfews, anti-gang loitering ordinances, and order-maintenance crackdowns as *milder alternatives* to the theory of incapacitation and increased incarceration. Their primary motive in proposing these initiatives is, in their words, "as much political as conceptual" (Kahan and Meares 1998b:806). They explain:

> Contemporary policies of criminal law, particularly those targeted at fighting inner-city crime, focus on severe punishments. This approach suffers from well-known defects, both practical and moral. Nevertheless, the public demand for "get-tough" law enforcement policies stems from deep-seated political, ideological, and even psychological dynamics. Scholarly works that merely criticize existing criminal law policies do nothing to alter these public views and are thus likely to prove politically inert.
>
> The emerging norm-focused scholarship, in contrast, generates an intensely practical agenda. Norms are created through social dynamics that are important enough to be worth regulating but discrete enough to be regulated efficiently. Understanding these dynamics suggests a variety of politically feasible and morally attractive alternatives to the severe punishments that now dominate America's inner-city crime-fighting prescriptions. (Kahan and Meares 1998b:806; see also 1999a:23)

It is precisely the modern incarceration frenzy that makes these milder order-maintenance strategies attractive and that renders the broken windows theory, the quality-of-life initiative, and the New Chicago School "new" and "progressive."

There is, however, a serious flaw in this story. As a preliminary matter, order-maintenance strategies are by no means "new." They hark back to the order-maintenance function of the police, and, more specifically, to the "legalistic" style of police management described well by James Q. Wilson in his 1968 book *Varieties of Police Behavior*. "The legalistic [police] department," Wilson explained, "will issue traffic tickets at a high rate, detain and arrest a high proportion of juvenile offenders, act vigorously against illicit enterprises, and make a large number of misdemeanor arrests. . . . The police will act, on the whole, as if there were a single standard of community conduct—that which the law prescribes—rather than different standards for juveniles, Negroes, drunks, and the like" (1968:172). Order-maintenance crackdowns, youth curfews, anti-loitering ordinances, mass searches, snitching policies, and shaming penalties have been around for a long time both in this country and abroad. In fact, order-maintenance disciplinary practices, as we will see, date back well before the 1950s to the early penitentiary model and beyond. But this, of course, is hardly an indictment. Few ideas are ever new.

The real problem is that, today, order-maintenance crackdowns are not an *alternative* but rather an *addition* to the severe penalties that dominate criminal justice. The broken windows theory, aggressive misdemeanor arrests, and intensive stops and frisks have become not a *substitute* but a *supplement*—a supplement that feeds into and itself produces a dramatic increase in detentions, arrests, and criminal records. What we are left with today is a system of severe punishments for major offenders and severe treatment for minor offenders and ordinary citizens, especially minorities, a double-barreled approach with significant effects on large numbers of our citizenry. The problem, in a nutshell, is that order-maintenance crackdowns permeate our streets and police station houses while severe sentencing laws pack our prisons. We are left with the worst of both worlds.

### The False Promise of Order Maintenance

Broken windows policing has not received enough critical attention. This book is intended to be a corrective. In this book I pose three simple questions about the order-maintenance approach. In Part I, I ask whether there is any evidence to support the broken windows theory or to argue that order-maintenance policing has brought about a decline in crime. After reviewing the available social-scientific data, replicating a key study, and closely scrutinizing the empirical evidence in New York City, Chicago, and other cities, I find that there is no good evidence to support the broken windows theory. In fact, the social science data reveal no statistically significant relationship between disorder and crime in four out of five tests. The existing data, in the words of Robert Sampson and Stephen Raudenbush, do "not match the theoretical expectations set up by the main thesis of 'broken windows'" (1999:637).

In Part II, I ask whether the order-maintenance approach is theoretically sound. I trace the genealogy of the approach to an intellectual tradition spawned by Edward C. Banfield and his student and later colleague James Q. Wilson. It is a tradition that seeks to enrich the classical model of criminology by supplementing it with conceptions of thicker propensities, human nature, and social norms and meaning. It is a tradition that emphasizes the social norm of orderliness and its influence on crime. The turn to norms and social meaning, I find, is a positive step in criminal justice; but in the hands of order-maintenance proponents, it leads to an uncritical dichotomy between disorderly people and law abiders—or, more generally, between order and disorder. The order-maintenance approach fails to explore how these notions of thicker propensities and human nature—how the categories of the disorderly and law abider—are themselves shaped by policing and punishment strategies. The result is that these categories mask the repressive nature of broken-windows policing and overshadow significant costs, including increased complaints of police misconduct, racial bias in stops and frisks, and further stereotyping of black criminality.

In Part III, I then ask how the order-maintenance approach—an approach without empirical foundation that does not withstand theoretical scrutiny—has become so popular, particularly when there are many alternatives to stops, frisks, arrests, and incarceration. After reviewing theories that have been advanced to explain the rise of the penal state, I offer as a supplement a rhetorical analysis. Order-maintenance proponents have deployed what is perhaps the most effective rhetorical move at the turn of century, namely, the turn to harm. The broken windows theory has transformed conduct that was once merely offensive or annoying into positively harmful conduct—conduct that causes serious crime.

My overarching goal is to critically examine the order-maintenance approach and to place order maintenance within the framework of two of the most interesting developments of late modernity: the social meaning turn and the turn to injury. These are both developments that I applaud and that, in this book, I hope to push even further. In the process, I offer a new vision of punishment and criminal justice that builds on the contributions of Banfield, Wilson, and the New Progressives and pays critical attention to the creation of the contemporary subject.

## A Pervasive Lack of Empirical Evidence

My starting point is the simple but startling fact that, decades after its first articulation in the *Atlantic Monthly*, the famous broken windows theory has never been verified. Despite repeated claims that the theory has in fact been "empirically verif[ied]" (Kelling and Coles 1996:24), there is no reliable evidence that the broken windows theory works. In fact, the existing social-scientific data suggest that the theory is probably not right.

Advocates of broken windows policing generally point to two social-scientific studies—Wesley Skogan's *Disorder and Decline* (1990) and a 1988 study by Robert Sampson and Jacqueline Cohen—and to the recent experience of falling crime rates in New York City to support their position. The problem is that these quantitative studies, as well as anecdotal evidence, do not come close to establishing the broken windows theory. Sampson and Cohen, in fact, recognize that studies of the direct effect of aggressive policing on crime are "sparse" and have had "mixed" results (1988:166–167). They acknowledge that their own model cannot establish the disorder-crime hypothesis (1988:185). Skogan's study is based on weak data. Worse yet, he fails to disclose to the public in *Disorder and Decline* or in his *Final Report to the National Institute of Justice* that his data reveal no statistically significant relationship between disorder and crime with regard to four out of five crime variables. Skogan only reveals and discusses the results of the one test that supports the broken windows theory—the statistical relationship between disorder and robbery victimization, with poverty, race, and neighborhood stability held constant. He fails even to mention that his data contain four other measures of crime—burglary, physical assault, rape, and purse-snatching/pocket-picking—and that these measures do *not* relate significantly to disorder when poverty, race, and neighborhood stability are held constant.

A more recent and thorough study of the crime-disorder nexus— a study which is based on careful data collection, including systematic social observation and official crime records—is Robert Sampson and Stephen Raudenbush's 1999 study, "Systematic Social Observation of Public Spaces: A New Look at Disorder in Urban Neighborhoods." On the basis of their research, Sampson and Raudenbush conclude that "the current fascination in policy circles on cleaning up disorder through law enforcement techniques appears simplistic and largely misplaced, at least in terms of directly fighting crime. . . . Attacking public order through tough police tactics may thus be a politically popular but perhaps analytically weak strategy to reduce crime" (1999:638).

New York City's spectacular drop in crime tells us little, if anything, about the broken windows theory. As a preliminary matter, large cities across the country have experienced a remarkable drop in crime since the early 1990s. Many large cities—including Boston, Houston, Los Angeles, St. Louis, San Diego, San Antonio, San Francisco, and Washington, D.C.—have experienced significant declines in crime, in some cases proportionally larger than New York City's. Yet many of these large cities have not implemented order-maintenance crackdowns and misdemeanor sweeps. More important, a large number of factors have led to the drop in crime in New York City, including a significant increase in the raw number of police officers on the beat, a shift in drug use patterns from crack cocaine to heroin, favorable economic conditions in the 1990s, new computerized tracking systems that speed up police response to crime, a dip in the number of eighteen- to twenty-four-year-old males, the arrest of several big drug gangs in New York, as well as possible changes in adolescent behavior (Karmen 1996; Fagan, Zimring, and Kim 1998; Butterfield 1998a). Many of these factors are significant, especially when they are combined, while there is no good reason to believe, by contrast, that increased neighborhood orderliness is what accounts for the drop in crime in New York City.

Even more important, there is no reason to believe—nor is there any evidence—that the broken windows theory is the *mechanism* that explains any contribution that the quality-of-life initiative may have made to the drop in crime. The brute fact is that misdemeanor arrests in New York City increased sharply since the inception of the police strategy, jumping by more than 50 percent in the first three years. Misdemeanor arrests reached 205,277 in 1996, up from 133,446 in 1993 (Farrell 1998a and 1998b). In contrast, the number of misdemeanor complaints for the period remained remarkably stable, with 421,116 misdemeanor complaints recorded in 1993 compared to 424,169 in 1996 (Farrell 1998b). The upward trend continued through 1998—the most recent available data. According to New York State statistics, total adult misdemeanor arrests stood at 215,158 in 1998, up a total of 66.3 percent from 129,404 in 1993 (New York State, Division of Criminal Justice Services 2000). The NYPD has also implemented an aggressive stop-and-frisk policy (Spitzer 1999), and replaced desk-appearance tickets with trips to the precinct for background checks. These enforcement mechanisms allow for enhanced surveillance—for increased arrests on outstanding warrants, gun searches, identification and fingerprint comparisons, interviews, and use of confidential informants.

Soon after the original strategy was first tested in the New York subways in 1990, Bratton realized the full potential of order-maintenance crackdowns and sweeps. "For the cops," Bratton exclaimed, they were "a bonanza. Every arrest was like opening a box of Cracker Jack. What kind of toy am I going to get? Got a gun? Got a knife? Got a warrant? Do we have a murderer here? Each cop wanted to be the one who came up with the big collar. It was exhilarating for the cops and demoralizing for the crooks" (1998:154). George Kelling also caught on quickly. "Restoring order reduces crime," Kelling wrote. But, he added, "crime is reduced at least in part because restoring order puts police in contact with persons who carry weapons and who commit serious crimes" (Kelling and Coles 1996:137). The fact is, even if the quality-of-life initiative contributed to some degree to the decline in crime in New York City, the primary mechanism is probably not the broken windows theory. The primary engine is probably the enhanced *power of surveillance* offered by a policy of aggressive stops and frisks and misdemeanor arrests.

There is also little if any evidence that other order-maintenance policing techniques are effective in combating crime. Although proponents of Chicago's anti-gang loitering ordinance contend that "law enforcement officials in Chicago . . . report dramatic reductions in violent offenses in neighborhoods in which that city's gang-loitering ordinance is most vigorously enforced" (Kahan and Meares 1998b:822), those same reports do not in fact substantiate their claim. University of Chicago law professors Stephen Schulhofer and Albert Alschuler have pored over the official reports and conclude that "whether judged in absolute terms or relative to crime trends elsewhere in Chicago, the number of violent offenses *did not* drop dramatically in the high-crime districts where the ordinance was most vigorously enforced. On the contrary, the most dramatic reductions occurred in the low-crime districts where the ordinance was *least* vigorously enforced" (2000:7; see also *Morales* 1999:50 n.7; Roberts 1999:794). As for the policy of encouraging juvenile snitching, there is simply no existing empirical evidence that the policy correlates with reductions in juvenile gun possession, or, more important, that the purported effect operates through a social norm mechanism. In other words, even if there were a correlation between enforcement of these policies and crime, the correlation alone would tell us little to nothing about whether it is social meaning, norms, or some other more traditional explanation that accounts for the relationship.

## A Genealogy of Order Maintenance

The order-maintenance approach to criminal justice does not fare better at the theoretical level. The surprising and somewhat ironic fact is that broken windows policing shares the same conceptual framework as its alternative, massive incarceration and the theory of incapacitation. The broken windows theory traces its intellectual roots to conservative origins in the second half of the twentieth century—primarily to the writings of James Q. Wilson and, before him, Edward C. Banfield, Wilson's professor and mentor at the University of Chicago and, later, co-author and colleague in the Government Department at Harvard University. What these different intellectual currents share—

Banfield and Wilson, on the one hand, and the New Chicago School, or the "New Progressives," as they have been called (Pildes 1999), on the other—is a common conceptual mission of building on and enriching the classical model of criminology while remaining faithful to the core insight of rational choice. More specifically, what unifies these intellectual currents is the *means* they employ to accomplish this conceptual task.

The classical model of criminology was grounded on the assumption of utility maximization. It was predicated on the idea that people pursue self-interest by trying to avoid pain and seek pleasure. It was based on the assumption that individuals have an ordered set of preferences and choose rationally among their opportunities to maximize satisfaction of those preferences—the two key elements of the classical model being preferences and opportunities. This is the fundamental assumption for Banfield and Wilson and the New Progressives. "There is an element of calculation—indeed, a very considerable one—in practically all criminal behavior," Banfield emphasized. "To be sure, impulse characteristically enters into some types of crime more than into others, but an element of rationality is hardly ever absent" (1974:181).

James Q. Wilson and his co-author Richard Herrnstein were equally clear: "Our theory rests on the assumption that people, when faced with a choice, choose the preferred course of action" (1985:43). Wilson and Herrnstein's conceptual project was precisely to enrich the classical model by infusing it with sociological and political insights, while retaining the premise of rational action. "It is a mistake to explain crime (or its absence) on grounds of profit maximization narrowly defined," they wrote. "A narrow economic explanation of crime is, to us, inadequate" (1985:59). It has to be supplemented with insight about people's propensity to commit crime. By critiquing the marginal deterrence model, Wilson and Herrnstein claimed to be building a more predictive theory of rational choice:

> Economists, concerned chiefly with estimating the marginal effects of
> employment opportunities or judicial sanctions on criminal behavior,
> concede that people differ in these ways [risk-aversion, competence
> at making calculations, present-orientedness], but dismiss such differ-
> ences as "tastes" that lie outside econometric models of how behavior

changes in response to changes in the net value of alternative courses of action. If one is interested only in discovering how behavior changes with changes in readily available policy instruments, that dismissal is often quite appropriate. But if one is interested in explaining individual differences in behavior, that dismissal is tantamount to discarding the most important set of explanatory variables. (1985:516–517)

The New Chicago School follows in these footsteps. It is "new" in the sense that it is a movement from within the classical law and economics writings of Guido Calabresi, Ronald Coase, Richard Posner, and others beginning in the 1960s and 1970s—what is often referred to as the Chicago School. The New Progressives build on this classical tradition by incorporating social norms and meaning into the study of rational choice in criminal law. Engaged primarily in a dialogue with classical law and economics, they too seek to enrich the marginal deterrence model by developing a thicker, more expressive conception of individual preferences. As Dan Kahan asserts:

Economic analyses of criminal law that abstract from social meaning fail, on their own terms, because social meaning is something people value. As individuals, they take the meaning of their actions into account in responding to the incentives created by law; as communities, they structure the criminal law to promote the meanings they approve of and to suppress the ones they dislike or fear. Economic analyses that ignore these expressive evaluations produce unreliable predictions and uncompelling prescriptions. (1998:610)

What is important, though, is that the New Progressives—like Edward Banfield and James Q. Wilson—remain solidly within the rational-choice paradigm. "This criticism," Kahan emphasizes, "is meant to be *internal to economic analysis*. My point isn't that taking social meaning into account reveals economics to be a bad way to think about crime; rather, it's that thinking about crime without taking social meaning into account is a *bad way to do economics*" (Kahan 1998:610, emphasis added).

Not only do Banfield, Wilson, and the New Progressives come out of the same intellectual tradition and share a common conceptual mission, but also, and more important, they deploy the *same means* for enriching the rational action model. Each, in his or her own way, develops a *thicker* understanding of preferences and broadens the repertoire of opportunities in order to gain greater leverage on the rational calculus that leads to crime. First, they thicken the notion of the propensity to commit crime. Banfield developed the idea of the "lower-class individual" who is present-oriented to a fault and unable to discount future benefits and costs. The attitudes, perceptions, and values of this "lower-class individual" are deeply embedded in his psyche and ways, and shape his behavior. Wilson focused on the notion of "human nature" and the "constitutional factors" that shape how we evaluate our options and act. "Wicked people exist," Wilson notoriously wrote. "Nothing avails except to set them apart from innocent people" (1975:209). The New Progressives develop the expressive nature of our preferences—the social meanings that people value—and accordingly divide the world into "committed law abiders" and "individuals who are otherwise inclined to engage in crime" (Kahan 1997a:370–371). The important insight for all three is that people in certain groups have certain character traits, patterns of behavior, values, tastes, and perceptions. These represent thick preferences that are not easily changed—ingrained class characteristics, human nature, or social meaning—and that researchers must factor into the equation of rational action if they are to develop predictive theories.

Second, all three, again each in his or her own way, increase the repertoire of opportunities in order to accommodate the thicker conception of propensities and to leverage these into behavioral consequences. A richer conception of preferences naturally means that they are less manipulable. It may no longer be cost-effective, for instance, to try to rehabilitate or otherwise reconfigure the present-oriented. In fact, it may no longer be possible. "The fact is," Banfield emphasized, "that no one knows how to change the culture of any part of the population—the lower class or the upper, whites or Negroes, pupils or teachers, policemen or criminals" (1974:263). As a result, policy making must focus on enlarging the range of manipulations and operations that can be performed on the inducement to commit crime, and on broadening our horizon regarding opportunities.

Banfield proposed, among other things, to eliminate the minimum wage and reduce the school-leaving age in order to remove impediments to the employment of the unskilled and unschooled. He advocated a negative income tax for the more competent poor and intensive birth-control guidance for the rest (1974:269–270). These policies were intended to change the situational inducements to crime by giving youths work and relieving poor women of the burdens of child rearing. More generally, he advocated "abridg[ing] to an appropriate degree the freedom of those who in the opinion of a court are extremely likely to commit violent crimes" (1974:270). In his essays in *Thinking about Crime,* James Q. Wilson picked up on this suggestion and strenuously argued for incarcerating a larger number of habitual offenders (1975:199). Drawing on his earlier study of police departments, Wilson also argued, in the later "Broken Windows" essay, for greater attention to neighborhood cues of order and disorder. The New Progressives enlarge the range of opportunities by focusing on social meaning and possible changes in meaning. Their idea is that social meaning may offer a better way to control behavior. The inner-city youth, for instance, who wants to be cool and admired at any cost may be willing to join a gang or carry a gun. It may not be possible to change the youth's preferences, these scholars suggest, so instead we should manipulate social meaning so as to change gun carrying or gang membership from something that is admired to something that is ridiculed.

What further unites Banfield, Wilson, and the New Progressives is a shared focus on the *norm of orderliness* and on public policies that achieve order through law enforcement. One of the central insights of these scholars is that the norm of order has social meaning and may influence behavior. It may, for example, influence the behavior of neighborhood residents and outsiders in such a way as to reduce the occurrence of serious criminal activity. Order, they suggest, means that the community has control of the neighborhood, that it will not tolerate criminality, and that it will enforce basic norms of civility. Order thus signifies security, safety, and control, which may help bring about behavior that discourages crime. Conversely, disorder means that the community tolerates crime, that the neighborhood is unsafe, and that disruptive persons and criminals can and will take over. The social meaning of disorder thus makes a neighborhood vulnerable to crime. "By shaping preferences for crime, accentuating the perceived status of lawbreaking, and enfeebling the institutions that normally hold criminal propensities in check," Kahan and Meares assert, "disorderly norms create crime" (1998b:806).

The Unexamined Categories of Order and Disorder

In this sense, the order-maintenance approach shares the same intellectual roots and has the same conceptual structure as the theory of incapacitation. It is precisely the thicker notion of propensities to commit crime that produces *both* the habitual serious criminal who must be incarcerated *and* the disorderly person who must be arrested, controlled, and relocated. Broken windows policing is therefore not an alternative to the theory of incapacitation. It is, instead, its twin.

And, as a result, running throughout the order-maintenance approach is the pervasive and familiar dichotomy between "committed law-abiders" and "individuals who are otherwise inclined to engage in crime" (Kahan 1997a:371); between "families who care for their homes, mind each other's children, and confidently frown on unwanted intruders," and "disreputable or obstreperous or unpredictable people: panhandlers, drunks, addicts, rowdy teenagers, prostitutes, loiterers, the mentally disturbed" (Wilson and Kelling 1982:31, 30). As James Q. Wilson wrote in 1968:

> A noisy drunk, a rowdy teenager shouting or racing his car in the middle of the night, a loud radio in the apartment next door, a panhandler soliciting money from passersby, persons wearing eccentric clothes and unusual hair styles loitering in public places—all these are examples of behavior which "the public" (an onlooker, a neighbor, the community at large) may disapprove of. (1968:16)

> A teenager hanging out on a street corner late at night, especially one dressed in an eccentric manner, a Negro wearing a "conk rag" (a piece of cloth tied around the head to hold flat hair being "processed"—that is, straightened), girls in short skirts and boys in long hair parked in a flashy car talking loudly to friends on the curb, or interracial couples—all of these are seen by many police officers as persons displaying unconventional and improper behavior. (1968:39–40)

These are the visible cues that might distinguish "the behavior of committed *law-abiders*" from the behavior of "lawbreakers" or "individuals who are otherwise inclined to engage in crime" (Kahan and Meares 1998b:823). These are the visible cues of public disorder. And hand in hand with this set of categories goes another ubiquitous dichotomy between order and disorder, between "norms of orderliness" and "[p]ublic drunkenness, prostitution, aggressive panhandling and similar behavior" (Kahan 1997a:371, 370), between a "stable neighborhood" and "an inhospitable and frightening jungle" (Wilson and Kelling 1982:31–32).

The order-maintenance approach is grounded in these categorical distinctions. The mechanisms of social influence assume these fixed categories. The central premise of the broken windows theory is that disorder operates on honest people and on the disorderly *in different ways*. Neighborhood disorder influences honest people to move *out* of the neighborhood or to lock themselves in their homes. "Law-abiding citizens are likely to leave a neighborhood that is pervaded by disorder. . . . Law-abiders who stick it out, moreover, are more likely to avoid the streets, where their simple presence would otherwise be a deterrent to crime" (Kahan and Meares 1998b:823). But neighborhood disorder influences the disorderly—and especially criminals—to move *into* the neighborhood and commit crimes. It is precisely in this disorderly environment that "individuals who are otherwise inclined to engage in crime are much more likely to do so. . . . And their decisions to commit crime reinforce the disposition of still others to do the same" (Kahan and Meares 1998b:823). Order and disorder thus operate *differently* on law-abiders and the disorderly.

But how is it that the line between the disorderly and law abiders is drawn? How is it, exactly, that the thicker propensities are determined? Why is it that eccentric clothes, youthful exuberance, or loitering is disorderly? What are the distinctions between difference, eccentricity, disorder, and criminality? How does police brutality map onto disorder? And why should we distinguish so sharply between street disorder and other forms of disorder? Everyday forms of tax evasion—paying cash to avoid sales tax, paying workers or household help under the table, using an out-of-state address—are also disorderly. Insider trading, insurance misrepresentation, police corruption, and police brutality: these are all disorderly. Yet they figure nowhere in the theory of order-maintenance policing. How come?

Moreover, what exactly is the meaning of disorder? To be sure, it may signal that a community is not in control of crime; but that is not the only possible or plausible meaning. After all, it could also signal an alternative subculture, political opposition, or artistic ferment. Similarly, an orderly neighborhood could be a sign of a commercial sex strip, wealthy neighbors, a strong Mafia presence, or a large police force. There may not be such a coherent message attached to order and disorder. On close examination, the meaning of order and disorder may not be as stable or as fixed as the order-maintenance approach suggests.

The important point is that the categories of the disorderly and the law abider do not have a preexistent fixed reality independent of the techniques of punishment that we implement as a society. The categories do not predate the policing strategies and punishment techniques. To the contrary, the notion of thick propensities or human nature is itself a reality produced by a certain method of policing and punishment. It is a reality shaped, in part, by the norm of orderliness and by policies of aggressive order maintenance. It is the product of techniques of punishment—misdemeanor arrests, enforced order, stops and frisks, order-maintenance crackdowns—that combine several different historical modalities, such as classical strategies of excessive force and modern disciplinary mechanisms of surveillance and spatial control. These techniques of punishment account for the category of the disorderly, and they shape the way we perceive, feel about, and judge people who are homeless, hustling, or panhandling. Michel Foucault's study *Discipline and Punish* focuses on how techniques of punishment shape us, and it is there, I suggest, that we should turn to better understand the central category of the disorderly, how it is informed by the norm of orderliness and how it simultaneously facilitates crackdown policing.

The category of the disorderly in the writings of the New Progressives and the "Broken Windows" essay, of the wicked in James Q. Wilson's *Thinking about Crime,* or of the lower-class and present-oriented in Edward Banfield's writings are not pre-political categories that exist in nature. They too are infused with social meaning and constructed in part through lengthy processes of punitive practices. The norm of strict orderliness—as well as the policing techniques of order-maintenance crackdowns—help shape both our understanding of the "disorderly" or the "wicked" or the "present-oriented" and the way we perceive and judge the people who are out of order, disheveled, or different. In other words, the very norm of orderliness and the policing and punitive practices that we employ help shape the thicker conception of propensities at the heart of the order-maintenance approach.

Moreover, this conception of thick propensities may in fact facilitate broken windows policing in a kind of feedback loop. The category of the disorderly may make order-maintenance policing natural and necessary. Once order is defined in terms of serious crime, there is little else to do but crack down on the disorderly. Once we are saddled with this thicker notion of propensities, there is little we can do but manipulate, in small ways, the situational inducements that promote or discourage crime. We have little alternative given that some people simply are "wicked" and others "disorderly."

In sum, order maintenance begins with a common notion of thick propensities and gravitates toward a policy orientation that focuses on manipulating inducements. What the approach fails to recognize, however, is that the conception of thick propensities may itself be constructed over lengthy periods of time by the practices and institutions that surround us. The proposed public policies, though perhaps addressed only to inducements, may themselves reinforce the thicker conception of propensities. When we engage in public policy analysis, we need to explore the way in which policing practices affect us as researchers and as contemporary subjects of society. Whether or not we decide to implement policies that seek to rehabilitate, reform, correct, or control the disorderly, we must analyze them all from the perspective of how they do and will create the subject.

The truth is that broken windows policing operates, in many cases, by means of aggressive disciplinary practices that are masked by the regularity of legal processes. In New York City, for instance, the quality-of-life initiative and the resulting orderliness have been produced, in large part, by a policy of stops and frisks and misdemeanor arrests, and have been accompanied by a significant increase in complaints of police misconduct. These policing practices have created, under the cover of law, something that may look like order to many residents. But that order may contain a lot of disorder. And the disorder may contain a lot of order; the disorderly, after all, are not chosen by lot. The orderliness of broken windows policing may be an *illusion of order.* Much of what the police may do to enforce order in the streets may not, in the words of Wilson and Kelling, "withstand a legal challenge"

(1982:31). Some of these order-maintenance practices may not "easily [be] reconciled with any conception of due process or fair treatment" (1982:35). Many of them cannot easily be reconciled with the norm of orderliness.

## The Turn to Injury in Late Modernity

How is it, then, that the order-maintenance approach to criminal justice—a theory without solid empirical or social-scientific foundation, a theory that has resulted in aggressive stops, frisks, arrests, and detentions of hundreds of thousands of citizens, a theory that has been accompanied by increased complaints of police misconduct—has come to be one of the leading criminal justice theories embraced by progressive reformers, many liberal New Yorkers, police chiefs, mayors, policy makers, and academics across the country? This is an important and puzzling question that deserves our attention. In part, the answer may parallel the explanations that have been offered to account for the other major turn-of-century trend in criminal justice—the incarceration mania. A number of scholars have advanced compelling analyses of this fundamental shift from a welfare state to a penal state (Garland 1996 and 2001; Becket 1997; Caplow and Simon 1998; Wacquant 1998 and 1999). In this book, I offer an additional dimension to that literature—the dimension of rhetoric—to help explain the power and popularity of order maintenance.

The category of the disorderly places the unattached adult, the panhandler, the rowdy children outside the norms of orderliness, due process, and fairness. In the writings of Banfield, Wilson, and the New Progressives, the present-oriented, the wicked and the disorderly are portrayed as abnormal—as being in need of normalization, control, and supervision. This makes it a lot easier for the rest of us—law abiders—to accept the aggressive policing and harsh punishment of the disorderly others. It also makes it a lot easier to ignore many of the other costs associated with the proposed policing initiatives. The meaning of orderliness, understood in terms of preventing serious crimes such as homicide and robbery, may blind us to some significant disadvantages of order-maintenance policing. Order maintenance, for instance, may hand over the power to define deviance to police officers and some citizens who are not representative of the community.

According to Wilson and Kelling, one rule of the patrol officer is that "[i]f a dispute erupted between a businessman and a customer, the businessman was assumed to be right" (1982:30). This rule may not reflect the voice of all members of the community. It may, in fact, reflect none. The businessman himself may live in a completely different neighborhood.

The order-maintenance approach turns disorderly persons into dangerous and threatening people. Once upon a time, the disorderly were merely the "losers" of society. They were hoboes, bums, winos—a nuisance to many, but not threatening or dangerous. The same was true of loitering, hustling, and panhandling. They were, again for many, a nuisance—irritating, particularly since they reminded many of us of our privilege, but something simply to ignore. Today, however, the disorderly are the agents of crime and neighborhood decline. The squeegee man, the peddler, the homeless—they are what *causes* serious crime. Loitering, panhandling, soliciting prostitution, graffiti writing—these activities foster serious criminality. As a result, disorder in itself has become a harm that justifies the criminal sanction. By appropriating harm in this way, the order-maintenance approach to criminal justice has disarmed the traditional progressive 1960s response of "no harm." This turn to harm, I argue, may account in part for the rhetorical power and overwhelming popularity of the approach. It may explain why so many progressive reformers—seeking an alternative to the traditional means of arrest, conviction, and incarceration—have ended up rallying behind order-maintenance crackdowns, zero tolerance, and other measures that fall back on stops, arrests, and detentions.

### A New Vision

In this book I explore the order-maintenance approach to criminal justice. I offer a critique of this approach—empirical and methodological in Part I, theoretical in Part II, and rhetorical in Part III. My critique, however, gives rise to an alternative approach and research agenda, which I set forth in Part IV. This alternative approach builds on the work of Banfield, Wilson, and the New Progressives. The turn to norm-driven hypotheses and social meaning *is* a positive development for criminal justice, and it is important not to discard these valuable insights. The fundamental problem with order maintenance is not that it rests on discussion of the norm and social meaning of orderliness, but rather that it fails to be critical about these categories—order, disorder, and the disorderly—and to consider the ways in which they are shaped by the policing practices that surround us. Order maintenance fails to explore how punishment techniques may shape our very conception of thicker propensities, human nature, and social meaning.

The alternative approach that I propose focuses not only on social meaning and short-term behavior and perception, but also, and more important, on the relationship between policing practices and the perceptions, thoughts, feelings, understandings, and relations of the contemporary subject. Law enforcement policies and punitive practices shape us—and it is here, I suggest, that we should begin to rethink and research our criminal laws and policing. This book is a critique of the order-maintenance approach to criminal justice, but it is also a prolegomenon to a new vision of punishment and criminal justice policy analysis.

# CHAPTER 2

# The Order-Maintenance Approach

Broken windows policing has swept the American criminal justice system at record speed. In the euphoria of support, it is sometimes easy to lose sight of the subtle distinctions between the various practices and theories. Order maintenance, broken windows, zero tolerance, community policing, social norms, social meaning, social influence: the terms begin to bleed into one another. How is it, precisely, that the broken windows theory relates to the legal scholarship of the New Chicago School or to New York–style policing? And how is it, exactly, that the more conservative writings of James Q. Wilson and Edward C. Banfield relate to the contemporary writings of the New Progressives? In this chapter I offer an interpretation of the different theories and practices that make up the order-maintenance approach to criminal justice. I begin with perhaps the most central doctrine of all, the broken windows theory.

## Broken Windows

The broken windows theory was first articulated in James Q. Wilson and George L. Kelling's short, nine-page article "Broken Windows," which appeared in the *Atlantic Monthly* in 1982. The theory is premised on the idea that "disorder and crime are usually inextricably linked, in a kind of developmental sequence" (Wilson and Kelling 1982:31). According to Wilson and Kelling, minor disorders (such as littering, loitering, public drinking, panhandling, and prostitution), if tolerated in a neighborhood, produce an environment that is likely to attract crime. They signal to potential criminals that delinquent behavior will not be reported or controlled—that no one is in charge. One broken window, left unrepaired, invites other broken windows. These progressively break down community standards and leave the community vulnerable to crime.

In the essay, disorder breeds crime in a highly scripted manner:

> A stable neighborhood of families who care for their homes, mind each other's children, and confidently frown on unwanted intruders can change, in a few years or even a few months, to an inhospitable and frightening jungle. A piece of property is abandoned, weeds grow up, a window is smashed. Adults stop scolding rowdy children; the children, emboldened, become more rowdy. Families move out, unattached adults move in. Teenagers gather in front of the corner store. The merchant asks them to move; they refuse. Fights occur. Litter accumulates. People start drinking in front of the grocery; in time, an inebriate slumps to the sidewalk and is allowed to sleep it off. Pedestrians are approached by panhandlers.
>
> At this point it is not inevitable that serious crime will flourish or violent attacks on strangers will occur. But many residents will think that crime, especially violent crime, is on the rise, and they will modify their behavior accordingly. They will use the streets less often, and when on the streets will stay apart from their fellows, moving with averted eyes, silent lips, and hurried steps. . . .
>
> Such an area is vulnerable to criminal invasion. Though it is not inevitable, it is more likely that here . . . drugs will change hands, prostitutes will solicit, and cars will be stripped. That the drunks will be robbed by boys who do it as a lark, and the prostitutes' customers will be robbed by men who do it purposefully and perhaps violently. (1982:31–32)

On the surface, the "Broken Windows" script privileges order over disorder. Whereas disorder attracts crime, order, by contrast, decreases criminal activity. The principal policy recommendation of the essay is that the police resume their "order-maintenance function"—a function that was essentially displaced by the "crime fighting function" during the 1960s (1982:33; see also Wilson 1968:16–34). The order-maintenance function focuses on integrating police officers into the community and teaching them to maintain the peace and order rather than solve crimes. It is symbolized by the foot-patrol officer on his beat, making his rounds, enforcing rules of civility, and maintaining good order.

This hierarchy of order over disorder is refracted throughout the essay. A typical community, for instance, is composed of citizens or "decent folk" on the one hand, and criminals and "disorderly people" on the other (1982:30). The disorderly people include "disreputable or obstreperous or unpredictable people: panhandlers, drunks, addicts, rowdy teenagers, prostitutes, loiterers, the mentally disturbed" (1982:30; see also Wilson 1968:16, 39). They are the rowdy children, the fighting teenagers, the slumped inebriates, and the marauding panhandlers in the script. And they are pitted against orderly citizens in a continual struggle of good versus evil. The disorderly are closely associated with vices such as drinking, prostitution, littering, and begging. They are the "ill-smelling drunk" or the "importuning beggar" (1982:34). They are often associated with youth or with "unattached adults" (1982:32).

This opposition of orderly and disorderly people cuts across a further pervasive insider-outsider dichotomy, in effect producing two categories of troublemakers—the disorderly insiders, who need to be controlled, and the disorderly outsiders, who need to be excluded. The scheme of the essay can be represented as follows:

|  | Regulars | Strangers |
|---|---|---|
| Ordered | Decent folk | Visitors |
| Disordered | Drunks and derelicts | Criminals |

According to the essay, it is "outsiders" or "strangers" who commit crimes (1982:36, 30). "Regulars," by contrast, tend not to cause real problems (1982:30). So, for instance, the essay recounts the views of a patrol officer, fictitiously named Kelly, who is assigned a beat in downtown Newark in a controlled experiment regarding community policing:

> The people were made up of "regulars" and "strangers." Regulars included both "decent folk" and some drunks and derelicts who were always there but who "knew their place." Strangers were, well, strangers, and viewed suspiciously, sometimes apprehensively. The officer—call

him Kelly—knew who the regulars were, and they knew him. As he saw his job, he was to keep an eye on strangers, and make certain that the disreputable regulars observed some informal but widely understood rules. Drunks and addicts could sit on the stoops, but could not lie down. People could drink on side streets, but not at the main intersection. Bottles had to be in paper bags. Talking to, bothering, or begging from people waiting at the bus stop was strictly forbidden. If a dispute erupted between a businessman and a customer, the businessman was assumed to be right, especially if the customer was a stranger. If a stranger loitered, Kelly would ask him if he had any means of support and what his business was; if he gave unsatisfactory answers, he was sent on his way. (1982:30)

Kelly's task, as he saw it, was to regulate the disorderly insiders and exclude the disorderly outsiders—a task that reflects the type of order-maintenance policing espoused in the essay. "We look for outsiders," reports a leader of a community watch group in the Silver Lake area of Belleville, New Jersey. "If a few teenagers from outside the neighborhood enter it, 'we ask them their business'" (1982:36).

The insider-outsider dichotomy is also reflected in the recurring reference to "criminal invasion" (1982:32–33). The term "invasion" reinforces the idea that crime comes from outside the community. The essay manages to sustain this fiction essentially by excluding delinquents. The insider teenager, for instance, who lives in a housing project and becomes a gang member simply loses his insider status. Though he may continue to live in the projects, he is no longer a "project resident," no longer a "citizen," and no longer has a legitimate voice (1982:35). In short, he no longer has a claim to membership in the community—especially in the face of competing claims by orderly residents who are struggling to "reassert control over [their] turf" (1982:33). "What the police in fact do," the essay asserts, "is chase known gang members out of the project" (1982:35). The essay does the same when it excludes gang members from the category of "residents."

The "Broken Windows" essay is premised, then, on a number of shared assumptions about the privilege of order over disorder and of insider over outsider, about the likelihood of criminal invasion in disorderly neighborhoods, and about the suspicious nature of the unattached adult, the importuning beggar, the unpredictable person—in sum, the disorderly. It is premised on a categorical distinction between the disorderly and the decent folk. The essay intimates that reducing crime is merely a question of details, that it requires only that we pick up litter, paint over graffiti, hide inebriates and panhandlers, and fix broken windows. The essay reflects an aesthetic of orderliness, cleanliness, and sobriety. And on these assumptions it tells a compelling story about crime and deterrence. The basic plot is simple: fighting minor disorder deters serious crime.

### Edward C. Banfield and the Lower Class

The "Broken Windows" essay reflects an approach to crime, urban issues, and politics that was shaped by the earlier writings of Edward C. Banfield—James Q. Wilson's mentor, colleague, and co-author in 1963 of *City Politics*. In a series of writings addressing the urban crisis in the 1960s and 1970s—especially in *The Unheavenly City* and the subsequent revision, *The Unheavenly City Revisited*—Banfield set forth a distinct perspective on crime and urban decay that, in many ways, made possible the later broken windows theory. Just as the broken windows theory describes an evolutionary—or devolutionary—spiral of decay, Banfield had articulated earlier a similar developmental model of neighborhood change that relied significantly on behavioral norms and economic necessity to explain crime and urban blight. Banfield's model of urban change was similarly premised on two important factors: first, what he called the "logic of growth"; and second, the norms and values of neighborhood residents, including, more specifically, the pathological traits of "lower-class" individuals.

According to Banfield, urban change reflected, in part, a natural evolutionary process—what he referred to as a "logic of growth." Downtown neighborhoods fall into the hands of the less well-off because the original, better-off property owners leave the central city for larger homes and more acreage in the suburbs. The well-off move to the suburbs not because of fear of crime or "white flight," but rather because they "wanted and could afford newer and more spacious houses and neighborhoods" and could also afford to commute (1974:36). They are not pushed out by urban decay, but rather are impelled by their own desire for more luxurious homes. For their part, the less well-off are glad to move into the downtown neighborhoods because of the proximity to jobs and stores, and also because of the relative improvement of central city housing over rural poverty, older tenements, or shanties. "The logic of growth," Banfield emphasized, "*does* require that, in general, the lowest-income people live in the oldest, highest-density, most run-down housing, which will be nearest to the factories, warehouses, stores, and offices of the inner city, or downtown, part of the central city" (1974:52).

Eventually, the neighborhoods vacated by the well-off begin to decay. The well-off perceive their old neighborhoods, sadly, as examples of urban "blight"—"lawns and shrubbery trampled out, houses unpainted, porches sagging, vacant lots filled with broken bottles and junk" (1974:35). In what might playfully be called the "broken bottle theory," Banfield suggests that the poor—or in his terms the "less well-off"—have an incentive to let their neighborhood decay:

> To the people who moved from old tenements and shanties into the housing that had been vacated by the relatively well-off people who moved to the suburbs, what was happening to the central city neighborhoods did not appear as "decay." Many of them cared little or nothing for lawns and had no objections to broken bottles; they knew, too, that the more "fixed up" things were, the higher rents would be. . . . To the least well-off, "blight" was a blessing. They were able, for the first time in their lives, to occupy housing that was comfortable. (1974:36)

According to Banfield, the logic of growth, however, does not explain fully the existence of squalid and crime-ridden slums. What accounts for these features is the second important factor, namely, behavioral norms and the concept of class (1974:52–53). By class, Banfield meant certain "patterns of perception, taste, attitude, and behavior" (1974:53). These patterns, according to Banfield, permeate all facets of an individual's life, including his or her "manners, consumption, child-rearing, sex, politics, or whatever" (1974:53). Banfield referred to these patterns as norms or values. He called them "ethos," which he defined as "the sum of the characteristic usages, ideas, standards, and codes by which a group is differentiated and individualized in character from other groups" (Banfield 1958:10 n.3).

For Banfield, class membership turns on the individual's psychological orientation to time—that is, whether he or she is present- or future-oriented. Banfield's central hypothesis was that "the many traits that constitute a 'patterning' are all consequences, indirect if not direct, of a *time horizon that is characteristic of a class*" (1974:54, emphasis added). The "lower-class" person is present-oriented to a fault. In contrast to the future-oriented upper-class individual, the lower-class individual lives "from moment to moment," and his behavior is governed by impulse. He is improvident and irresponsible, and, as a result, "likely also to be unskilled, to move frequently from one dead-end job to another, to be a poor husband and father" (1974:61, 54).

The lower-class individual resembles, in many ways, the disorderly in Wilson and Kelling's "Broken Windows" essay. Like the unattached adult, the lower-class individual in Banfield's writings "is unable to maintain a stable relationship with a mate; commonly he does not marry" (1974:62). Like the aggressive panhandler, the lower-class individual is "aggressive yet dependent" (1974:62). And like the prostitute or slut, the lower-class person has loose sexual morals. "His bodily needs (especially for sex) and his taste for 'action' take precedence over everything else—and certainly over any work routine" (1974:61). The lower-class person is unemployed and "drifts from one unskilled job to another, taking no interest in his work" (1974:61). He is abusive and often violent. Lower-class households, Banfield contends, are "usually female-based." The women heads of household are "characteristically impulsive," and "once children have passed babyhood they are likely to be neglected or abused" (1974:61).

The lower-class person has a lot in common with his environment. "The lower-class individual lives in the slum," Banfield notes, "which, to a greater or lesser extent, is an expression of his tastes and style of life" (1974:71). He develops a symbiotic relationship with the ghetto that reinforces his own lower-class norms as well as the urban decay:

> [T]he indifference ("apathy" if one prefers) of the lower-class person is such that he seldom makes even the simplest repairs to the place that he lives in. He is not troubled by dirt and dilapidation and he does not mind the inadequacy of public facilities such as schools, parks, hospital, and libraries; indeed, where such things exist he may destroy them by carelessness or even by vandalism. . . . [T]he slum is specialized as [a site] for vice and for illicit commodities generally. Dope peddlers, prostitutes, and receivers of stolen goods are all readily available there,

within easy reach of each other and of their customers and victims. . . .
In the slum, one can beat one's children, lie drunk in the gutter, or go
to jail without attracting any special notice; these are things that most
of the neighbors themselves have done and that they consider quite
normal. (1974:72)

According to Banfield, it is precisely the norm of present-
orientedness, characteristic of lower-class individuals, that gives rise
to crime and delinquency, poverty and squalor, broken families and
illegitimacy. Banfield was surprisingly blunt, at least by contemporary standards. Lower-class people, he stated, "generate social problems—violent crime, for example" (1974:240). In *The Unheavenly City
Revisited,* Banfield explained that "since the benefits of crime tend to
be immediate and its costs (such as imprisonment or loss of reputa-
tion) in the future, the present-oriented individual *is ipso facto more dis-
posed toward crime than others*" (1974:183, emphasis added). Similarly, in
his later essay "Present Orientedness and Crime," Banfield wrote that
"a cohort of present-oriented persons could as a rule be expected to
commit a good many more crimes of certain types than a matched cohort of persons who are not present oriented" (1991:320–321). Banfield did not shy away from provocation.

The norm of present-orientedness, in conjunction with the logic of
growth, operates to perpetuate urban decay and blight. In turn, these
problems of crime and poverty reinforce present-orientedness in what
Banfield described as a "feedback loop" (1991:319). It is thus the mix
of class culture and the logic of growth that determines the crime rate
and housing conditions in central city neighborhoods (1974:74). The
norm of present-orientedness, in conjunction with urban evolutionary
norms, *causes crime.* Banfield's "feedback loop" can be graphically illustrated as shown in Figure 2.1.

In effect, Banfield explained crime on the basis of two interrelated
factors—class and situation. He summarized his view as follows:

[C]rime, like poverty, depends primarily upon two sets of variables.
One set relates mainly to class culture and personality (but also to sex
and age) and determines an individual's *propensity* to crime. The other
relates to situational factors (such as the number of policemen on the
scene and the size of the payroll) and determines his *inducement.* The
probability that he will commit crimes—his *proneness* to crime—de-

pends upon propensity *and* inducement. A city's *potential* for crime may be thought of as the average proneness of persons in various "sex-age-culture-personality" groups times their number. (1974:180)

According to Banfield, present-orientedness contributes not only to serious crime, such as assault, robbery, and rape, but also to antisocial behavior more generally. It causes what Wilson and Kelling refer to as "disorder"—in Banfield's words, "behavior that is antisocial without being illegal, or that is merely unsocial." This behavior, in turn, threatens "the 'quality-of-life' or, as it used to be called *civilization*" (Banfield 1991:315).

The focus on the norm of present-orientedness to explain larger social phenomena is characteristic of Banfield's thought more generally. In his earlier work *The Moral Basis of a Backward Society*, Banfield focused on the behavioral norm of "amoral familism" to explain the extreme poverty and "backwardness" of southern Italian society (1958:9). "Amoral familism" is the tendency to care only about the short-term material advantages of one's nuclear family and to disregard all other, larger interests, such as the interest of one's community, city, or nation. The behavioral norm of amoral familism undermines the ability of southern Italians to act together to promote the general welfare, to create organizations to better society, or to cooperate in such a way as to improve living conditions. Banfield argued that the family-centered ethos explains the economic and social conditions of southern Italy. While he conceded that other factors were also important—such as "poverty, ignorance, and a status system which leaves the

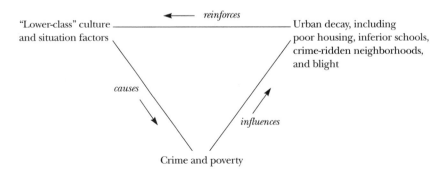

**Figure 2.1** Banfield's feedback loop of class, crime, and urban decay

peasant almost outside the larger society" (1958:155)—he nevertheless maintained that "for purposes of analysis and policy the moral basis of a society may usefully be regarded as the strategic, or limiting factor. That is to say, the situation may be understood, or altered, better from this standpoint than from any other." This "very simple hypothesis," Banfield contended, could "make intelligible *all* of the behavior about which questions have been raised and will enable an observer to predict how the Montegranesi [villagers] will act in concrete circumstances" (1958:155, 83, emphasis added).

Behavioral norms—present-orientedness in the lower classes in American society and family-orientedness in southern Italian society—are, for Banfield, the key to understanding social phenomena such as crime, urban decay, bad schools, lack of associations, and so on. They reflect what others, such as Wilson, would call "human nature" (Wilson and Herrnstein 1985). And, by and large, they have to be taken for granted in policy analysis. From a policy perspective, Banfield argued, there is no point in trying to change individuals' propensity to commit crime because these cultural and personality traits are practically immutable.

Banfield was deeply pessimistic about the possibility of changing class characteristics. "The fact is," he emphasized, "that no one knows how to change the culture of any part of the population" (1974:263). Even if we could change psychological orientation to time, he suggested, it would take several generations: class characteristics in any individual change very slowly, if at all, and can be discussed only from a multigenerational perspective (1974:238–239). Moreover, "even if one *did* know how, there is good reason to suppose that doing so would be infeasible on other grounds; for example, it might require unconstitutional methods, such as taking infants from their parents at birth, or entail other disadvantages that more than offset its advantages" (1974:263). As a result, the Banfieldian policy maker has to focus on the environment and inducements rather than class and propensity. "[T]he policy maker usually must take certain cultural and psychological traits as given," Banfield wrote. "If he is to change a city's potential for crime it must be by manipulating situational factors, which is to say inducements" (1974:180, 195–196). This could be done "either by raising the costs of crime or by raising the benefits of noncrime" (1974:196).

The truth is, Banfield was not very sanguine about the possibility of doing anything about the urban problem—and in fact sounded sometimes as if he believed the problem itself was not a real issue. Banfield emphasized, in *The Unheavenly City Revisited,* that "[t]he import of what has been said in this book is that although there are many difficulties to be coped with, dilemmas to be faced, and afflictions to be endured, there are very few problems that can be solved; it is also that although much is seriously wrong with the city, no disaster impends unless it be one that results from public misconceptions that are in the nature of self-fulfilling prophecies" (1974:285).

Banfield's list of policy proposals was, accordingly, short and somewhat limited (1974:268). He recommended repealing the minimum wage, reducing the school-leaving age, enacting a negative income tax for the "competent" poor, and providing intensive birth-control guidance to the "incompetent poor"—whom he defined as "the insane, the severely retarded, the senile, the lower class (inveterate 'problem families'), and unprotected children" (1974:269–270). In terms of policing, Banfield proposed, first, regulating police practices in such a way as to give victims a greater incentive to take reasonable precautions to prevent crime; second, intensifying patrols in high-crime neighborhoods and permitting police to stop and frisk; and third, reducing the time from arrest to conviction and punishment. In addition, as noted earlier, he recommended that society "abridge to an appropriate degree the freedom of those who in the opinion of a court are extremely likely to commit violent crimes" (1974:270). For Banfield, the policy focus was on manipulating opportunities rather than propensities.

### James Q. Wilson and Human Nature

Banfield's writings had a significant influence on Wilson and Kelling's "Broken Windows" essay at a number of different levels. Just as the disorderly and obstreperous person in Wilson and Kelling's work bears a sharp resemblance to the lower-class individual, the natural devolution of a disorderly neighborhood is also reminiscent of the logic of growth. In addition, the policy orientation of both works—the focus on modifying situational factors and inducements rather than class values or propensity—is very similar.

Not surprisingly, Banfield also influenced, more generally, the other writings of James Q. Wilson. Wilson's prolific writings on crime can be grouped into three periods: the first period includes the more policy-oriented writings such as the "Broken Windows" essay and others anthologized in *Thinking about Crime* (1975), as well as his work on policing, *Varieties of Police Behavior* (1968); the second involves more traditional criminological writings, especially his treatise *Crime and Human Nature* (1985), co-authored with his colleague at Harvard University, Richard Herrnstein; the third includes his more recent writings on moral theory reflected in works such as *The Moral Sense* (1993). All three periods reflect, in different ways and to different degrees, Banfield's influence.

In his earlier policy-oriented writings, Wilson, like Banfield, argued strenuously against trying to remedy the deep environmental causes of crime, such as poverty, or the psychological roots of crime, such as impulsiveness and present-orientedness. Instead, Wilson proposed more modest policies aimed at changing the situational factors that allow or encourage lawbreakers to commit crime—modest in the sense of the goal to achieve, not the consequences of the policies. Wilson's principal recommendations, other than order maintenance, included the increased use of incarceration, especially for serious and repeat offenders, more rapid trials and administration of punishment, mandatory sentencing, and reduced prosecutorial discretion over whom to charge (Wilson 1975:199–201, 208). Wilson also advocated aggressive arrest practices as a way to lower crime rates (Wilson and Kelling 1982; Wilson and Boland 1978 and 1981).

In these early writings, Wilson drew a sharp distinction between the criminologist's task of discovering the causes of crime and the policy analyst's task of proposing politically feasible measures that would have some impact on the crime rate. "Policy analysis, as opposed to causal analysis, begins with a very different perspective," Wilson wrote (1975:53). It begins with a perspective that focuses on feasible and measurable change. In contrast to Banfield—who, in a somewhat self-deprecating way, repeatedly emphasized that hardly any of his policy proposals were politically acceptable (1974:269, 285)—Wilson was highly concerned with political feasibility. Wilson's policy orientation was mostly the product of a genuine desire to offer *workable* policy prescriptions—a desire shared by the New Chicago School. "Though intellectually rewarding, from a practical point of view it is a mistake to think about crime in terms of its 'causes' and then to search for ways to alleviate those causes," Wilson noted. "We must think instead of what it is feasible for a government or a community to do, and then try to discover, by experimentation and observation, which of those things will produce, at acceptable costs, desirable changes in the level of criminal victimization" (1975:207–208).

In other words, for Wilson, it was the imperative of *political feasibility*—rather than pessimism about changing class culture—that was the driving force behind his policy orientation. To be sure, Wilson shared with Banfield both a thick conception of human nature and deep skepticism about changing human nature. In fact, in many passages in *Thinking about Crime*, Wilson, like Banfield, suggested that it may well be impossible to change human nature (see, e.g., Wilson 1975:209). Nevertheless, Wilson's principal motivation for situation-oriented policies was the desire to change the real world by proposing politically practicable policies. And his principal prescription was to incapacitate a larger number of habitual offenders (1975:199).

In the second period—in his more criminological writings—Wilson developed with Richard Herrnstein a comprehensive theory of crime that, like Banfield's, emphasized human nature but also focused on situational factors. In contrast to his earlier writings, Wilson with Herrnstein distanced himself from the conception of class that was so central to Banfield's writings. Whereas, in the earlier period, Wilson wrote about "lower-class persons" in a very Banfieldian way, suggesting that they are preoccupied with "immediate gratification" and are "inclined to uninhibited, expressive conduct" (1975:37), Wilson and Herrnstein recognized in their treatise in 1985 that "this argument continues to be controversial, and so it seems inappropriate to begin an explanation of criminality by assuming that it is based on class" (1985:28). They nevertheless developed a notion of present-orientedness that played a similar role as in Banfield's writings. They referred specifically to the concept of "present-oriented[ness]" and discussed it in similar terms of "discounting" future rewards (1985:62). In fact, a central principle of their comprehensive theory of crime was that "people differ in the rate at which they discount the future" (1985:61).

More generally, Wilson and Herrnstein developed a conception of human nature as playing an important role in determining crime.

"The argument of this book," they explained, "is that there *is* a human nature that develops in intimate settings out of a complex interaction of constitutional and social factors, and that this nature affects how people choose between the consequences of crime and its alternatives" (1985:508). As with Banfield, Wilson and Herrnstein's focus on human nature differentiated their work from sociological writings on crime, especially theories of strain, control, and cultural deviance, which traditionally emphasized social processes and their influence on crime (1985:63). Although Wilson and Herrnstein's comprehensive theory of crime attempted to accommodate, to some extent, sociological emphases on social processes and norms, it focused to an important extent on psychological, biological, and environmentally caused predispositions to crime. In other words, like Banfield, Wilson and Herrnstein constructed a theory of crime that focused on propensity—what they refer to as "constitutional" and "developmental" factors, or "subjective" states of the person—but that also implicated inducement—what they refer to as "social context," objective factors, or contingencies. Like Banfield, Wilson and Herrnstein maintained that it is "very hard for society to change, by plan, the subjective state of large numbers of persons" (1985:377). In contrast to the earlier Wilson, though, they reached this conclusion less because of the distinction between policy analysis and criminology, and more because of criminological "truth."

In his more recent writings on moral theory, Wilson focuses increasing attention on the purported breakdown of morality in the modern age, and the resulting global increase in crime. This is a departure from his earlier writings. In *Thinking about Crime*, for instance, he emphasized that "[m]y strong inclination is to resist explanations for rising crime that are based on the alleged moral breakdown of society, the community, or the family. I resist in part because most of the families and communities I know have not broken down, and in part because, had they broken down, I cannot imagine any collective action we could take consistent with our civil liberties that would restore a moral consensus" (1975:206).

In his 1993 work *The Moral Sense*, however, Wilson maintains that moral relativism in the twentieth century contributed, to some extent, to an increase in crime rates. He suggests that global crime patterns today respond more to cultural circumstances than, as they did formerly, to material circumstances, and that one important cultural circumstance is "the collapse in the legitimacy of what once was respectfully called middle-class morality but today is sneeringly referred to as 'middle-class values'" (1993:10). Wilson argues that worldwide moral relativism may contribute to the global increase in crime "by replacing the belief in personal responsibility with the notion of social causation and by supplying to those marginal persons at risk for crime a justification for doing what they might have done anyway" (1993:10). Banfield too attributed some of the increase in crime to moral relapse. He suggested that upper- and middle-class persons became more crime-prone during the 1960s because "these classes have come to have less respect for authority, including the authority of the law . . . [and because] their conventional morality has been weakened and partially destroyed" (1974:193). Wilson's discussion of the "moral sense" is also influenced by Banfield's focus on ethos—as in the ethos of amoral familism that characterizes southern Italian villagers. Overall, though, Banfield's influence may be less apparent here than in the first two periods.

## The New Chicago School

What emerges from the Banfield-Wilson tradition is a common effort to enrich classical doctrine with a thicker notion of class culture or human nature, as well as a policy orientation that focuses on the environmental and situational cues that encourage people to commit crime. And it is here that the Banfield-Wilson tradition intersects with the writings of the New Chicago School. Dan Kahan, Tracey Meares, and others share Wilson's orientation to policy analysis. In their own words, they are generating "an intensely practical agenda" of law enforcement policies, and their motivations are "as much political as conceptual" (Kahan and Meares 1998b:806).

In sharp contrast to Wilson, however, these legal scholars do not advocate lengthier and more severe terms of incarceration. Quite to the contrary. In this respect they are writing *against* James Q. Wilson. They affirmatively promote what they refer to as "milder public-order alternatives," such as youth curfews, anti-gang loitering ordinances, and order-maintenance crackdowns (Kahan and Meares 1999a:23). These, they contend, are "politically feasible and morally attractive" substitutes for extended incarceration (Kahan and Meares 1998b:806). At the same time, though, their policy proposals draw heavily on the logic of Wilson's broken windows theory. Kahan in fact relies on the theory (1997a:369), as do other social norm theorists (see, e.g., Ellickson 1996:1171–73, 1177–79, 1182; Livingston 1997:581–591).

Social norm scholarship in criminal law, I would suggest, is best understood as a type of constructivist social theory. The emerging literature attempts to explain behavior by focusing on shared interpretations of social practices. These shared interpretations are socially constructed, and they move social actors to behave in certain ways. As Lawrence Lessig explains, "The regulatory effect of norms comes not from something physical or behavioral. The regulatory effect comes from something *interpretive*" (1998:680, emphasis added).

Socially constructed meaning is at the heart of social norm theorizing. With regard to each and every policy recommendation, social meaning plays a pivotal, if not *the* pivotal, role. The reverse sting strategy (the strategy of setting up and arresting purchasers rather than drug dealers), for example, purportedly changes "the social meaning of drug-law policy" (Kahan and Meares 1998b:818–819). At present, the meaning stigmatizes African-Americans as lawbreakers because they are the predominant targets of sting operations. By redistributing the impact of drug convictions outside the inner city, reverse stings "can affect the social meaning of drug offending in ways that encourage residents of minority communities to cooperate with police officers and with each other to reduce crime" (1998b:818–819). Anti-gang loitering ordinances and youth curfews allegedly affect behavior by changing the social meaning of gang membership: "The level of gang activity reflects whether individual juveniles believe that others value and expect gang membership" (1998b:819). Ordinances and curfews change the perception among juveniles that peers value gang criminality by reducing, for instance, the expressive function of the behavior: "[B]eing out at night becomes a less potent means of displaying toughness because fewer of one's peers are around to witness such behavior" (1998b:821). Order-maintenance policing purportedly works because of the social meaning of order. Since order means that a neighborhood is in control, changing a neighborhood from disorderly to orderly will reduce crime (1998b:823). The policy of encouraging juvenile snitching, it is argued, works by changing the social meaning of carrying guns. By rewarding kids who turn in their peers, the strategy "interferes with norms that give guns their meaning" (1998b:825). Finally, church-police cooperation (such as the Eleventh District prayer vigil in Chicago) is purportedly effective in part because it changes the social meaning of the police by casting them in a new light within the social fabric of the community, and changes police officers' perceptions of suspects (1998b:829–830).

All of these proposed policing strategies operate on social meaning. In this regard, social norm scholarship in criminal law traces back, primarily, to Lawrence Lessig's 1995 essay "The Regulation of Social Meaning." Although Lessig did not originate the social norm turn—others, most notably Robert Ellickson (1991) and Jon Elster (1989) preceded him in this respect—Lessig nevertheless initiated the focus on *social meaning* as the lens through which we understand social norms (Lessig 1995, 1996, and 1998; Ellickson 1998:549; Posner 1998a:563). The social norm scholarship in the criminal law area adopts the social meaning lens, and, in this respect, traces back most directly to Lessig's work.

In his 1995 essay, Lessig positions his conception of social meaning within the framework of constructivist theory. Lessig offers, in the margin, the following intellectual background to his use of the term "social meaning":

> It is constructivism that defines modern social theory. Emile Durkheim is one start: "(S)ocial reality is constructed by the operation of the society itself. . . . Social facts are the product of the group life of the total operation of a society." In our own time, the notion was advanced most forcefully in sociology by Peter L. Berger and Thomas Luckman's work, *The Social Construction of Reality: A Treatise in the Sociology of Knowledge*, and in law most importantly by Roberto Unger. Unlike some of the earlier theorists, moderns think less about "society itself" constructing itself and more about how the actions of individuals and collectivities work to construct it. Nevertheless, the tradition has maintained its view about social reality's source: "Human reality is not provided at birth

by the physical universe, but rather must be fashioned by individuals out of the culture into which they are born." (1995:949 n.19, citations omitted)

Both Dan Kahan and Tracey Meares rely in important respects on Lessig's conception of social meaning (Kahan 1997a:351 n.7; Kahan 1997b:2478 n.8; Kahan 1998:611; Kahan and Meares 1998a:1181; Kahan and Meares 1998b:815). On its basis, they offer explanations for the purported effectiveness of the proposed policing strategies. They make predictions, as evidenced by their claim that "disorderly norms create crime" (Kahan and Meares 1998b:806), and they endorse policy prescriptions. But they are candid about the fact that they are focusing on shared *interpretations* (1998b:815). In this sense, they are proposing "an interpretive turn" (Lessig 1996:2184)—a movement away, however slight, from behavioralism or more traditional economic modeling (Lessig 1998:682). This movement, interestingly, mirrors a larger intellectual shift toward interpretivism in the human sciences (Foucault 1970:359).

Lessig illustrates the social meaning approach with a discussion of New York City's various strategies toward panhandling. During the late 1980s and early 1990s, the city sought to ban panhandling by passing a law prohibiting loitering for the purpose of begging (Lessig 1995:1039). That law was struck down by the federal courts under the First Amendment and, as a result, was not given the chance to change the social meaning associated with giving to panhandlers.[1] The Transit Authority then took a different tack, Lessig explains, and, through an advertising campaign, communicated to passengers that it was wrong to give money to panhandlers because it made them less likely to seek help. That campaign, Lessig reports, was effective and succeeded in changing the social meaning associated with giving to beggars. Lessig writes:

Before the Transit Authority started this poster campaign, the refusal of a passenger to give any money to a panhandler had a relatively unambiguous meaning—identifying the passenger as coldhearted, or cheap, or uncaring. Thus, the refusal to give was costly for the passenger. But the Authority's poster campaign ambiguated this meaning. Now, the refusal could either be because the passenger is coldhearted, etc., or because the passenger is concerned to do what is best for the panhandler. What is best for the panhandler is for the passenger to say no to the panhandler. Thus the posters succeeded in making it less costly for the passenger not to give to the panhandler by ambiguating the social meaning of a refusal to give. (1995:1040)

By changing the social meaning (through ambiguation), the Transit Authority attempted to change the patterns of giving to panhandlers and thereby reduce the number of panhandlers.

To say that social norm theory is "constructivist" or "interpretive," however, calls for more specificity, since there are today so many different types of social construction theories. Contemporary constructivist theories range from the historical or ironic, to the unmasking or reformist, to the more rebellious or revolutionary (Hacking 1999:19–21). I would characterize the social norm scholarship as moderate, instrumental, and at times reformist. First, it is moderate insofar as it does not suggest that *all* social meanings are constructed. As Lessig asserts, "[S]ome social meanings are constructed" (1995:949). Moreover, he maintains, even though more than one construction may be possible, not every construction is possible (1995:949 n.19). Second, it is instrumental insofar as it seeks primarily to change social meaning in order to affect behavior. As discussed earlier, most of the proposed policing strategies operate in this way—most, but not all. And for this reason, third, it has an ambivalent relationship to reform. Again, most of the time, but not all, it questions, criticizes, or seeks to change social meaning. To make this clear, I will review here three of the concrete policy proposals that social norm scholars advocate.

## Juvenile Snitching Policies

One of the earliest and longest-lived recommendations of social norm scholars is the policy of rewarding, in their own words, "juvenile snitching" as a way to reduce juvenile gun possession (Kahan 1997a:364; Kahan 1998:611–612; Kahan and Meares 1998b:824–825; Kahan 1999a:1867). Kahan and Meares begin their analysis by suggesting that guns have social meaning among youths. This, of course, is undoubtedly true. (See, e.g., Pattillo and May 1994:16–29; Fagan 1999:29–31.) Specifically, Kahan and Meares maintain that "[g]un possession can confer status on the carrier because it expresses confidence and a willingness to defy authority. Failure to carry a gun, on the other hand, may signal fear and thus invite aggression" (1998b:824).

Kahan and Meares suggest that we should develop policies to discourage juvenile gun possession that take account of this meaning. They argue that the traditional policy of rewarding juveniles who voluntarily give up their weapons and severely punishing those who do not is doomed to fail because the policy *supports* the present social meaning of gun possession. It "reinforce[s] the message of defiance associated with carrying guns and thus *increase*[s] the expressive value of that behavior" (1998b:825).

In contrast, Kahan and Meares endorse a policy of rewarding juveniles who turn in their classmates who are carrying guns:

> When students fear that their peers will report them, they are less likely to display their guns; when students are reluctant to display them, guns become less valuable for conveying information about attitudes and intentions. In addition, the perception that onlookers are willing to sell out possessors counteracts the inference that possessors enjoy high status among their peers. Encouraging snitching thus reduces the incidence of gun possession both by deconstructing its positive meaning and by disrupting behavioral norms—including the ready display of guns—that are essential to that activity's expressive value. (1998b:825)

The policy of encouraging juvenile snitching, Kahan and Meares argue, changes the social meaning of gun possession and thereby lowers the incentive to carry. It works on the inducement to commit crime by decreasing the attractiveness of guns.

## Anti-Gang Loitering Ordinances

Kahan and Meares also propose enforcing anti-gang loitering ordinances. Their analysis begins with the proposition that gang membership has social meaning—which, again, is undoubtedly true. Specifically, Kahan and Meares argue, in high-crime neighborhoods a majority of teens believe that their peers predominantly admire gang activity. Therefore, in order to reduce gang activity, "the law should regulate the sources of social meaning that construct th[ese] impression[s]" (1998b:819). They advocate, on these grounds, the use of anti-gang loitering ordinances, such as the ordinance that was enacted by the city of Chicago in 1992 (held unconstitutionally vague in 1999 by the United States Supreme Court in *City of Chicago v. Morales*). Kahan and Meares explain:

> A potentially more effective approach is to attack the public signs and cues that inform juveniles' (mis)perception that their peers value gang criminality. That's what gang loitering laws attempt to do. . . . By preventing gangs from openly displaying their authority, such laws counteract the perception that gang members enjoy high status in the community. As that perception recedes, the perceived reputation pressure to join and emulate them should diminish. (1998b:820–821)

Here, the norm-focused hypothesis is that anti-gang loitering ordinances change the social meaning of gang membership, reducing its attractiveness and thereby reducing the amount of gang activity.

## Order-Maintenance Policing

Kahan and Meares also endorse the police strategy of order maintenance. Their analysis, again, starts with social meaning, here the meaning of order and disorder. Kahan writes that "[t]he effect of disorder on crime can be understood in terms of the effect that *social meaning* has on the mechanisms of *social influence*" (Kahan 1997a:370). Order, according to Kahan and Meares, means that the community has control of the neighborhood, that it will not tolerate criminality, and that it will enforce basic norms of civility. Conversely, disorder means that the community tolerates crime, that the neighborhood is unsafe, and that disorderly persons and criminals can and will take over. The social meaning of disorder makes a neighborhood vulnerable to crime. "By shaping preferences for crime, accentuating the perceived status of lawbreaking, and enfeebling the institutions that normally hold criminal propensities in check," Kahan and Meares argue, "disorderly norms create crime" (1998b:806).

The three key concepts, then, are social meaning, social norms, and social influence. The *social meaning* in question is the meaning of order and disorder. So, for instance, Kahan writes that "[d]isorder is . . . pregnant with meaning: Public drunkenness, prostitution, aggressive panhandling and similar behavior *signal* . . . that the community is unable or unwilling to enforce basic norms" (Kahan 1997a:370). Social meanings can have *social influence*, which is to say they can influence the behavior of individuals in society. In the order-maintenance context, the social meaning of disorder influences the disorderly to commit crimes and law abiders to leave the neighborhood. Conversely, the social meaning of order influences the disorderly to resist their inclination to commit crime, and influences law abiders to walk more freely in the streets at night. It is in this sense that Kahan writes: "Visible disorder . . . tells individuals that their own forbearance is unlikely to be reciprocated. . . . The meaning of disorder can also influence the behavior of committed law-abiders in a way that is likely to increase crime." In contrast, Kahan explains, "[w]hen citizens obey norms of orderliness—and when authorities visibly respond to those who don't—onlookers see that the community is intolerant of criminality. This message counteracts the inferences that point social influence in the direction of crime" (1997a:371). To take advantage of social influence, the *social norm* of orderliness must be enhanced. The idea is, as the previous passage suggests, that social influence may sway citizens to "obey norms of orderliness" (1997a:371). The norm of orderliness operates through social meaning to influence the kind of good behavior on the part of disorderly and honest people that will reduce crime. Social influence then has a feedback effect on social norms, influencing people to act in a more orderly manner. In this way, changing a social meaning may change social norms.

In the context of order-maintenance policing, then, order itself brings about a dynamic relationship between meaning and influence, a relationship that is illustrated in Figure 2.2. It is important to emphasize that there is a feedback mechanism in this explanation. Orderliness has a social meaning, which, by means of social influence, effectively promotes the norm of orderliness itself. The social norm explanation, accordingly, loops through the figure over and over.[2]

At the level of provocation, the New Progressives also take a page out of the Banfield-Wilson repertoire. In their writings, Kahan and Meares confront, head-on, the traditional racial coalitions of the civil rights era. They claim to speak on behalf of the African-American community *against* the American Civil Liberties Union. "[C]ircumstances have changed since 1960," they emphasize. "Today African-

Americans exercise considerable political clout in our nation's inner-cities; and far from being terrorized by anti-loitering laws, curfews and building searches, many inner-city residents *support* these measures as potent weapons against the crime that drastically diminishes their economic and social prospects" (Kahan and Meares 1999a:8). The New Progressives claim to speak for inner-city residents and to express what is really an unspoken and unrecognized majority within that minority. They have challenged liberal stereotypes and aggressively promoted a provocative, alternative vision of justice. They have been called "New Progressives" (Pildes 1999) precisely because they claim to advance the interests of inner-city residents and of the African-American community by challenging the central orthodoxies of the Warren Court and the civil rights movement.

And, not surprisingly, they elicit sharp responses. Some cheer them on enthusiastically. "In the lingo of the 1960s," Jean Bethke Elshtain writes, "right on!" (1999:11). Wesley Skogan calls them "brave" (1999:15). Others, however, read their work as neoconservative. "The measures that Meares and Kahan advocate are not so much about expanding black self-determination," Margaret Burnham writes, "as they are about expanding an already discredited approach to crime" (1999:17). Or, to borrow the title of Mark Tushnet's response essay, "Everything Old Is New Again" (1998). Whether "New Progressive" or neoconservative, they certainly share with Wilson and Banfield a knack for being provocative.

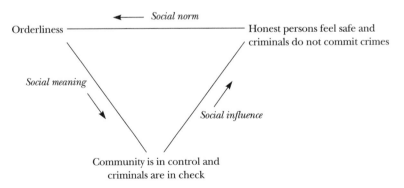

**Figure 2.2** Order-maintenance policing

## The "Revolution in American Policing"

The order-maintenance approach has not been limited to scholarly books, law review articles, and academic conferences. A number of the policy proposals have been implemented in large cities, including New York, Chicago, and Boston, and in smaller cities and rural areas. In many cases, in fact, it is new policing strategies that have triggered social norm theorizing, not the other way around. And the combination of theory and practice has been truly combustible. It has ignited what has been dubbed the "Blue Revolution," a "revolution in American policing" (Massing 1998:32; Nifong 1997).

At the outset, it is important to distinguish between these policing initiatives—order-maintenance crackdowns, anti-gang loitering ordinances, and youth curfews—and what is referred to as "community policing." Public officials, journalists, and commentators often blur the distinctions between these policing techniques, sometimes calling the social norm proposals "community policing," at other times drawing sharp distinctions. The slippage requires some attention.

"Community policing," at its most general level, stands for the idea that police officers can prevent crimes by integrating themselves into the community and solving community problems, rather than by merely responding to emergency calls. Community policing is prevention-oriented, in contrast to the earlier reform model—the model of professional crime fighting—which centered on the 911 strategy. It seeks to share with the public the tasks of problem identification, problem solving, and crime control. It is a means of developing increased communication between the police and the community (Fielding 1995:25; Kelling and Coles 1996:239; Moore, Trojanowicz, and Kelling 2000:53–55). In essence, community policing "consists of two complementary core components, community partnership and problem solving" (Community Policing Consortium 2000:118). It rests on the idea that "effective crime-fighting is based upon a 'partnership' between police and the residents of the immediate community they serve" (Spitzer 1999:47).

The difficulty is that "community policing" comes in a wide variety, and, as Kelling and Coles concede, "has come to mean all things to all people" (1996:158). Some understand community policing as a type of order maintenance whereby police officers maintain neighbor-hood order by aggressively arresting low-level offenders. Kelling and Coles, for instance, have characterized New York City's quality-of-life initiative as "community policing," though they are acutely aware of the tension (1996:109, 145, 161–163). Others understand community policing as a style of community integration in which the beat cop specifically withholds enforcement as a way to build community contacts. So, for instance, in Chicago, some police officers on the beat reportedly tolerate disorder so as to ingratiate themselves with the community (Eig 1996:63; see generally Skogan and Hartnett 1997).

The variations on the theme of community policing are wide. This may explain why community policing has swept police departments in the United States and abroad in the past few decades. In a 1994 National Institute of Justice survey of police departments, more than 80 percent of police chiefs polled stated that they were either implementing or intended to implement some aspect of community policing (McEwen 1995:27; see also Murphy 1992). The truth is, however, that the popularity and success of community policing is attributable in large part to the vagueness of the definition, to the national decline in crime beginning in the early 1990s, and to the fact that the expression "community policing" is far more effective for public relations purposes than other terms such as "aggressive misdemeanor arrests," "stop and frisk," or "mass building searches." It is important, then, to distinguish carefully between the specific types of community policing that are being discussed. For this reason, I will try to avoid using the term as much as possible, and turn instead to the more specific techniques of policing that make up the order-maintenance approach to criminal justice.

## New York City's "Quality-of-Life Initiative"

Rudolph Giuliani was elected mayor of New York City in 1993 on a platform that focused largely on crime, disorder, and quality-of-life issues, especially on the notorious "squeegee men." Giuliani appointed William Bratton police commissioner in December 1993, and together they soon began implementing a policing strategy called the "quality-of-life initiative," expressly premised on the broken windows theory

(Giuliani and Bratton 1994e:6). Both Giuliani and Bratton cite the "Broken Windows" essay as the main source of their initiative (Bratton 1995; Bratton 1996:785–789; Bratton 1998:138–139, 152, 192; Giuliani 1998 and 1999). In Bratton's words, the essay "articulated and put into beautiful words what I had found from experience. I supported what [Wilson and Kelling] wrote because I had already lived it" (Bratton 1998:139).

The quality-of-life initiative was modeled on Bratton's work in the New York subways. Bratton had first been appointed head of the New York Transit Police under Mayor David Dinkins in April 1990—recruited by George Kelling to implement a strategy of order maintenance based on the broken windows concept (Bratton 1998:140). From 1990 to 1992, Bratton implemented an aggressive policy of misdemeanor arrests in the subways. "We began to apply this ["Broken Windows"] concept to crime in the subways," he writes. "Fare evasion was the biggest broken window in the transit system. We were going to fix that window and see to it that it didn't get broken again" (1998:152). Bratton aggressively pursued turnstile jumpers with subway station mini-sweeps. In addition, he changed the procedure for arrests. Instead of issuing what were known as "desk-appearance tickets"—summonses which were generally disregarded—police officers began booking and processing suspects on the spot. Bratton initiated the "Bust Bus," a city bus that was "completely retrofitted . . . into an arrest-processing center" (1998:155). He made a number of other changes at the Transit Police, including revamping radio equipment, moving the force to nine-millimeter semiautomatic weapons, and designing new uniforms. These changes were all part of a $40 million infusion into the Transit Police in 1990 from Governor Mario Cuomo (1998:172–176).

As a result, ejections and arrests for misdemeanors both tripled within a few months of Bratton's appointment—and, in fact, continued to escalate through at least 1994 (Kelling and Coles 1996:132–133). As Bratton soon discovered, "many of those caught committing these small crimes were also guilty of larger crimes. One out of seven fare evaders had prior warrants out for their arrest. One out of 21 was carrying a handgun" (Kaplan 1997). The result was a sharp increase in arrests on outstanding warrants and gun possession (Purdy 1997). While the rate of arrests for felonies did not change, reported crimes in the subway declined by about 50 percent from 1990 to 1995 (Lardner 1995:56).

When Bratton took over as police commissioner in early 1994, he began implementing a similar policy aimed at creating public order by aggressively enforcing laws against quality-of-life offenses such as public drunkenness, loitering, vandalism, littering, public urination, panhandling, turnstile jumping, prostitution, and other minor misdemeanor offenses (Giuliani and Bratton 1994e:6).

Like the subway strategy, the quality-of-life initiative focused on aggressive arrests for minor misdemeanors (Giuliani and Bratton 1994e:39–40). And, as in the subways, Bratton implemented a change in arrest procedures at the citywide level (Giuliani and Bratton 1994e:9)—with similar results. "Very shortly into our program of dealing with squeegee operators—and I remember this—after the first group of arrests," Giuliani recalls, "Police Commissioner Bratton came back to me and said that some very large percentage—don't remember the exact percentage—of the squeegee operators had warrants for other crimes, a number of them being violence crimes" (Onishi 1998). As in the subways, the order-maintenance strategy began netting a lot of other arrests.

The quality-of-life initiative was one of a number of policing strategies that Bratton implemented during his two years as police commissioner. Other strategies targeted gun possession, school violence, drug dealing, domestic violence, auto theft, and police corruption (Giuliani and Bratton 1994a, 1994b, 1994c, 1994d, and 1994f; Bratton 1998:227–230). One other important initiative, for example, was called Operation Juggernaut, a strategy of flooding drug-infested neighborhoods with large numbers of police officers carrying out buy-and-bust operations, quality-of-life enforcement, and stops and frisks (Bratton 1998:272–278). Bratton shook up the NYPD in numerous other ways. He eliminated several layers of bureaucracy, appointed young and ambitious managers to top positions, and created a bottom-line mentality. He implemented a business school management-theory approach that brought him "a coterie of business school admirers" ("NYPD, Inc." 1995; see also Lardner 1995; Bratton 1998:224). He increased the power of precinct commanders and instituted biweekly meetings, known as Crime Control Strategy Meetings or Compstat (for computer-statistics) meetings, where the top administrators would grill precinct commanders on crime on their beat (Kelling and Coles 1996:146; Bratton 1998:233). But, in the words of Bratton himself, the quality-of-life initiative was the "linchpin strategy" (1998:228; see also Giuliani and Bratton 1994e:7).

Bratton's successor, Howard Safir, continued the strategy of aggressive misdemeanor arrests, and also promoted a more aggressive stop-and-frisk policy. In 1997 Safir tripled the size of the Street Crime Unit (SCU)—originally a small, specialized plainclothes enforcement unit created in the 1970s under Police Commissioner Patrick Murphy, which was refocused on gun-oriented policing under Bratton (Giuliani and Bratton 1994a:12, 16)—to about 400 officers, and sharpened even further its focus on getting guns off the street by means of aggressive stop-and-frisk procedures. Safir credited the unit with about 40 percent of all illegal gun confiscations in New York City in 1998. During 1998, the SCU, with only 435 officers out of a 40,000-member police force, was responsible for more than 10 percent of documented stop-and-frisk encounters citywide (Spitzer 1999:59). The unit stopped and frisked at least 45,000 people in 1997 and 1998 (Cooper 1999; Rosen 2000:26)—a conservative estimate based on *reported* searches only, which suggests that the real number was higher. The SCU received notorious attention in 1999 as a result of the shooting death of an unarmed man, Amadou Diallo, by four of its members. It has undergone changes since then, including a return to uniforms and an increase in the number of minority officers.

New York City's quality-of-life initiative has variously been called "order-maintenance policing," "community policing," "broken windows," and "zero tolerance."[3] Very little, though, turns on the question of nomenclature. Both Giuliani and Bratton have used the various terms interchangeably since the inception of the policing initiative. Clearly, the initiative was originally premised on the broken windows theory. Equally clearly, the implementation of the initiative revealed *other* justifications for its continued use. It has been continuously implemented in New York City in part because, it is believed, it promotes the broken windows theory and has produced increased orderliness in the city, but also because it has resulted in the arrest of suspects on outstanding warrants, as well as suspects linked to other crimes, and because it has functioned as a type of gun-oriented policing. In this sense, the most appropriate label for New York City's quality-of-life initiative is "order-maintenance" or "broken windows" policing.[4]

## Chicago's Anti-Gang Loitering Ordinance

In June 1992 the city of Chicago enacted an anti-gang loitering ordinance. The ordinance prohibited any person from loitering with one or more other persons whom the police reasonably believed to be a member of a street gang. Specifically, the ordinance provided that "[w]henever a police officer observes a person whom he reasonably believes to be a criminal street gang member loitering in any public place with one or more other persons, he shall order all such persons to disperse and remove themselves from the area. Any person who does not promptly obey such an order is in violation of this section." The ordinance defined loitering as "to remain in any one place with no apparent purpose." The ordinance subjected any violator to a fine, to imprisonment for not more than six months, to community service, or to some combination of the three (Chicago Municipal Code §8-4-015 [added June 17, 1992]).

The Chicago Police Department adopted implementing regulations in 1992, and began enforcing the ordinance gradually in 1993 through most of 1995. During the three-year period of implementation, the police issued over 89,000 orders to disperse and arrested over 42,000 persons under the ordinance (*Morales* 1999:49; Schulhofer and Alschuler 2000:7). In 1995 alone, the police made over 22,000 arrests under the ordinance (Schulhofer and Alschuler 2000:13).

Enforcement of the ordinance was enjoined in December 1995, when a state appellate court in Illinois ruled that the ordinance was unconstitutional for its vagueness, its overbreadth, and the fact that it criminalized the status of being a gang member (*Youkhana* 1995). The Illinois Supreme Court and the United States Supreme Court affirmed (*Morales* 1997 and 1999). Despite the temporary litigation setback, however, the city council of Chicago quickly got back to work on a new anti-gang loitering ordinance. Their task was made easy by Justice Sandra Day O'Connor, who, in a somewhat unusual maneuver for the Supreme Court, had telegraphed to the city council, in a concurring opinion in *Morales,* how they might redraft the ordinance. "The term

'loiter,'" O'Connor wrote, "might possibly be construed in a more limited fashion to mean 'to remain in any one place with no apparent
purpose other than to establish control over identifiable areas, to intimidate others from entering those areas, or to conceal illegal activities. Such a definition," O'Connor pregnantly suggested, "would avoid
the vagueness problems of the ordinance as construed by the Illinois
Supreme Court" (*Morales* 1999:68).

Not surprisingly, the revised draft of the anti-gang loitering ordinance, which was passed by the city council in February 2000, by a vote
of 44 to 5 (Fingeret 2000), defines "gang loitering" as remaining in any
one place when the purpose is "to enable a criminal street gang to
establish control over identifiable areas, to intimidate others from entering those areas, or to conceal illegal activities" (Chicago Municipal Code §8–4–015[d][1] [added February 16, 2000]). The revised
ordinance limits enforcement to high-crime neighborhoods, as designated by the police superintendent. It specifies the time period—
three hours—during which the dispersal order remains in effect. And
it adds a sentence enhancement for repeat offenders. The sentencing
provision of the ordinance was revised to read:

(e) Any person who fails to obey promptly an order [to disperse] under
section (a), or who engages in further gang loitering within sight or
hearing of the place at which such an order was issued during the three
hour period following the time the order was issued, is subject to a fine
of not less than $100 and not more than $500 for each offense, or imprisonment for not more than six months for each offense, or both. A
second or subsequent offense shall be punishable by a mandatory minimum sentence of not less than five days imprisonment.

In addition to or instead of the above penalties, any person who violates this section may be required to perform up to 120 hours of community service. (§8–4–015[e])

The Chicago police started arresting people under the new ordinance in August 2000 (Belluck 2000). In addition, the Chicago council passed, at the same time, a narcotics-related anti-loitering ordinance very similar to the anti-gang ordinance. It too provided for a
sentence enhancement for habitual offenders (Chicago Municipal
Code §8–4–017 [added February 16, 2000]). These are but two of

dozens of targeted anti-loitering ordinances that were enacted in the 1990s (Johnson 2000:A14).

## Youth Curfews

Youth curfews are another very popular measure. In a 1997 survey of 347 cities conducted by the United States Conference of Mayors, 276 were found to have enacted a youth curfew; 190 of those had been enacted within the previous ten years (U.S. Conference of Mayors 1997; Beaumont 1998). Since 1990, 90 cities with populations over 100,000 have either enacted a new curfew or modified an existing one. Moreover, four out of five cities with a population over 30,000 have curfews today (Privor 1999:420).

Youth curfews are especially popular among mayors and city officials. When these officials were polled in the Conference of Mayors survey, 93 percent of the cities surveyed responded that curfews are useful. About 80 percent reported that curfews had made the streets safer for residents, and most had found that the curfews had resulted in decreased traffic at night, increased security for residents, and a decline in graffiti and vandalism. More than 80 percent of cities surveyed stated that the curfews helped to curb gang violence. These cities found that the curfews were an effective tool to reach potential gang members and that the curfews had helped to educate parents as to the signs of gang membership. Only nineteen surveyed cities reported that curfews were not useful. Twelve percent of the cities surveyed reported that curfews had no impact on street safety, noting that it is people over the age of seventeen who commit the most serious crime, and that the curfews are typically not enforced owing to lack of city resources (U.S. Conference of Mayors 1997).

## Other Policy Initiatives

Police departments, municipalities, and courts have experimented with other order-maintenance and norm-focused strategies. In Chicago, for instance, the Housing Authority (CHA) began conducting mass building searches in September 1988. Between 1988 and 1994, the CHA, with the aid of the Chicago police and other law enforcement agencies, conducted searches of at least sixty buildings (Kirby

1994). In 1993 the CHA instituted an unwritten policy of conducting warrantless searches of entire buildings if random gunfire occurred in the area. This resulted in the warrantless searches, in the summer of 1993, of several public housing projects, including the Robert Taylor Homes and Stateway Gardens (O'Connor 1994). The searches prompted the American Civil Liberties Union to file a federal lawsuit. On February 14, 1995, United States District Judge Wayne Anderson issued a temporary injunction barring the searches, and on August 16, 1995, the injunction was made permanent ("Injunction Forbids Sweeps by CHA" 1995). According to the *Chicago Tribune*, the CHA has been attempting to get residents to agree formally to allow searches of their apartments as a rider to the standard lease, though residents were not being denied housing for failing to sign the agreement. The ACLU was planning to challenge this effort (Crawford 1994).

In Charleston, South Carolina, the chief of police implemented a juvenile snitching policy specifically designed to keep firearms away from schools. The *New York Times* reported, "With money from several local businesses, the Charleston police will now pay $100 to any student who provides information on a person who has an illegal handgun in a public place" (Butterfield 1996). Other cities, including Boston, have also implemented order-maintenance crackdowns as part of larger strategies to combat juvenile gun carrying (Kennedy 1998:5).[5]


These are some of the diverse strands that together make up the order-maintenance approach to criminal justice. There are, of course, important differences between the various theories and practices. The New Progressives, for example, do not advocate, like James Q. Wilson, incapacitating increased numbers of repeat offenders for lengthier periods of time. In fact, it is precisely *against* this trend in criminal justice that Kahan and Meares revolted. Similarly, the New Progressives do not talk about "lower-class" individuals—even with the caveat, which Banfield repeatedly insisted upon, that "lower-class" is not a proxy term for "black" or "poor" (1974:235). To the contrary, the New Progressives boldly speak on behalf of inner-city residents and the African-

American community. They claim to represent these communities and to be working on their behalf to improve their living conditions.

Despite these important differences, the tradition of Banfield and Wilson and the New Progressives have a lot in common, especially at the conceptual level. What they share is the desire to build on and enrich the classical model of criminology. They all seek to enrich the economic notion of preferences. Banfield accomplished this with concepts such as "lower-class individuals," "present-orientedness," and "amoral familism"; Wilson by focusing on "human nature"; social norm theorists by developing social meaning and expressive preferences. They also all seek to broaden the range of opportunities. Banfield and Wilson oriented their policy discussions toward reshaping situational factors; the New Progressives enrich the conception of opportunities by focusing on social meaning and possible changes in meaning. In addition, these various intellectual traditions share an important focus on the social norm and meaning of orderliness. Their central insight is that order in a community may influence the behavior of neighborhood residents and outsiders in such a way as to improve the quality of life in the neighborhood and decrease serious criminal activity. And their insights have met with overwhelming popularity.

# PART I

# Empirical Critique

Broken windows policing has become conventional wisdom in this country and is being exported abroad to Australia and to countries in Europe, South America, Asia, and Africa (Dixon 1999; Wacquant 1999:22–27). The national and international allure of order maintenance is truly astonishing. In 1998 alone, representatives of over 200 police departments—more than 150 of them from foreign countries—visited the New York Police Department for briefings and instruction in New York–style policing. During the first ten months of 2000, another 235 police departments—85 percent of them from abroad—sent delegations to police headquarters in New York City (Gootman 2000).

Journalists, academics, policy makers, and many in the general public believe that the broken windows theory has been proven. Many proponents specifically claim that the theory has been empirically established (Giuliani and Bratton 1994e:6; Kelling and Coles 1996:24–25; Kahan 1997a:369; Kahan and Meares 1998b:822). The surprising fact, though, is that the broken windows effect has never been verified. More important, as I will demonstrate in Chapter 3, the existing social-scientific data suggest that the theory is probably not right.

Now, it is important to place this empirical discussion in context. The truth is that many theoretical accounts in politics, criminal justice, and public policy are not validated, but that usually does not stop us from implementing those policies. I do not intend to hold the broken windows theory to an unrealistically high empirical standard. My purpose, instead, is to begin to get the facts straight and to place the theoretical discussion of order maintenance on its proper empirical footing. The fact is that the order-maintenance approach *does* generate a number of significant empirical questions. Is it true that order-maintenance policing reduces the level of serious criminal activity in a neighborhood? If it does reduce serious crime, is it really the social meaning of order, and not some other feature of order-maintenance policing, that causes the decline in crime? Is there any evidence that anti-gang loitering ordinances or juvenile snitching policies reduce criminal gang activity or juvenile gun possession? These are important issues that raise both empirical and methodological questions. It is fair and appropriate to ask at this point exactly how much evidence supports the order maintenance approach. I turn first, in Chapter 3, to an empirical assessment of the social-scientific evidence supporting the broken windows theory. I then review, in Chapter 4, the evidence concerning specific police initiatives, including New York City's quality-of-life initiative, Chicago's anti-gang loitering ordinance, and Charleston's juvenile snitching program. I also assess there the empirical evidence from a larger methodological perspective.

# CHAPTER 3

# The Broken Windows Theory

Order maintenance advocates generally refer to two social science studies to support the broken windows theory. The first is Wesley Skogan's 1990 *Disorder and Decline: Crime and the Spiral of Decay in American Neighborhoods*. The second is a 1988 study by Robert Sampson and Jacqueline Cohen titled "Deterrent Effect of the Police on Crime: A Replication and Theoretical Extension." In this chapter I review and assess these two studies and then turn to a more recent study on the disorder-crime nexus, Robert Sampson and Stephen Raudenbush's "Systematic Social Observation of Public Spaces: A New Look at Disorder in Urban Neighborhoods" (1999).

## Replicating Skogan's 1990 Study

Working with Wesley Skogan's data, which are available through the Inter-University Consortium for Political and Social Research at the University of Michigan (Skogan 1988), I was able to assess his data and replicate his analysis. The discussion of the replication is somewhat technical, and in order to facilitate the transition to statistics, I will begin by summarizing in lay terms the thrust of my assessment of Skogan's study, before turning in more detail to the regression analysis.

The portion of Wesley Skogan's study that is of particular interest to the broken windows debate is his discussion of the relationship between neighborhood disorder and crime victimization. To get at that relationship, Skogan explored whether neighborhoods that were perceived as disorderly by residents also suffered from high levels of criminal activity. The idea was to see if there was a statistical connection between the level of disorder in a neighborhood and the amount of crime in that same neighborhood. To measure disorder, Skogan relied on surveys that asked neighborhood residents whether they thought that certain physical and social disorders—such as litter or vandalism—were a problem in their neighborhoods. To measure crime, Skogan relied on surveys that asked neighborhood residents whether they had been the victim of different types of crime—burglary, robbery, rape, assault, and purse-snatching. Overall, Skogan found that there was a strong connection between residents' perceptions of neighborhood disorder and their robbery victimization, even when he took account of the level of poverty and stability in the neighborhood and the race of the residents. He concluded from this finding that disorder played an important role in neighborhood crime and urban decline.

I have a number of reservations about the data and about the design of Skogan's study. As a preliminary matter, Skogan's data are weak. Skogan patched together his data from five separate studies that were not entirely consistent, and as a result the study is missing a large amount of information. Robbery victimization is available in only thirty neighborhoods, and the disorder information is missing on average 30 to 40 percent of the time. The first point, then, is that the data are not reliable.

But even more troubling is the fact that Skogan failed to disclose that there is no real connection between disorder and crime with regard to the other four crime variables in his study. Skogan focused on robbery victimization—where he found a connection with disorder—but failed to reveal that there is no similar connection between disorder and burglary, rape, physical assault, or purse-snatching victimization. In other words, in four out of five tests, there is no real connection between disorder and crime. Moreover, on close analysis, it turns out that the one place where there is a connection—the disorder-robbery nexus—is itself questionable. First, the survey question that was posed to neighborhood residents about robbery victimization was not neighborhood specific. In other words, the question did not specify that the robbery victimization had to occur in the neighborhood in question, so as a result, it may have occurred in another neighborhood. Second, and more important, there is a set of five neighbor-hoods in Newark that exert excessive influence on Skogan's findings. When we take away those Newark neighborhoods, the tenuous connection to robbery disappears.

As a result, Skogan's study does not support the broken windows hypothesis. In four out of five tests, there is no real connection between disorder and various crimes. In the only test where there is a connection, the nexus is itself highly questionable. It is fair to conclude that Skogan's study does not prove a connection between disorder and crime in general. As I suggested earlier, the details of this analysis are somewhat technical in nature. I summarize this discussion at the end of this chapter, as well as at the beginning of Part II, for those readers who may wish to move ahead to the discussion of New York City's quality-of-life initiative in Chapter 4 or to social theory in Chapter 5.

## Skogan's Method and Findings

On the basis of data collected in five separate studies between 1977 and 1983, Skogan found, inter alia, that neighborhood disorder had a statistically significant relationship with the level of robbery victimization. This finding is only one piece of a much larger work on disorder and urban decline. With regard to crime, Skogan discusses and verifies several other hypotheses, for instance, that there is a link between disorder and fear of crime victimization,[1] as well as a link between disorder and perception of crime problems.[2] But I will treat exclusively the disorder-crime nexus, since this is the finding that relates most directly to and, according to proponents, empirically establishes the broken windows theory.

Skogan's data come from five previously existing studies, which he aggregates and merges to produce neighborhood-level data of disorder, crime rates, and socioeconomic factors (Skogan 1987:8). The five existing data sets consist of thirteen thousand personal and telephone interviews conducted between 1977 and 1983 (1987:6, 97). The respondents were residents of forty different neighborhoods in six cities: Chicago, Newark, Houston, Philadelphia, San Francisco, and Atlanta. Random-digit dialing was used to select respondents for the telephone interviews, and random selection from address lists for the personal interviews (1987:99 fig. 25; 1990:190).

Skogan performs two analyses to assess the disorder-crime nexus.

First, he regresses the rate of robbery victimization on the level of disorder. Second, he regresses the rate of robbery victimization on the level of disorder taking into account the level of poverty, residential stability, and the racial composition of the neighborhoods.

### The Disorder-Robbery Regression Analysis

With regard to the simple regression of robbery victimization on the level of disorder, Skogan finds that "levels of crime victimization were strongly related (+.80) to levels of disorder in the 30 areas for which robbery victimization was measured" (1987:53; 1990:73). He does not report his coefficients, but does include a graph showing the regression line running through the observations on a scatter plot: x-axis level of disorder, y-axis percent victims of robbery (1990:74 fig. 4–2). The scatter plot indicates a positive relationship between disorder and robbery victimization.

### The Other-Explanatory-Variables Analysis

Skogan then conducts further analysis to take into account the effect of neighborhood poverty, stability, and race. The measures of poverty and stability are indices composed of weighted factors such as average length of residence, percentage of rental dwellings, and percentage of incomes over $20,000 (1987:22 fig. 4; 1990:192 table A–3–1). Race is measured by the variable corresponding to respondents' answers about their race, and reflects the percentage of minorities in the community (1987:25–19; 1988:14). Skogan finds that the correlation between robbery victimization and disorder remains high (+.54) even when these three other explanatory variables are taken into account (1987:53; 1990:73–74).

### Skogan's Conclusion

Skogan prefaces his findings with a significant caveat. In effect, he begins by saying that the data do little to illuminate the causal relationship:

> Ironically, the data from the 40 neighborhoods cannot shed a great deal of light on the details of the relationship between disorder and crime, for the measures all go together very strongly. With only 40 cases to untangle this web, the high correlation between measures of victimization, ratings of crime problems, and disorder make it difficult to tell

whether they have either separate "causes" or separate "effects" at the area level. (1990:73; see also Skogan 1987:49)

Nevertheless, in response to the broad question "Does disorder cause crime?" Skogan ultimately concludes: "These data support the proposition that disorder needs to be taken seriously in research on neighborhood crime, and that both directly and through crime it plays an important role in neighborhood decline. 'Broken windows' do need to be repaired quickly" (1990:75; see also Skogan 1987:53).

Despite his initial caveat, then, Skogan asserts that there is a causal relationship between levels of neighborhood disorder and rates of crime, and so concludes:

> The evidence suggests that poverty, instability, and the racial composition of neighborhoods are strongly linked to area crime, but a substantial portion of that linkage is through disorder: their link to area crime virtually disappears when disorder is brought into the picture. This too is consistent with Wilson and Kelling's original proposition, and further evidence that direct action against disorder could have substantial payoffs. (1990:75)

Not surprisingly, Skogan's study has been consistently interpreted by broken windows proponents as establishing the disorder-crime nexus.

## Skogan's Findings: A Replication

Before turning to a critique of Skogan's study, I will first set forth his findings in greater detail. In order to do this, it is necessary to replicate the study because Skogan does not provide most of the quantities of interest in either the more technical *Final Report* or in his book *Disorder and Decline* (1987:52–53; 1990:73–75).

### The Disorder-Robbery Regression

Although Skogan does not share his regression coefficients or standard errors, it is possible to estimate them by replication and verify them by comparing the scatter plot that he published in *Disorder and Decline* (1990:74 fig. 4–2) with the one that I obtain using his data. The scatter plot that I obtain is, in all pertinent respects, identical to Skogan's.[3] The replicated graph is shown in Figure 3.1.

Given that the scatter plots are identical, I am comfortable using

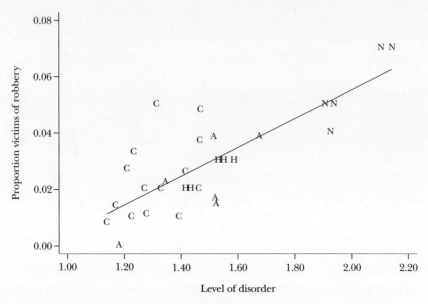

**Figure 3.1** Replication of Skogan's figure 4–2

my replication to estimate the coefficients and standard errors of Skogan's analysis. What the regression reveals is that, for every one-unit increase in the level of disorder (where, as I discuss later, a unit is one of three unit measures of the level of disorder felt by the respondents), the proportion of victims of robbery in the neighborhood can be expected to increase by 0.05 (5 percent) on average, with a standard error of plus or minus 0.007. The 95 percent confidence interval has, as a result, a small range, with a lower bound of 0.036 and an upper bound of 0.066. The p-value (which is the probability of observing a t-statistic of 6.953, assuming that the null hypothesis is true) is extremely small in this case—less than 0.001—which means that it is extremely unlikely that there is no statistical relationship. As a result, we can conclude that there is a near-zero probability that an estimate of 0.05 could have arisen by chance alone if there truly were no linear relationship between Skogan's variables for disorder and crime.[4]

*The Other-Explanatory-Variables Analysis*
Skogan's second analysis takes account of the level of poverty, stability, and racial composition of the neighborhoods. In this case, Skogan did publish his coefficients and levels of significance, and I have been able

to reproduce them substantially (1990:193 table A–4–1). A comparison of Skogan's and my results is given in Table 3.1.

Skogan interprets his results as follows: "The correlation between *residual* values for robbery victimization and disorder, once the effects of poverty, stability, and racial composition had been removed statistically from each, was still high (+.54)" (1990:73). He concludes that "ignoring these demographic factors, there still was quite a strong tendency for crime and disorder to 'go together'" (1990:74; see also 1987:53).

The replication confirms that Skogan's disorder index remains statistically significant when multiple regression is conducted with his indices for poverty, stability, and race. The replicated regression indicates that, if we hold those three other variables constant, for every one-unit increase in the level of disorder, the proportion of victims of robbery in the neighborhood can be expected to increase by 0.038 on average (3.8 percent), with a standard error of plus or minus 0.012. The 95 percent confidence interval has, as a result, a small range, with a lower bound of 0.014 and an upper bound of 0.062.

## Problems with the Data and Certain Design Decisions

Certain problems with the data and some design decisions undermine my confidence in Skogan's findings and conclusions. I begin with the issue of missing values.

### Missing Values

A number of the underlying surveys are missing values for most of the important variables relating to the disorder-crime nexus. For instance,

Table 3.1: Replication of Skogan's table A–4–1

| | Robbery victimization | | | | |
|---|---|---|---|---|---|
| | Skogan | | Replication | | |
| Measure | Standardized coefficient | Significance | Coefficient | Standardized coefficient | Significance |
| Poverty score | .05 | .78 | .00 | .04 | .78 |
| Stability score | −.04 | .82 | .00 | −.04 | .79 |
| Percent minority | .23 | .20 | .01 | .23 | .19 |
| Disorder | .58 | .008 | .04 | .60 | .004 |

the 1981 study by Skogan and Michael Maxfield—which is the only study that covers neighborhoods in Philadelphia and San Francisco—does not have any values for noise, litter, trash, gangs, public drinking, and insults, which are among the main variables in Skogan's index of physical and social disorder (Skogan 1987:18). With a few rare exceptions, missing values actually plague all of the studies and all of the relevant variables to different degrees, as evidenced in Table 3.2. As this table reflects, the data are missing values, on average, for between 30 and 40 percent of the variables, which is a high percentage given the small sample size (forty neighborhoods in all).

The more traditional way of dealing with this problem of missing values would be to disregard completely the neighborhoods for which values are missing But that is not possible with this data set. In the case of Skogan's indices of physical and social disorder, it is impossible because there is not one single neighborhood that has all the values for the relevant variables. As a result, Skogan does not disregard any neighborhood, but rather constructs his indices "by summing the

**Table 3.2** Missing values in Skogan's data set

| | | Physical disorder | | | |
|---|---|---|---|---|---|
| | Noise | Abandoned buildings or vehicles | Litter | Trash | Total |
| No. missing | 20 | 0 | 24 | 16 | 60 |
| % missing | 50 | 0 | 60 | 40 | 37.5 |

| | | | Social disorder | | | |
|---|---|---|---|---|---|---|
| | Loitering | Drugs | Vandalism | Gangs | Public drinking | Insults | Total |
| No. missing | 8 | 6 | 24 | 24 | 24 | 10 | 96 |
| % missing | 20 | 15 | 60 | 60 | 60 | 25 | 40 |

| | | Crime victimization | | | |
|---|---|---|---|---|---|
| | Purse-snatching | Assault | Burglary | Robbery | Rape | Total |
| No. missing | 24 | 10 | 0 | 10 | 16 | 60 |
| % missing | 60 | 25 | 0 | 25 | 40 | 30 |

component items which were available for each area and then dividing that sum by the number of available items" (1988:8; see also Skogan 1987:108). In other words, Skogan simply averages the values that are available—which raises another problem discussed later. Aggregation, however, does not resolve the problem of missing values.

It is equally difficult to disregard the observations where crime victimization data are missing because to do so would leave us with only sixteen neighborhoods—just 40 percent of our original small sample. This, however, is essentially what Skogan does with regard to victimization, using only the robbery victimization variable and therefore narrowing his study to only thirty available observations (Skogan 1990:73–75; see also Skogan 1987:50–53). The result is that, at least with regard to the disorder-crime nexus, Skogan's is a study of a small sample of neighborhoods with many missing values of disorder.

*Selecting the Independent Variable*
The independent variable that Skogan employs is also problematic and may include, in my opinion, elements of the dependent variable. Skogan's independent variable is called "disorder," and he constructs it by averaging two multi-item scales, "social disorder" and "physical disorder" (Skogan 1988:7–8). These are both constructed by averaging the values of a number of variables, each of which corresponds to respondents' answers (on a scale of 1 to 3) to a question assessing the extent to which a certain type of disorder is perceived by them as a problem in their neighborhood (Skogan 1988:6–8). The variables included in the two multi-item scales[5] are the following:

| Social disorder | Physical disorder |
| --- | --- |
| Loitering | Noise |
| Drug use and sale | Abandoned buildings or vehicles |
| Vandalism | Litter |
| Gang activity | Trash in vacant lots |
| Public drinking | |
| Insulting language | |

So, for instance, in the case of the litter variable, respondents would have been asked to assess the extent to which "garbage or litter on the streets and sidewalks" is a problem in the neighborhood (Skogan 1988:7). For all of these variables, the possible values range from 1 ("no problem") to 2 ("some problem") to 3 ("a big problem") (1988:6). The two multi-item scales were constructed "by summing the component items which were available for each area and then dividing that sum by the number of available items" (1988:8).

Using respondents' assessment of drug trafficking or gang activity, however, presents a significant problem given that the dependent variable is supposed to be the level of *serious* criminal activity. In this respect the analysis would be tautological, because some of these disorderly activities—such as drug trafficking or certain gang activities— would be considered by respondents to be major crimes in themselves and are thus likely to trigger responses that assess the level of crime in the neighborhood.

To be precise, the broken windows theory suggests that minor disorder, both physical (in the sense of litter and broken windows) and social (in the sense of minor misdemeanor offenses) is causally related to serious crime. Therefore, the independent variable (disorder) should not include—or should exclude as much as possible—serious criminal activity. Some degree of overlap is inevitable, given that the respondents may be thinking about criminal activity when they assess, for instance, the problem of abandoned buildings, which have become a symbol of the crack house. It is crucial, however, to reduce the overlap as thoroughly as possible. Accordingly, it would probably be best to eliminate drug trafficking and gang activity from the independent variable.

A second problem with Skogan's independent variable results from missing values. Creating the index by simply averaging the existing values for the set of variables may produce bias. For instance, the mean for the noise variable is 1.3, while the mean for the public drinking variable is 1.8. As a result, neighborhoods for which there is no value for noise may end up having higher values for the disorder index than they would otherwise, whereas neighborhoods for which there is no value for public drinking may end up having lower values for the disorder index than they would otherwise. This potential for bias could be resolved by standardizing the variables on their means.

Third, Skogan excluded from his indices four measures of disorder that were available from the data. These were the variables "smut" (adult movies and bookstores); "prostitution"; "dogs" ("barking loudly or relieving themselves near your home"); and "garbage" ("[p]eople

not disposing of garbage properly or leaving litter around the area")
(Skogan 1988:6–7). He compiled these four variables under the head-
ing "Measures of Disorder," but did not include them in his index for
two reasons. With regard to the commercial sex variables, Skogan discovered that they were independent measures of disorder. He writes:

> At the individual level, reactions to these problems [prostitution and
> smut] formed a separate factor in every area in which they were in-
> cluded. A separate index of the extent of *commercial sex problems* was
> formed, but—as the status of the items as a separate factor hints—it was
> correlated only +.18 with the summary disorder measure and was not
> related to other neighborhood factors in the same fashion as either so-
> cial or physical disorder. . . . As a result, this cluster of (very interesting)
> problems will not be considered in any detail in this report. (1987:19)

In addition, Skogan suggests that the questions were asked in too few
cases.

Yet neither of these reasons for excluding the commercial sex variables from the index of disorder is compelling. The fact that the commercial sex variables are independent of the other indices of disorder
is not a reason to ignore those variables. The broken windows theory
includes prostitution in its conception of disorder. In fact, the "Broken
Windows" essay repeatedly refers to prostitutes and street prostitution.
As we saw in Chapter 2, they are an integral part of the disorderly and
of disorder. The fact that these "very interesting"—I would say fascinating—findings about commercial sex are at odds with the broken windows theory is not a reason to discard the variables, particularly when
one is testing the theory's validity.[6] Moreover, the smut and prostitution variables contain sixteen observations each, the same number as,
for instance, litter, public drinking, or vandalism. The dogs and garbage variables are missing only two more observations. I therefore
would not exclude those variables.

*Selecting the Dependent Variable*
The biggest problem with Skogan's design, however, concerns the selection of the dependent variable. Skogan is interested in measuring
the impact of disorder on *crime,* and throughout his book he claims
to be studying the relationship between disorder and *crime.* The passage in his book is, after all, titled "Disorder, Crime, and Fear," and

the principal paragraph is captioned "Disorder and Common Crime" (1990:73). The repeated reference to the statistical findings are to the "crime-disorder connection" or the "relationship between disorder and crime" (1990:73–74). Another caption reads "Does Disorder Cause Crime?" (1990:75). It would appear from all this that Skogan's study relates to general crime levels.

Skogan, however, selects as the dependent variable only *one* crime, namely robbery, even though the data include a number of other crimes, such as purse-snatching, physical assault, burglary, and sexual assault. This is especially troubling because robbery victimization, it turns out, is one of the crime victimization variables with the *highest* relationship to neighborhood disorder, and, even more important, is the *only* crime victimization variable that remains statistically significantly related to disorder when neighborhood poverty, stability, and race are held constant.

With regard to the crime-disorder regression, robbery, burglary, and physical assault have extremely low p-values, which suggests that they are statistically significantly related to disorder. Sexual assault has a very high p-value (0.66), which signifies that in all likelihood it is not related to disorder; purse-snatching/pocket-picking appears to be only marginally related to disorder, but in an inverse relationship, which suggests that, if anything, it might be inversely related to disorder. This is demonstrated in Table 3.3.

What is even more troubling, however, is that the statistical relationships regarding physical assault and burglary *vanish* if neighborhood poverty, stability, and race are held constant. Robbery victimization is the *only* variable that remains related to disorder if we take socioeco-

Table 3.3 Coefficients for Skogan's index of disorder and individual crimes

| Crime | Skogan's index of disorder | | | | |
|---|---|---|---|---|---|
| | Coefficient | Standard error | P-value | 95% Conf. interva |  |
| Purse snatching | −0.025 | 0.017 | 0.160 | −0.061 | 0.011 |
| Physical assault | 0.055 | 0.014 | 0.000 | 0.027 | 0.08￼ |
| Burglary | 0.076 | 0.025 | 0.004 | 0.026 | 0.126 |
| Robbery | 0.051 | 0.007 | 0.000 | 0.036 | 0.066 |
| Sexual assault | 0.001 | 0.003 | 0.659 | −0.005 | 0.008 |

nomic factors into account. The coefficients are reproduced in Table 3.4. As this table demonstrates, it would be improper to conclude from the data that, as a statistical matter, general levels of *crime*—or *common crime*—and disorder are related. Even if we put aside all the problems with the data set, the data suggest that only *one* particular crime, namely *robbery*, may be statistically related to disorder.

Skogan justifies using robbery victimization exclusively as an index of local levels of crime for the following reasons: "Methodological research suggests it is reliably measured; it tends to correspond better than many other victimization measures with comparable official crime statistics; aggregate city-level studies indicate it is linked to fear of crime; and comparable measures of robbery victimization were included in 30 of the areas surveyed" (1990:195 n.1, chap. 4). On close scrutiny, however, these arguments are not entirely persuasive.

First, robbery victimization is not the only measure that corresponds well with comparable official crime statistics. Burglary does, too. This is generally explained by the fact that the most powerful predictor of whether a crime is reported to the police appears to be the seriousness of the offense (Gove, Hughes, and Geerken 1985:479, 468). Second, with regard to rape and physical assault, victimization surveys substantially underreport incidences among acquaintances, friends, and relatives, and they therefore measure very different things than do the Uniform Crime Reports (Gove, Hughes, and Geerken 1985:464–465). But this fact does not address the *cross-jurisdictional reliability* of victimization surveys for rape or physical assault. The same biases might affect cross-jurisdictional comparisons of victimization surveys and of

**Table 3.4** Coefficients for Skogan's index of disorder and individual crimes holding constant neighborhood poverty, stability and race

| Crime | Skogan's index of disorder | | | | |
|---|---|---|---|---|---|
| | Coefficient | Standard error | P-value | 95% Conf. interval | |
| Purse snatching | −0.013 | 0.027 | 0.639 | −0.072 | 0.046 |
| Physical assault | 0.014 | 0.019 | 0.459 | −0.025 | 0.054 |
| Burglary | −0.006 | 0.035 | 0.875 | −0.078 | 0.066 |
| Robbery | 0.038 | 0.012 | 0.004 | 0.014 | 0.062 |
| Sexual assault | 0.006 | 0.006 | 0.341 | −0.007 | 0.019 |

official crime statistics (Gove, Hughes, and Geerken 1985:466). The issue presented here is not the comparability of victimization surveys and official crime statistics, which is what Skogan discusses. The issue is the comparability of victimization surveys across neighborhoods. It is the cross-jurisdictional reliability of victimization surveys.[7] Third, as a technical matter, there are *no* missing values for burglary victimization in the data, whereas there are ten missing values for robbery—and as many for physical assault. This fact would militate in favor of using burglary as the dependent variable.

Fourth, and most important, it appears from the *Final Report* and the *Codebook* (Skogan 1987 and 1988) that the measure of robbery victimization is *not* neighborhood specific. Whereas the typical purse-snatching question[8] and assault question[9] explicitly referred the interviewee to acts committed "in the neighborhood where you live now," and whereas the typical burglary question was by definition neighborhood specific, the robbery question[10] and the rape question[11] apparently did not specify the location of the attack. In other words, it is possible that the robbery and rape questions could have been interpreted by the interviewee as referring to incidents that happened *outside* their neighborhood. This militates even more in favor of using the burglary variable.

Skogan's arguments do not fully address these concerns. In my opinion, if we are going to draw conclusions about the effect of disorder on *common crime* or *general levels of crime,* it may be more conservative to look at each substantive crime for which we have data and make a more nuanced assessment of the disorder-crime relationship.

*The Newark Effect*

As noted earlier, all of Skogan's statistically significant relationships between disorder and the individual substantive crimes vanish when neighborhood poverty, stability, and race are held constant, *except for robbery.* The only reason robbery remains statistically significant, it turns out, is Newark. If you look at Skogan's figure 4–2, or my replication in Figure 3.1, you will notice that the five Newark neighborhoods, in contrast to the other city neighborhoods, are clustered together (Skogan 1990:74 fig. 4–2). If you disregard those five Newark observations and look at the other twenty-five neighborhoods, the relationship between disorder and robbery victimization seems much less obvious.

And, in fact, it is. If the same three explanatory variables (poverty, stability, and race) are held constant, there is *no significant relationship* between disorder and robbery victimization when the five Newark neighborhoods are excluded. I call this the Newark Effect, and it is summarized in Table 3.5. In fact, without the Newark neighborhoods, the relationship between robbery victimization and disorder vanishes if race alone is held constant; see Table 3.6.

As Tables 3.5 and 3.6 demonstrate, the statistically significant relationship between disorder and robbery in the data is principally due to the five Newark neighborhoods that are clustered together. In contrast, the other neighborhoods from the three other cities for which data are available (Atlanta, Chicago, and Houston) are pretty well distributed in the remaining group of observations. What this means is that, when the five Newark neighborhoods are included in a data set that contains only twenty-five other neighborhoods, Newark has a significant impact on the equation. In fact, if we take account of the *city effects* on the neighborhood data, the statistical relationship between

le 3.5  The Newark Effect: coefficients for Skogan's index of disorder and robbery victimization excluding Newark neighborhoods and holding constant poverty, stability and race

| planatory variables | Robbery | | | | |
| --- | --- | --- | --- | --- | --- |
| | Coefficient | Standard error | P-value | 95% Conf. Interval | |
| sorder | .011 | .025 | .670 | −.042 | .063 |
| verty | .001 | .003 | .741 | −.006 | .008 |
| bility | −.002 | .003 | .517 | −.008 | .004 |
| ce | .014 | .008 | .109 | −.003 | .031 |

le 3.6  The Newark Effect: coefficients for Skogan's index of disorder and robbery victimization excluding Newark neighborhoods and holding only race constant

| planatory variables | Robbery | | | | |
| --- | --- | --- | --- | --- | --- |
| | Coefficient | Standard error | P-value | 95% Conf. interval | |
| sorder | .021 | .018 | .256 | −.016 | .058 |
| ce | .015 | .007 | .056 | .000 | .030 |

disorder and robbery disappears (again, holding constant poverty, stability, and race). If we hold constant the effects of the different cities on the neighborhood data by using dummy variables for the cities, the relationship simply vanishes: if we assign a dummy variable to each city, the p-value rises to 0.195, and if we assign a dummy variable to Newark alone, the p-value reaches 0.436. Clearly, there is something about the city of Newark that is unduly influencing the relationship between disorder and robbery victimization at the neighborhood level.

Is it fair, then, to exclude the Newark neighborhoods, given that there are only thirty observations in all? I think so. Given the small number of observations, it is especially important to eliminate cases that exert too much influence on the findings.[12] The Newark data seem to do just that. The point here is that it is not an individual neighborhood per se but the Newark cluster that excessively influences the results. What does it mean to have the relationship between disorder and robbery depend entirely on whether the Newark neighborhoods are in or out of the data set? It suggests that certain characteristics about Newark are skewing the results.[13] It means that there is a *city* effect, rather than a *neighborhood* effect. But that stretches the broken windows theory too far. In the end, it is more conservative to exclude the Newark neighborhoods than it is to conclude from these data that disorder and crime are causally related.[14]

## Making the Best of the Data

I attempt here to redress some of the design decisions that I disagree with—at least those that can be corrected—in order to test the broken windows hypothesis. With regard first to the independent variable disorder, I propose to create a new multi-item index of neighborhood disorder that incorporates only those variables that are not themselves serious criminal activities (in other words, that are not part of the dependent variable). I therefore exclude the variables related to drug trafficking and gang activity. I follow Skogan's lead and create a corrected index for social disorder and one for physical disorder and then average the two.[15] I refer to the new multi-item index as "corrected disorder." In addition, I include the four other measures of disorder that were available from the data but that Skogan omitted from his indices—the first two (smut and prostitution) in the social disorder index and the second two (dogs and garbage) in the physical disorder index. The variables included in the two corrected multi-item scales thus consist of:

| Social disorder | Physical disorder |
| --- | --- |
| Loitering | Noise |
| Vandalism | Abandoned buildings or vehicles |
| Public drinking | Litter |
| Insulting language | Trash in vacant lots |
| Smut | Dogs |
| Prostitution | Garbage |

With regard to the problem of missing values, I propose to standard-ize these twelve variables on their respective means.[16] This avoids the problem of bias resulting from missing values (discussed earlier). It is, of course, impossible to determine what the missing values would ac-tually have been. In this case I am not entirely comfortable imputing values by means of multiple imputation because of the large number of missing values. I hesitate possibly to inject additional biases into this already weak data set. I assume that Skogan may have felt the same way, which may explain why he did not impute values for the missing data. In any event, standardizing the variables on their means is a more con-servative approach.

In effect, what standardizing the variables does is turn them into *comparable* measures of relative disorder. Let's take, for instance, two variables in the social disorder index: public drinking and insults. At present, the values for each observation correspond to the respon-dents' perception of these as problems in the neighborhood on a scale of 1 to 3. The mean for the public drinking variable is 1.8. The mean for the insults variable is 1.3. A neighborhood for which there are no data on public drinking but there are data on insults is likely to have a lower value for social disorder because of the missing data. By stan-dardizing the two variables on their means, however, we create, instead of an absolute value for the variable, a relative weight of disorder. So a neighborhood for which there are no data on public drinking will have a value for social disorder equal to the relative orderliness or dis-orderliness of the neighborhood in terms of insults. Each variable will become a comparable relative indicator of the level of disorder. By av-eraging the available values, we will obtain a good indicator of the relative level of disorder in each neighborhood. In addition, the use of standardized values essentially substitutes for multiple imputation, insofar as it does similar work as the algorithms commonly used for imputation.

## The Corrected Results Using Skogan's Data

### The Corrected Disorder-Crime Regression Analysis

If we look only at "corrected disorder" and the various crimes, it appears that the corrected disorder variable continues to be statistically significantly related to three of the five crimes: physical assault, burglary, and robbery. At this preliminary stage, however, we can already conclude that purse-snatching/pocket-picking and rape are not significantly related to disorder. This is reflected in Table 3.7.

### The Other-Explanatory-Variables Analysis

With the single exception of robbery, however, these statistically significant relationships between individual crimes and disorder simply disappear when the socioeconomic factors are taken into account. In fact, with regard to purse-snatching, if stability alone is held constant, the p-value is 0.978.

PHYSICAL ASSAULT. If we use Skogan's indices for poverty, stability, and race, and hold these variables constant, neighborhood disorder is no longer statistically significantly related to the number of residents victimized by physical assault in their neighborhood. When we hold these three variables constant, a one-unit increase in corrected disor-

Table 3.7  Regression coefficients for corrected disorder and various crimes

| Crime | Corrected disorder | | | | |
|---|---|---|---|---|---|
| | Coefficient | Standard error | P-value | 95% Conf. interv |
| Purse-snatching | −.054 | .033 | .126 | −.125 | .017 |
| Physical assault | .112 | .029 | .001 | .053 | .17( |
| Burglary | .137 | .051 | .011 | .033 | .24) |
| Robbery | .107 | .015 | .000 | .077 | .137 |
| Sexual assault | .001 | .007 | .901 | −.013 | .015 |

der tends to increase physical assault by 0.007 on average, with a standard deviation of 0.04. The 95 percent confidence interval therefore has a lower bound of −0.08 and an upper bound of 0.09, which suggests that a good portion of estimated values will be inversely related to increases in disorder. The p-value is very high, standing at 0.873. This is reflected in Table 3.8.

BURGLARY.  The relationship between burglary victimization and corrected disorder also disappears when neighborhood poverty, stability, and race are taken into account. With these variables held constant, neighborhood disorder is no longer significantly related to the number of residents victimized by burglary in their neighborhood. This is reflected in Table 3.9.

As a result, it is only robbery that remains significantly related to disorder, with Skogan's other explanatory variables held constant. When we exclude the five Newark neighborhoods and hold constant the explanatory variables, even the robbery relationship vanishes. This is reflected in Table 3.10.

**ıble 3.8** Regression coefficients for physical assault and the explanatory variables

| xplanatory variables | Physical assault | | | | |
|---|---|---|---|---|---|
| | Coefficient | Standard error | P-value | 95% Conf. interval | |
| orrected disorder | .007 | .042 | .873 | −.081 | .094 |
| overty | .013 | .005 | .014 | .003 | .022 |
| ability | −.014 | .005 | .009 | −.024 | −.004 |
| ace | −.002 | .013 | .856 | −.028 | .024 |

**ıble 3.9** Regression coefficients for burglary and the explanatory variables

| xplanatory variables | Burglary | | | | |
|---|---|---|---|---|---|
| | Coefficient | Standard error | P-value | 95% Conf. interval | |
| orrected disorder | −.059 | .069 | .401 | −.199 | .081 |
| overty | .022 | .007 | .004 | .008 | .036 |
| ability | −.029 | .007 | .000 | −.043 | −.014 |
| ace | −.010 | .020 | .636 | −.050 | .031 |

Table 3.10 The Newark Effect: Coefficients for robbery and the explanatory variables excluding Newark neighborhoods

|  | Robbery | | | | |
| Explanatory variables | Coefficient | Standard error | P-value | 95% Conf. interva |  |
| --- | --- | --- | --- | --- | --- |
| Corrected disorder | .060 | .039 | .141 | −.022 | .141 |
| Poverty | .000 | .003 | .988 | −.006 | .006 |
| Stability | .001 | .003 | .794 | −.006 | .008 |
| Race | .014 | .008 | .089 | −.002 | .030 |

## Conclusion

My findings using the corrected disorder index essentially track my earlier replication using Skogan's index for disorder. They suggest that, in the final analysis, there are *no* statistically significant relationships between disorder and purse-snatching, physical assault, burglary, or rape when other explanatory variables are held constant, and that the relationship between robbery and disorder also disappears when the five Newark neighborhoods are set aside. In the end, the data do not support the broken windows hypothesis.

### The Sampson and Cohen Study

Advocates of order maintenance cite one other quantitative study, Robert Sampson and Jacqueline Cohen's 1988 "Deterrent Effects of the Police on Crime," as further evidence of the broken windows effect. This study, however, is by no means conclusive. To the contrary, the study takes a far more nuanced approach and, in the end, supports the argument that the social-scientific evidence for the broken windows theory is lacking. As Sampson and Cohen acknowledge, research on the relationship between disorder and crime is "sparse," as is research on the relationship between proactive policing and crime, and the results thus far have been "mixed" (1988:167, 166).

Sampson and Cohen's study makes a useful contribution to the controversy over the benefits of aggressive policing strategies on crime prevention. The debate was triggered, in part, by James Q. Wilson's 1968 work, *Varieties of Police Behavior,* and by his study with Barbara

Boland on the effects of aggressive police arrest practices on crime (Wilson 1968; Wilson and Boland 1978 and 1981; see also Boydstun 1975). Wilson and Boland hypothesized that aggressive police patrols, involving increased stops and arrests, have a deterrent effect on crime (1978:373–374). A number of contributions ensued, both supporting (see, e.g., Whittaker et al. 1985) and criticizing these findings (see, e.g., Jacob and Rich 1981; Decker and Kohfeld 1985). The controversy was slightly different in focus from the Skogan study and the debate over the broken windows theory, since it centered more on aggressive police behavior and heightened stops and arrests. Nevertheless, since the control of disorder feeds into policies of aggressive arrest and order-maintenance crackdowns, as I have argued, the study is relevant to our debate.

In their study, Sampson and Cohen focus on two possible mechanisms—only one of which reflects the broken windows hypothesis—by which aggressive, proactive policing strategies might be related to lower crime rates. The first mechanism, which they refer to as "indirect," operates by increasing the arrest/offense ratio (1988:164). Aggressive, proactive policing results in an increased number of police-civilian exchanges, which in turn increases the likelihood of solving crimes: "By stopping, questioning, and otherwise closely observing citizens, especially suspicious ones, the police are more likely to find fugitives, detect contraband (such as stolen property or concealed weapons), and apprehend persons fleeing from the scene of a crime" (1988:164). Under the first hypothesis, aggressive policing affects crime "by changing the actual probability that an arrest is made (e.g., by increasing the arrest/offense ratio)" (1988:164). The second mechanism, which they refer to as "direct," operates by influencing community perceptions regarding the certainty of punishment (1988:165). The heightened police presence and interventions that accompany proactive policing communicate to potential criminals that they are more likely to be caught if they commit a crime. This second mechanism—increasing certainty of arrest—is the one that is explicitly linked to the broken windows theory. The authors make this link by using as the measure of aggressive policing "the number of arrests per police officer for disorderly conduct and driving under the influence (DUI)" (1988:169).

With regard to the indirect effect, Sampson and Cohen report that proactive policing appears to have a differential effect on robbery and burglary arrest certainty rates. Arrest certainty appears to have a significant inverse effect on the rate of robberies—second only to that, believe it or not, of the divorce rate (1988:176). Arrest certainty, by contrast, has only a marginally significant effect on burglary rates. With regard to the direct effect, proactive policing appears to have a very weak effect on burglary, and for that reason the authors focus the remainder of their study on robbery, where there does appear to be a significant inverse effect.[17] With regard to robbery, the authors find that "[t]he magnitude of the effect is clearly much less than that of divorce, but it is similar to that of region, income, and [population] size" (1988:176). The direct effect also varies by age and race of the offender. "[P]olice aggressiveness has a much larger (inverse) effect on black adult robbery offending than on white adult robbery offending. . . . Similarly, the effect of police aggressiveness on white juvenile robbery is insignificant, while the corresponding effect for black juvenile robbery is significant and almost double in magnitude" (1988:177).

In the end, however, the authors acknowledge that their study does not establish whether aggressive policing affects the robbery rate by means of the direct or the indirect mechanism: "[O]ur analysis was not able to choose definitively between the two alternative scenarios [indirect or direct] posed by Wilson and Boland (1978). One cannot determine empirically the direct effects of *both* police aggressiveness and the arrest/offense ratio on crime in a simultaneous equation model because such a model is unidentified."[18] Sampson and Cohen favor the direct mechanism interpretation, in large part because of the sharp criticisms that have been leveled against the indirect deterrence literature. But in the final analysis the study is inconclusive.

### The 1999 Sampson and Raudenbush Study

As of this writing, the most comprehensive and thorough social scientific evidence on the relationship between disorder and crime is the 1999 study by Robert J. Sampson and Stephen W. Raudenbush titled "Systematic Social Observation of Public Spaces: A New Look at Disorder in Urban Neighborhoods." Their findings closely replicate my conclusions about Skogan's data, and provide further evidence that the broken windows theory has not been verified. In fact, their study suggests that the broken windows theory may simply be wrong—that disorder may not be the "active ingredient" in crime, but instead that crime and disorder may have "common origins" that trace back to "structural disadvantage and attenuated collective efficacy" (Sampson and Raudenbush 1999:638). Sampson and Raudenbush offer a compelling alternative to the broken windows theory, an alternative theory that emphasizes the role of collective efficacy and structural constraints on crime.

Before turning to the intricate details of their study, though, I want to begin at the very end, where Sampson and Raudenbush summarize their findings in relation to the broken windows theory. Their comments are particularly apposite. In the continued interests of full disclosure, I will quote them at length. Sampson and Raudenbush conclude from their study that

> observed disorder did not match the theoretical expectations set up by the main thesis of "broken windows." Disorder is a moderate correlate of predatory crime, and it varies consistently with antecedent neighborhood characteristics. Once those characteristics were taken into account, however, the connection between disorder and crime vanished in 4 out of 5 tests—including homicide, arguably our best measure of violence. . . .
>
> Although our results contradict the strong version of the broken windows thesis, they do not imply the theoretical irrelevance of disorder. After all, our theoretical framework rests on the notion that physical and social disorder comprise highly visible cues to which neighborhood observers respond. According to this view, disorder may turn out to be important for understanding migration patterns, investment by businesses, and overall neighborhood viability. . . .
>
> What we would claim, however, is that the current fascination in policy circles on cleaning up disorder through law enforcement techniques appears simplistic and largely misplaced, at least in terms of directly fighting crime. Eradication of disorder *may* indirectly reduce crime by stabilizing neighborhoods, but the direct link as formulated by proponents was not the predominate [sic] one in our study. What we found instead is that neighborhoods high in disorder do not have higher crime rates in general than neighborhoods low in disorder once

collective efficacy and structural antecedents are held constant. Crime and disorder are not even that highly correlated in the first place. . . . Put differently, the active ingredients in crime seem to be structural disadvantage and attenuated collective efficacy more so than disorder. Attacking public disorder through tough police tactics may thus be a politically popular but perhaps analytically weak strategy to reduce crime, mainly because such a strategy leaves the common origins of both, but especially the last, untouched. (Sampson and Raudenbush 1999:637–638)

I turn now to the details of their study.

## Data Collection

Sampson and Raudenbush designed an extremely, but justifiably, labor-intensive study that departs, in several important respects, from the design of the Skogan study. First, in order to assess neighborhood disorder, Sampson and Raudenbush engage in "systematic social observation" rather than relying on the impression of neighborhood residents. Systematic social observation (SSO) traces to the early Chicago school of urban sociology and the work of Albert J. Reiss, Jr. SSO represents direct and recorded observation by trained observers that results in data that can be replicated. It produces a permanent visual record that can be later reexamined, recoded, and reinterpreted in light of new theoretical insights. The key features of SSO are, first, the systematic and independent measurement of social phenomena that, second, are permanently recorded and thereby, third, can later be replicated by other researchers.[19]

In this particular study, Sampson and Raudenbush used videotaped recordings of Chicago streets made in 1995 by "observers trained at the National Opinion Research Center (NORC) [who] drove a sports utility vehicle (SUV) at a rate of five miles per hour down every street in 196 Chicago census tracts" (1999:615). A random sample (representing 15,141 street sides) was then selected, and the videotapes were viewed and coded. During the videotaping, two trained observers also recorded their observations and added audio commentary to the videotape. All in all, 126 variables were coded, including physical conditions, social interactions, housing characteristics, and land use. The physical disorder scale included observations such as whether there were cigarettes, litter, empty beer bottles, graffiti of different types, abandoned cars, condoms, or hypodermic needles on the streets. The social disorder scale included observations such as whether there was loitering, public drinking, gang indicators, public intoxication, adults fighting, selling of drugs, or prostitution on the streets (1999:615–618).

In order to assess "collective efficacy," structural factors such as poverty, and neighborhood levels of crime, Sampson and Raudenbush used police records, vital statistics, and census data. They also conducted a survey in late 1994 and 1995 of 3,864 adults chosen from households within the 196 tracts (1999:620). The official documents and survey were thus obtained completely independently of the SSO disorder data.

For the crime variables, Sampson and Raudenbush obtained official crime data from the Chicago police and vital statistics. Specifically, they obtained "the incidents (not arrests) of homicide, robbery, and burglary in the years 1993 and 1995, geocoded from records of the Chicago Police Department and aggregated to the census tract of occurrence." They also obtained homicide victimization data from vital statistics (1999:621).

For the "collective efficacy" variable, they relied on their survey data. "Collective efficacy" represents the capacity of a social unit to regulate itself and realize collective goals. It encompasses informal mechanisms of social control. Sampson and Raudenbush define it as "the linkage of cohesion and mutual trust with shared expectations of intervening in support of neighborhood social control" (1999:612–613). They obtained their collective efficacy data from a survey they conducted which asked multiple questions that addressed, first, shared expectations for informal social control and second, social cohesion and trust. The two measures were then combined to create a measure of "collective efficacy" (1999:620–621).

Sampson and Raudenbush also obtained census data at the tract level for three structural constraint scales: "concentrated disadvantage" (including variables for poverty, public assistance, unemployment, and female-headed families), "concentrated immigration" (including variables for percentage Latino, percentage foreign-born, and density of children); and "residential stability" (including variables for owner-occupied homes and percentage living in the same house as five years earlier). They also obtained census data for land use (the mix of residential and commercial uses) and population density (1999:621–622).

In addition, in order to check the reliability of the SSO disorder data and the official crime reporting data, Sampson and Raudenbush asked questions regarding crime victimization ("violent victimization" and "household burglary or theft victimization") and perceptions of disorder, both physical and social (1999:620).

## Research Findings

Having collected this large and methodologically diverse data set, Sampson and Raudenbush then engaged in several analyses to determine the statistical relationships among disorder, structural constraints, collective efficacy, and crime.

As a preliminary matter, they found a moderately strong correlation between SSO disorder (both physical and social) and concentrated poverty ($r = .50$), as well as between SSO disorder and collective efficacy ($r = -.49$ for social disorder and $r = -.47$ for physical disorder). With regard to the disorder-crime nexus, they found that "physical disorder measured in the SSO is only moderately correlated with rates of predatory crime measured by police-recorded rates of homicide ($r = .27$), robbery ($r = .45$), and burglary ($r = .24$). The relationships with survey-reported victimization are weaker: $r = .21$ for violence, and $r = .06$, NS, for burglary. A similar pattern of correlation appears with respect to social disorder" (1999:623). From this finding they preliminarily remarked that "the correlations of SSO disorder with crime rates, although positive, are not at the levels one might expect from the broken windows thesis" (1999:623).

Sampson and Raudenbush also preliminarily conducted two separate multivariate regression analyses to determine, first, the relationships between SSO disorder and other potential active ingredients of crime, and second, the association of collective efficacy with SSO disorder. With regard to the first, they found that "concentrated disadvantage is the single most important predictor of disorder in Chicago neighborhoods" (1999:625). With regard to the second, even controlling for prior crime rates and perceived (as opposed to SSO) disorder, they found that there is a persistent negative association of collective efficacy with SSO disorder (1999:626).

Sampson and Raudenbush then addressed, head-on, the broken windows theory. They set up two separate models corresponding to their two competing theories: first, the broken windows theory (Model 1), and second, their alternative theory that both disorder and crime are the product of weakened collective efficacy and structural constraints (Model 2). Under Model 1, they regressed crime victimization on SSO disorder and prior crime rates. Under Model 2, they regressed crime victimization on SSO disorder and prior crime rates, as well as collective efficacy, structural constraints, mixed land use, and population density. They ran those two model tests using both the survey-reported victimization data and the official crime data.

With regard to the survey-reported crime victimization data, they found a positive but weak statistical relationship with regard to violent victimization in Model 1, and no relationship with regard to household burglary. Nevertheless, even the weak relationship between SSO disorder and violent victimization simply vanished when they held constant, in Model 2, structural antecedents and collective efficacy. In other words, there was, in their words, a "spurious association of disorder with predatory crime" (1999:627).[20] In fact, the authors observed, the statistical relationship between SSO disorder and survey-reported violent victimization vanishes when collective efficacy alone was held constant.

With regard to the official crime data, Sampson and Raudenbush first found that SSO disorder is significantly statistically related to all three categories of crime in Model 1. When structural constraints and collective efficacy are taken into account in Model 2, however, the statistical relationship vanishes with regard to burglary. With regard to homicide, the estimated coefficient for disorder drops by half, but remains significant at the 0.05 level. With regard to robbery, however, the estimated coefficient remains large (0.31) and remains significant at the 0.01 level. Moreover, when prior levels of relevant crime are held constant—Sampson and Raudenbush develop a third model (Model 3) for this purpose—the relationship between SSO disorder and homicide also disappears.

In contrast to SSO disorder, concentrated disadvantage and collective efficacy are consistent predictors of crime at the 0.01 level across all three categories of crime. The estimated coefficient of collective efficacy with regard to the homicide count is the most robust, standing at −1.97. Sampson and Raudenbush conclude, "[T]he key result is that the influences of structural characteristics and collective efficacy on burglary, robbery, and homicide are not mediated by neighborhood disorder" (1999:629).

## Sampson and Raudenbush's Conclusions

With regard to the disorder-crime nexus, Sampson and Raudenbush find that their data do not support the strong version of the broken windows theory. Disorder and predatory crime are only moderately correlated, and when antecedent neighborhood characteristics are taken into account, the connection between disorder and crime "vanished in 4 out of 5 tests—including homicide, arguably our best measure of violence" (1999:637). They nevertheless suggest that disorder may have indirect neighborhood effects on crime by influencing "migration patterns, investment by businesses, and overall neighborhood viability" (1999:637).

Sampson and Raudenbush did find "a significant albeit modest association of disorder with officially measured robbery" (1999:637). As they explain, however, the aggregate-level correlation was not high: it did not exceed 0.5 (1999:638). They suggest several possible explanations that could minimize the importance of these findings. First, areas with a high level of disorder may be more attractive venues for robbers because the disorder may increase "the potential pool of victims without full recourse to police protection, such as those involved in drug trafficking and prostitution" (1999:630). The authors observe that recent research "has indicated that robbery offenders are especially attuned to local drug markets, where they perceive drug dealers and their customers as prime targets with cash on hand" (1999:630). Second, Sampson and Raudenbush leave open the possibility that the correlation is "an artifact of official data" (1999:638 n.35). As indicated earlier, none of the crime survey data, including the data on violent crime victimization, were significantly statistically related to disorder. "It is possible," they observe, "that citizen calls to the police or police accuracy in recording robberies is greater in areas perceived to be higher in disorder. That there was no disorder link for official homicide or burglary is perhaps telling" (1999:638).

Despite these possible caveats, Sampson and Raudenbush suggest that robbery may be induced by neighborhood disorder. They note that disorder may entice robbers, in turn undermining collective efficacy and thereby promoting both more disorder and more robbery. Nevertheless, they conclude that the single correlation with robbery, which is itself weak, does not overshadow the strong findings of a relationship between collective efficacy, structural disadvantage, and crime. "In this sense, and bearing in mind the example of some European and American cities (e.g., Amsterdam, San Francisco) where visible street level activity linked to prostitution, drug use, and panhandling does not necessarily translate into high rates of violence, public disorder may not be so 'criminogenic' after all in certain neighborhood and social contexts" (1999:638).

Because of the consistent and strong relationship between disorder, collective efficacy, and structural disadvantage across all crime variables, Sampson and Raudenbush conclude from their study that "public disorder and most predatory crimes share similar theoretical features and are consequently explained by the same constructs at the neighborhood level, in particular the concentration of disadvantage and lowered collective efficacy" (1999:637).

## Assessing the Sampson and Raudenbush Study

As of the date of this writing, Sampson and Raudenbush's data had not yet been prepared for public use, and I was therefore not able to replicate their study (communication with Robert J. Sampson, May 30, 2000). Nevertheless, their study raises very few questions or concerns, in large part because they have so thoroughly presented their data and findings and evenhandedly assessed the evidence. Sampson and Raudenbush set forth all of their quantities of interest and offer a full opportunity to assess their work. As a result, I have only two minor reservations about the study design.

First, in reviewing Wesley Skogan's disorder index, I argued that it was not appropriate to include in the social disorder scale disorderly behavior such as drug use and gang activity that signals major criminal activity. While I agree with Sampson and Raudenbush—and with my colleagues Michael Gottfredson and Travis Hirschi—that it may not make sense to think about these different acts as if they had a different etiology and were caused by different factors, it is nevertheless important to distinguish, insofar as possible, between minor disorder and major crime when we are trying to assess the broken windows theory. It is important to make every possible effort to keep minor and serious offenses separate. Otherwise, the broken windows theory itself becomes tautological.

Sampson and Raudenbush include in their disorder scale both "selling drugs" and "peer group with gang indicators" (1999:618), factors I would exclude from the social disorder scale. Nevertheless, positive observations for both variables were exceedingly rare: of 15,111 observations, there were only twelve for "selling drugs" and twenty for "peer group with gang indicators." The more frequent positive observations were for loitering (861 positive observations) and for physical disorder more generally (1999:618). As a result, including the two variables in this study had an insignificant effect.

Second, I am left thinking that it is quite unfortunate that both modern technology (videotaping) and more traditional techniques (observing with the naked eye) made it necessary to do all the observations between 7 A.M. and 7 P.M. It would have been preferable to conduct the research during the evening, since a good deal of neighborhood disorder takes place after sunset. Nevertheless, there is apparently little that can be done to resolve this problem. This is, again, a minor concern, and in this case one that seems unavoidable.[21]

Overall, the Sampson and Raudenbush study offers compelling evidence that the broken windows theory has not been established. It confirms my replication of the Skogan study. And it is uncontradicted by the Sampson and Cohen study.

### The Broken Windows Theory: "Simplistic and Largely Misplaced"

It is fair to conclude from the existing social-scientific data that neighborhood disorder is not significantly related to homicide, burglary, physical assault, rape, or purse-snatching/pocket-picking victimization when antecedent neighborhood characteristics (such as poverty, stability, race, and collective efficacy) are held constant. Insofar as the broken windows theory is a theory about common crime or generalized levels of crime, it is not supported by the evidence.

The connection between disorder and robbery is less clear. Skogan's data—though weak and somewhat unreliable—retain significance when the five Newark neighborhoods are included, but not when they are excluded. Sampson and Raudenbush's survey data reveal no significant relationship with violent victimization (which would include robbery) when antecedent neighborhood conditions are held constant. Their data do reveal a significant relationship with official robbery data, but the correlation is not great. Perhaps their data indicate some relationship between disorder and robbery. As Sampson and Raudenbush suggest, "[A]reas with greater cues of disorder appear to be more attractive targets for robbery offenders, perhaps because disorder increases the potential pool of victims without full recourse to police protection" (1999:630). However tenuous, there may be a link between disorder and robbery. To suggest from that, however, that the broken windows theory has been empirically verified is a veritable leap. At most, we can conclude that there may be some connection, not between disorder and "serious crime," but rather between disorder and robbery. And even here I am being generous. As I explain in Chapter 4, the bare correlation between disorder and robbery itself—however weak or strong—is not proof of a *causal* relationship between the two, nor is it proof that the causal *mechanism* is the *social meaning* of disorder.

# Policing Strategies and Methodology

The media, policy makers, and public officials point to New York City's quality-of-life initiative as evidence of the broken windows effect. The implementation of the initiative in early 1994 coincided with a remarkable drop in crime in New York City, a decline that initially outpaced that in many other large cities. The sharp rate of decline, some argue, is attributable to the policing strategy. In this chapter I assess that claim. I also review and assess the empirical evidence concerning several other policing initiatives, including Chicago's anti-gang loitering ordinance and Charleston's juvenile snitching policy.

I then turn to the larger question of methodology. I explore, more generally, the *type* of empirical evidence that the order-maintenance approach principally relies on. I suggest that the approach depends excessively on purported correlations between the enforcement of proposed policing practices and a drop in crime rates. The problem is not simply that the purported correlations do not hold up under close scrutiny—which is, indeed, a significant weakness. The greater problem is that purported correlations do not begin to address the causal mechanisms—in this case the social norm pathways—that are at the heart of the order-maintenance approach.

## New York City's Quality-of-Life Initiative

Crime rates in New York City plummeted in the 1990s, a period that coincided, by and large, with the implementation of the quality-of-life initiative. In 1997 Dan Kahan tallied the numbers as follows: "Since 1993, the murder rate [in New York City] has come down nearly 40 percent, the robbery rate more than 30 percent, and the burglary rate more than 25 percent" (Kahan 1997a:367). William Bratton also emphasized "the turnaround," noting, "Crime is down by more than 50 percent from 1990. Murders are down by 63 percent." As a result, he observed in 1997, "[t]here will be 200,000 fewer victims of major crimes this year than there were in 1990" (Bratton 1997). Moreover, in the period 1993–1996, the crime rate in New York City fell more sharply than in most other large cities (Kahan 1997a:367–368). The only thing that can account for the difference, many argue, is the quality-of-life initiative.[1]

Here again, however, the empirical evidence does not withstand scrutiny. As a preliminary matter, crime rates declined nationally for eight straight years, from 1991 to 1999. By 1999, the murder rate in the United States had dropped to 5.7 per 100,000 persons, the lowest level since 1966 (Butterfield 2000c). A number of large U.S. cities—Boston, Houston, Los Angeles, San Diego, San Francisco, among others—experienced significant drops in crime in the 1990s, in some cases even larger proportionally to the drop in crime in New York City, many without implementing the same type of aggressive order-maintenance policing. Applying a variety of different tests, one study found that New York City's drop in homicides, though not very common, is not unprecedented either. Houston's drop in homicides of 59 percent between 1991 and 1996 outpaced New York City's 51 percent decline over the same period, and both were surpassed by Pittsburgh's 61 percent drop in homicides between 1984 and 1988 (Fagan, Zimring, and Kim 1998:1280–86). Another study looked at the rates of decline of homicides in the seventeen largest U.S. cities from 1976 to 1998 in comparison to each city's cyclical peaks and troughs, using a method of indexed cyclical comparison. With regard to the most recent cyclical drop in homicides, the study found that New York City's decline, though above average, was the fifth largest, behind San Diego, Washington, D.C., St. Louis, and Houston (Joanes 1999:303–304). Moreover, a straight comparison of homicide and robbery rates between 1991 and 1998 reveals that, although New York City is again near the top, with declines in homicide and robbery rates of 70.6 and 60.1 percent, respectively, San Diego experienced larger declines (76.4 and

62.6 percent, respectively), Boston experienced a comparable decline in its homicide rate (69.3 percent), Los Angeles a greater decline in its robbery rate (60.9 percent), and San Antonio a comparable decline in its robbery rate (59.1 percent). Other major cities also experienced impressive declines in both homicide and robbery rates, including Houston (61.3 and 48.5 percent, respectively) and Dallas (52.4 and 50.7 percent, respectively) (Butterfield 2000a:A11, compiled by Alfred Blumstein).

What is particularly striking is that many of these cities did not implement New York–style order-maintenance policing. San Diego and San Francisco exhibit perhaps the greatest contrast. The San Diego Police Department adopted a radically different approach focusing on community-police relations. The police began experimenting with problem-oriented policing in the late 1980s, retraining the force to respond better to community concerns. They put in place a strategy of sharing responsibility with citizens for identifying and solving crime. They encouraged neighborhood watch and citizen patrol groups and collaborated with community organizations and local business groups to clean up specific areas that repeatedly attracted drug dealers, prostitutes, and gangs. They trained more than one thousand citizen volunteers to perform crime prevention and victim assistance services. Overall, while recording remarkable drops in crime, San Diego also posted a 15 percent drop in total arrests between 1993 and 1996, and an 8 percent decline in total complaints of police misconduct filed with the police department between 1993 and 1996 (Greene 1999:182–185).

San Francisco also focused on community involvement and experienced decreased arrest and incarceration rates between 1993 and 1998. San Francisco's felony commitments to the California Department of Corrections dropped from 2,136 in 1993 to 703 in 1998, while other California counties either maintained or slightly increased their incarcerations. San Francisco also abandoned a youth curfew in the early 1990s and sharply reduced its commitments to the California Youth Authority from 1994 to 1998 (Taqi-Eddin and Macallair 1999:7–8 table 9, 10–11 table 14). Despite this, San Francisco experienced greater drops in its crime rate for rape, robbery, and aggravated assault than did New York City for the period 1995–1998. In addition, San Francisco experienced the sharpest decline in total violent crime—sharper than in New York City or Boston—between 1992 and 1998 (Taqi-Eddin and Macallair 1999:4 table 3, 5 table 4).

Boston has implemented a number of different strategic interventions—including some order-maintenance policing. Operation Ceasefire, for instance, involves a team problem-solving approach to youth firearm violence. A number of different agencies—including the Boston Police Department, the Bureau of Alcohol, Tobacco, and Firearms, the federal and county prosecutors' offices, the departments of probation and parole, counselors and city-employed gang outreach and mediation specialists—work together to communicate directly with gang leaders and at-risk youth. The thought behind the project is that at-risk juveniles do not generally read about harsh sentencing penalties in the newspapers, and therefore need to be addressed directly (Kennedy 1997:2). Operation Night Light involves police-accompanied probation checks to ensure that young at-risk probationers, often youth gang members, are complying with court restrictions during high-risk evening hours. The Strategic Planning and Community Mobilization Project focuses on increased contact between community residents and police for purposes of local problem solving. These programs focus on coalition building and teamwork (National Crime Prevention Council 1998).

Other cities, such as Los Angeles, Houston, Dallas, and San Antonio, also experienced significant drops in crime without as coherent a policing strategy as in other large cities (Butterfield 2000a). The fact is, there has been a remarkable—and wonderful—decline in crime in several major cities in the United States since the early 1990s. Depending on the specific time frame of the "before and after" comparison, New York City's drop in crime can be characterized as anywhere from the largest decline to a very high performer. Time frames can be easily manipulated, and I do not want to engage in that kind of exercise. My point, simply, is that New York City has experienced a remarkable decline in its crime rate, as have several other major U.S. cities, and that these cities have employed a variety of different policing strategies. It would be far too simplistic to attribute the rate of the decline in New York City to the quality-of-life initiative.

Moreover, although New York City preceded many large cities in posting a drop in homicides and other violent offenses in the early 1990s, by the end of the decade it also seemed to be at the forefront of a possible cyclical rebound. Preliminary reports indicate that the number of murders in New York City increased by 6 percent from 633 in 1998 to 671 in 1999 ("Preliminary Annual Uniform Crime Report"

1999:5). Moreover, during the first six months of 2000, there were 269 homicides, compared with 248 at the same point in 1999, a further increase of 8.5 percent. (Blair 2000:A12; Butterfield 2000b:A12). At the time of writing, it is unclear whether this temporary rebound in homicides will continue or is, rather, a blip in a longer-term decline. One can only hope that it is the latter. But in any event, it simply underscores the fact that different cities experience different cycles, and that cross-jurisdictional comparisons of this type are fraught with danger.

More important, criminologists have suggested a number of possible factors that may have contributed to declining crime rates in New York City. These include a significant increase in the New York City police force, a general shift in drug use from crack cocaine to heroin, new computerized tracking systems that speed up police response to crime, favorable economic conditions in the 1990s, a dip in the number of eighteen- to twenty-four-year-old males, an increase in the number of offenders currently incarcerated in city jails and state prisons, the arrest of several big drug gangs in New York, as well as possible changes in adolescent behavior (Karmen 1996; Fagan, Zimring, and Kim 1998; Butterfield 1998a). Many of these factors are significant. None may singlehandedly account for the trend. But each one must be taken seriously. Here again, the devil is in the details.

The Growing NYPD

In 1992 Mayor Dinkins hired over 2,000 new police officers under the Safe Streets, Safe City program. By 1998, Mayor Giuliani had hired another 4,000 officers and merged about six thousand Transit and Housing Authority officers into the ranks of the NYPD (Bratton 1997 and 1998:198). As a result, the NYPD force almost doubled during that period, up by about 12,300 police officers (including those transferred from Transit) from a force of 26,856 police officers in 1991 to 39,149 in 1998. Excluding the Transit merger, the police force grew by almost a quarter (Uniform Crime Reports 1991: table 78; Uniform Crime Reports 1998: table 78).

A close inspection of the number of police officers per capita in the ten largest cities in the country reveals that, although New York City had been among the leading players in the previous decade, it jumped to the front of the pack in the mid-1990s. In 1980 and 1990, New York was elbow to elbow in a tight cluster of the top-ranked large cities in terms of its police force. This is illustrated in Table 4.1.[2] During the 1990s, however, New York City gradually began to lead its peers. The sustained spending over many years, plus the accelerated investment in police officers since 1992, had a significant impact on the numbers. This is reflected in Table 4.2.[3] As a result, on October 31, 1998, the NYPD had about 39,149 police officers on its payroll—the largest police force in the country, with the highest ratio per civilian by far.

## Changing Drug Consumption

Another factor that may account in part for the sharp drop in crime in New York City is the substitution by drug users of heroin for crack cocaine. One of the more authoritative studies on the relationship between crack cocaine and homicides in New York City found that, in the late 1980s, crack dealing significantly contributed to the homicide rate (Goldstein et al. 1989). In fact, 26 percent of the homicides in New York City in 1988 were estimated to have been crack-related systemic events—systemic, that is, to crack dealing (1989:682). During an eight-month period in 1988, 52.7 percent of homicides in New York City were projected to have been drug related, and of those, 60 percent involved the use of or trafficking in crack (1989:681). In contrast, only three of the 414 homicides in the study were primarily related to the use of or trafficking in heroin (1989:683).

The study suggested that the contribution of crack to the homicide rate was primarily through trade-related, or systemic effects, including

Table 4.1 Top five police departments in terms of total number of police officers per 10,000 citizens from among the 10 largest U.S. cities, 1980 and 1990 (ranked from highest ratio)

| Rank | 1980 | 1990 |
|------|------|------|
| 1 | Philadelphia (44) | Detroit (44) |
| 2 | Chicago (41) | Chicago (43) |
| 3 | Detroit (35) | Philadelphia (42) |
| 4 | New York (32) | New York (37) |
| 5 | Dallas (25) | Dallas (27) |

**Table 4.2** Top five police departments in terms of total number of police officers per 10,000 citizens from among the 10 largest U.S. cities, 1993–1998 (ranked from the highest ratio)

| Rank | 1993 | 1994 | 1995 | 1996 | 1997 | 1998 |
|---|---|---|---|---|---|---|
| 1 | Chicago (43) | Chicago (46) | New York (51) | New York (50) | New York (50) | New York (53) |
| 2 | Philadelphia (41) | New York (41) | Chicago (48) | Chicago (46) | Chicago (48) | Philadelphia (48) |
| 3 | New York (40) | Philadelphia (40) | Philadelphia (43) | Philadelphia (44) | Philadelphia (46) | Chicago (48) |
| 4 | Detroit (38) | Detroit (38) | Detroit (38) | Detroit (39) | Detroit (42) | Detroit (41) |
| 5 | Houston (27) | Houston (28) | Houston (29) | Houston (29) | Houston (29) | Houston (30) |

territorial disputes among crack dealers (1989:656). Of the 118 homicides that were traced primarily to crack involvement, 100 (85 percent) were attributed to the crack trade (1989:656, 664 table 2). Three
of the crack-related homicides were attributed to the psychopharmacological consequences of ingesting crack (increased violence, excit-
ability, and irrationality), and eight homicides were attributed to the
economic compulsion to engage in crime in order to subsidize drug
use. The fact that these homicides were predominantly related to the
crack trade rather than to the psychopharmacological consequences
of using crack, however, does not minimize the contrast between
crack-related and heroin-related homicides in New York City during
that period. The stark contrast is illustrated well in Table 4.3 (see
Goldstein et al. 1989:663–664 tables 1 and 2).

The important corollary is that cocaine use declined in New York

**Table 4.3** Drug-related homicides in four representative patrol zones in New York City,
March 1–October 31, 1988

| | Number | Psycho-pharmacological | Economic compulsive | Systemic | Multi-dimension |
|---|---|---|---|---|---|
| Total number of homicides | 414 | | | | |
| Primarily drug-related homicides[a] | 218 | 31 | 8 | 162 | 17 |
| Primary drug: | | | | | |
| Crack | 118 | 3 | 8 | 100 | 7 |
| Cocaine | 48 | 1 | 0 | 44 | 3 |
| Alcohol | 21 | 21 | 0 | 0 | 0 |
| Marijuana | 7 | 1 | 0 | 6 | 0 |
| Heroin | 3 | 0 | 0 | 2 | 1 |
| Combinations (non-heroin) | 18 | 5 | 0 | 7 | 6 |
| Combinations (with heroin) | 0 | 0 | 0 | 0 | 0 |
| Unknown | 3 | 0 | 0 | 3 | 0 |

a. This is a conservative estimate. Any case for which there was not sufficient evidence was classified "not drug-related" even if the police suggested that the cases were *probably* drug related
(Goldstein et al. 1989:662).

City during the 1990s, and some suggest that heroin use was being substituted.[4] In Manhattan, the percentage of youthful arrestees testing positive for cocaine dropped from 70 percent in 1987 to 21 percent in 1996 (Witkin 1998:36; see also Butterfield 1997:A12). In addition, a number of studies suggested that crack markets became increasingly dominated by "an older, mostly male group of heavy users," possibly resulting in fewer homicides "because this age group is less prone to violence, and many of these users have long-term, stable relationships with their suppliers" (Witkin 1998:36).

In contrast to New York City, mid-size cities—cities with populations of several hundred thousand, such as Louisville, Kentucky, or Nashville, Tennessee—suffered delayed effects of increased crack use and, as a result, defied the national downward trend in crime rates in the 1990s. These smaller cities were apparently going through the urban crisis that hit the bigger cities in the 1980s and were experiencing a resulting crime wave. In Louisville, for instance, according to federal and local authorities, homicides in 1997 jumped to a seventeen-year high (Janofsky 1998; Witkin 1998:36).

## Changes at the NYPD

Another important contributing factor is the NYPD's use of computer technology to compile crime statistics and to convert the data into maps and charts that inform the police about crime patterns in different precincts. The data allow the police to target their enforcement to changing crime trends. A sergeant at the NYPD explains: "Let's say we're having a problem with Laundromat robberies in Brooklyn. I can pull from the CD all the listed Laundromats in Brooklyn, map them, shade in color the ones that are already robbed and see if we can spot a pattern. There's a lot of possibilities" (Newcombe 1997). According to experts such as David Kennedy at Harvard's John F. Kennedy School of Government, these new technologies have contributed to the falling crime rates in New York City.[5]

Moreover, as we have seen, beginning in January 1994, Mayor Giuliani and his police commissioner, William Bratton, instituted major changes at the NYPD. The computerized crime statistics and biweekly Compstat meetings were just part of an overall reinvigoration of the department. Bratton shook up his management team, cut out

layers of bureaucracy, aggressively promoted younger and more ambitious managers, and delegated more authority to precinct commanders ("NYPD, Inc." 1995; Lardner 1995; Bratton 1998). In addition,
Giuliani and Bratton implemented a number of different police strategies—including gun-oriented policing and enhanced drug enforcement initiatives (Giuliani and Bratton 1994a and 1994c). It is within
this larger framework that the quality-of-life initiative—the "linchpin
strategy" (Bratton 1998:228)—must be understood.

*The Impact of the NYPD Changes*
The first question, then, is whether the changes at the NYPD really had
an effect on crime. A thorough analysis of the relationship between
New York City's policing initiatives and serious crime is offered by
Fagan, Zimring, and Kim in "Declining Homicide in New York City: A
Tale of Two Trends" (1998). The authors analyze a large number of
potential explanations for the sharp 52 percent drop in homicides in
New York City during the five-year period 1992–1996. The major finding of the study is that the trend in homicide rates has been different
for firearm and non-firearm homicides. Whereas firearm homicides
first increased in the late 1980s and early 1990s and then declined
sharply, non-firearm homicides steadily declined after 1987. "What the
gun trends obscure," they emphasize, "is the steadiest long-term trend
in New York City—a downward movement in homicides by all means
other than gun that begins after 1986 and gathers momentum steadily
throughout the late 1980s and early 1990s" (1998:1289).

The study thus suggests that the new policing initiatives in New York
City in all likelihood did not affect this category of non-firearm homicides: "The consistent decline in nongun homicide . . . starts too early
and continues too evenly throughout the period under study to have
any plausible linkage to changes that come into the city two or three
years into the 1990s" (1998:1319). As a result, "the nongun declines
are in all probability not the consequence of policing changes or any
other process that was not in effect until the 1990s" (1998:1322). And
it is worth emphasizing that non-firearm homicide is not a trivial category of major crime. In 1995 there were 675 such killings, in contrast
to 834 firearm homicides.

With regard to firearm homicides, though, the study is less conclusive. The authors observe that "[t]he temporal fit between policing

changes and gun homicide declines is a good one" (1998:1319). They suggest a number of factors that may also have contributed to the decline, including a certain amount of regression from peak rates in 1990, an increase in the police force, and social trends. The primary competing explanation for the sharp decline in gun killings is regression from abnormally high rates. Nevertheless, the authors write, "while the entire gun homicide drop of 1991 to 1996 is within the boundaries of regression possibility, the more prudent view is to regard the convergence of cyclical variation, social trends in risk and exposure, and law enforcement changes as jointly responsible" for the decline (1998:1322). The further complication is to disentangle the many changes at the NYPD—including "gun interventions, general increases in police enforcement resources, strategic targeting of police efforts through computer mapping, and precinct-level management accountability for crime trends" (1998:1322), as well as the quality-of-life initiative.

Overall, the authors conclude on a cautionary note:

> We have already learned that attributing nongun homicide declines to law enforcement changes was premature and unjustified. Rather than risk more precipitous error in the interpretation of the city's homicide trends, our current understanding of the period from 1985 to 1996 suggests caution. If the downward trend in gun killings continues far past the 1978 and 1985 levels, the probable role of the mid-1990s changes will loom larger with each further decline. If the nongun homicides also continue in their post-1986 pattern, however, even the best statistical views about New York homicide will not yield easy answers on causation. (1998:1323)

*The Broken Windows Theory?*
Even if we were prepared to attribute to the quality-of-life initiative an important role in the drop in crime in New York City—that is, despite all the other major cities that have experienced sharp drops in crime without instituting similar policing, and the numerous other factors that have contributed to the decline in crime in New York City—there is one *final* question we need to pose: Is it the broken windows theory or the enhanced surveillance afforded by a policy of aggressive stops and frisks and arrests that most likely explains the impact of the qual-

ity-of-life initiative on crime rates? The answer has to be enhanced surveillance.

The brute fact is that misdemeanor arrests in New York City increased dramatically once Mayor Giuliani took office. The reason, simply, is that the quality-of-life initiative expressly targeted enforcement
of existing laws against disorderly conduct, harassment, damage to
property, graffiti writing, and other minor misdemeanors (Giuliani
and Bratton 1994e:38–40). According to the NYPD, misdemeanor arrests in New York City jumped by more than 50 percent from 1993
to 1996: misdemeanor arrests reached 205,277 in 1996, up from
133,446 in 1993 (Farrell 1998a and 1998b). In contrast, the number
of misdemeanor complaints for the period remained remarkably stable—with 421,116 misdemeanor complaints recorded in 1993 compared to 424,169 in 1996 (Farrell 1998b). The upward trend continued in 1997—with arrests for the first six months of 1997 standing at
117,698 (Farell 1998a)—and in 1998 as well. According to New York
State statistics, total adult misdemeanor arrests stood at 215,158 in
1998, up a total of 66.3 percent from 129,404 in 1993 (New York State,
Division of Criminal Justice Services 2000).

The policy of aggressive misdemeanor arrests provides the police
with enhanced powers of surveillance. What the quality-of-life initiative gives the NYPD is a legitimate reason to seize, search, and run
checks on persons committing or suspected of committing minor offenses. This practice has important consequences for the detection
and prevention of crime, powerfully demonstrated in the case of John
Royster. Royster was accused of fatally beating a flower shop owner
on Park Avenue, as well as several brutal assaults on women, including an infamous assault on a piano teacher in Central Park that left
her severely impaired. Royster was fingered, literally, when he was arrested for turnstile jumping at a New York subway station. Upon arrest,
Royster was fingerprinted, and a computer matched his prints with
fingerprints left at the scene of the Park Avenue murder (Purdy 1997;
Rosen 2000).

The first quality-of-life experiment in the New York City subways
demonstrated early on the benefits of aggressive misdemeanor arrests.
Many of those arrested for turnstile jumping had warrants out for
their arrest; many were carrying guns (Kelling and Coles 1996:134;
Bratton 1998:154). With misdemeanor arrests up more than 50 per-

cent in New York City, and with routine fingerprinting and record checking, the quality-of-life initiative produced, by 1996, a 39 percent increase in arrests on outstanding warrants (Purdy 1997). Misdemeanor arrests are also a way to take a suspicious person into custody when there may not otherwise be sufficient cause. This occurred in another notorious incident in 1998, when police officers arrested a suspicious man for jaywalking. Since he was not carrying identification, he was transported back to the police station, where he was put in a lineup and identified by two robbery victims (Onishi 1998).

Order-maintenance policing also enhances surveillance by facilitating the transfer of information. "Most citizens like to talk to a police officer," Wilson and Kelling explain. "Such exchanges give them a sense of importance, provide them with the basis for gossip, and allow them to explain to the authorities what is worrying them" (1982:34). Having patrol officers walk a beat makes it easier for citizens to pass information on to them. Wilson and Kelling write:

> You approach a person on foot more easily, and talk to him more readily, than you do a person in a car. Moreover, you can more easily retain some anonymity if you draw an officer aside for a private chat. Suppose you want to pass on a tip about who is stealing handbags, or who offered to sell you a stolen TV. In the inner city, the culprit, in all likelihood, lives nearby. To walk up to a marked patrol car and lean in the window is to convey a visible signal that you are a "fink." (1982:34)

Order-maintenance policing not only facilitates communication but also may create more confidential informants by criminalizing more people. Commissioner Bratton understood this well. In New York City, the quality-of-life initiative was expressly joined with an aggressive push to generate confidential informants. Arrests were accompanied by interrogation, with the intended purpose of converting arrestees into informants (Bratton 1998:219–221; see also Giuliani and Bratton 1994a:14). Not surprisingly, it worked. As Bratton explains, "[P]eople like to talk" (1998:220). Kelling and Cole add:

> A person arrested for urinating in a park, when questioned about other problems, gave police information that resulted in the confiscation of a small cache of weapons; a motorist cited for not wearing a helmet, on closer inspection, was carrying a nine-millimeter handgun,

had another in his sidebag, and had several high-powered weapons in his apartment; a vendor selling hot merchandise, after being questioned, led police to a fence specializing in stolen weapons. . . . Just as every farebeater was not a felon, not every petty criminal is a serious criminal; yet enough are, or have information about others who are, that contact with petty offenders alerts all criminals to the vigilance of the police and gives police legitimate access to information about more serious problems. (Kelling and Coles 1996:146)

Order-maintenance policing New York–style enables the police to collect more identifying information. It increases the opportunity for checking records, fingerprints, DNA, and other identifying characteristics. And it facilitates information gathering from informants. These are all important mechanism of crime detection and prevention.

In the final analysis, there are a number of significant factors that have pushed down the crime rate in New York City. Criminologists, policy makers, and legal scholars are engaged in a hotly contested debate about the causes of the decline in New York City and nationally. Some experts, including James Alan Fox at Northeastern University, argue that the crime rate in New York would have dropped regardless of the quality-of-life initiative (Beiser 1995:39–40). To be sure, no one force conventionally assumed to drive down crime rates in New York City is solely responsible for the drop in crime. Nevertheless, the combined effect of numerous causal factors—such as the increased size of the police force, shifting drug use patterns, new computerized tracking systems, demographics, and other factors—may account for the rate of the decline. Our present understanding of the causes is too tentative—and too contested—to suggest that the quality-of-life initiative accounts for *the* difference in New York City's rates.

The quality-of-life initiative probably has contributed to some degree to the decline in crime in New York City. To whatever degree, though, the mechanism is probably not a reduction in litter, fixing broken windows, or beautifying neighborhoods—although all of these may have some minor positive neighborhood effects. The primary engine of order-maintenance policing is probably the enhanced power of surveillance offered by a policy of aggressive misdemeanor arrests. Even Kelling, perhaps the strongest broken windows proponent, seems to recognize this. When he explains the four reasons why the broken windows strategy purportedly works, he has little to say about the social meaning of disorder. What order maintenance is really about, he suggests, is putting the police in contact with criminals and the disorderly. What it is really about is increased surveillance and police contact "with troublemakers and serious offenders" and the "hard-core '6 percent' of youthful offenders" (Kelling and Coles 1996:243–254).

## Chicago's Anti-Gang Loitering Ordinance

Proponents of Chicago's anti-gang loitering ordinance argue that there is a "respectable body of evidence documenting the effectiveness" of the law. Specifically, they contend, "law enforcement officials in Chicago . . . report dramatic reductions in violent offenses in neighborhoods in which that city's gang-loitering ordinance is most vigorously enforced" (Kahan and Meares 1998b:822). Enforcement of the ordinance has purportedly coincided with significant reductions citywide, in the districts in which the ordinance was most vigorously enforced, and specifically in Chicago's most crime-ridden area, the Eleventh District (Meares 1998a:235; Kahan and Meares 1998b:822).

Once again, however, the empirical evidence does not withstand close scrutiny. Stephen Schulhofer and Albert Alschuler at the University of Chicago have reexamined the data and demonstrate in excruciating detail that there is in fact no such correlation. They conclude, from their review of the Chicago police data, that the "claim of a dramatic reduction in violent crime is simply untrue. None of the three crime trends [Kahan and Meares] describe actually occurred" (Schulhofer and Alschuler 2000:6). Let's look at the evidence.

### Citywide Data

As noted in Chapter 2, the ordinance was passed on June 17, 1992. The Chicago Police Department adopted implementing regulations in 1992, and began enforcing the ordinance gradually in 1993 through most of 1995. During that period, with the exception of 1995, the principal measures of gang-related crime increased sharply at the citywide level: gang-related homicides, for instance, rose from 116 in 1992 to 291 in 1994, and then fell to 218 in 1995, which is still 88 percent higher than in 1992 when the ordinance was enacted (Schulhofer and Alschuler 2000:12). Moreover, as Justice Stevens observed, writing for the majority in *Morales,* "gang-related homicides [in Chicago] fell by 19% in 1997, over a year after the suspension of the ordinance" (*Morales* 1999:50 n.7; Roberts 1999:794). Thus, unless one assumes a delay of two or more years in social influence, the correlation is absent at the citywide level.[6]

The other two principal measures of gang-related activity—narcotics-related homicide and aggravated battery (Meares 1998a:235)—similarly increased during enforcement of the ordinance at the citywide level. Narcotics-related homicides jumped from 13 in 1992 to 102 in 1995, an increase of 685 percent. Similarly, aggravated battery rose 58 percent from 1992 to 1995 citywide (Schulhofer and Alschuler 2000:13).

## District Data

The district data are no more supportive. As Schulhofer and Alschuler demonstrate, "whether judged in absolute terms or relative to crime trends elsewhere in Chicago, the number of violent offenses *did not* drop dramatically in the high-crime districts where the ordinance was most vigorously enforced. On the contrary, the most dramatic reductions occurred in the low-crime districts where the ordinance was *least* vigorously enforced" (2000:7).

Murder and aggravated assault are the two types of crime that are considered most significantly related to gang activity. Yet from 1992 to 1995, the number of murders fell by 55 percent in the districts where the ordinance was least actively enforced, but rose by 3 percent in the districts of most active enforcement (Schulhofer and Alschuler 2000:8). With regard to aggravated assaults, while the citywide numbers fell by just under 5 percent between 1992 and 1995, "the number of aggravated assaults fell more sharply (by 15%) in the districts of least active enforcement. In the districts of most active enforcement, aggravated assaults registered a 5% decline, mirroring the city-wide trend" (Schulhofer and Alschuler 2000:8–9).

Schulhofer and Alschuler present these district-level data obtained from the Chicago Police Department in two tables, which I consolidate and summarize in Table 4.4. During the years of enforcement (1992–

Table 4.4  Schulhofer and Alschuler's tables 1 and 2: murder and aggravated assault by Chicago police district

| | Murder | | Aggravated Assault | |
|---|---|---|---|---|
| District | Net change 1992–95 | Net change 1995–97 | Net change 1992–95 | Net chang 1995–97 |
| *High-Enforcement Districts* | | | | |
| District 11 | −6.4% | −21.6% | +1.4% | −20.2% |
| District 13 | +3.1% | −21.2% | −21.6% | −5.8% |
| District 10 | +20.4% | −23.7% | −8.3% | −11.1% |
| Subtotal | +2.9% | −22.2% | −5.4% | −15.5% |
| *Low-Enforcement Districts* | | | | |
| District 18 | −57.9% | −25.0% | −11.6% | −4.5% |
| District 16 | −62.5% | +100.0% | −25.5% | −6.5% |
| District 1 | −33.3% | 0% | −7.0% | +0.4% |
| Subtotal | −54.5% | −6.7% | −15.0% | −4.4% |

1995), the districts where the ordinance was least enforced generally experienced greater declines in murder and aggravated assault, in contrast to the districts where the ordinance was most enforced. And the years of nonenforcement (1995–1997) witnessed mostly sharp declines in both categories of crimes across the board.

Now, of course, we have no idea how much worse crime would have been in the districts of high enforcement if there had been no anti-gang loitering ordinance. It is possible that murders and aggravated assaults in some districts would not have decreased, and in others would have increased at a far greater pace. As Schulhofer and Alschuler remark, it is not possible to conclude from these data that the ordinance had no effect (2000:10–11 and 13). But, plainly, the purported statistical correlation between enforcement of Chicago's anti-gang loitering ordinance and a drop in gang-related crime has not been established.

### Charleston's Juvenile Snitching Policy

Charleston, South Carolina, police chief Reuben Greenberg implemented a juvenile snitching policy in the 1990s whereby the police department offered a $100 bounty to anyone who reported an illegal handgun. According to proponents of the policy, it is believed to have been effective. "This tactic works," it is claimed, "not just because it facilitates seizure of weapons, but also because it interferes with norms that give guns their meaning" (Kahan and Meares 1998b:825). Proponents cite three references for their argument: Blumstein and Cork (1996); Harrington-Lueker (1992); and Butterfield (1996) (see Kahan and Meares 1998b:825 and n.27; Kahan 1998:612 n.8; Kahan 1999a:1867 and n.29).

The problem is that these references do not provide any empirical evidence that snitching policies correlate with reductions in juvenile gun possession. The excellent study by Alfred Blumstein and Daniel Cork, "Linking Gun Availability to Youth Gun Violence," does not purport to prove or even address the efficacy of snitching policies. The study examines trends in crime rates in the United States from 1972 to 1995. It disaggregates the data by age, weapon used, race, and offense, and then performs time-series and regression analyses of the data. The study concludes, first, that homicides committed by youthful offenders have risen dramatically since 1985, and second, that "an important factor in that growth has been a significant increase in the availability of guns to young people" (Blumstein and Cork 1996:5). In conclusion, the study discusses the policy implications, the first and foremost being the need to reduce gun availability among juveniles. It lists many approaches that "have been tried with considerable success" (1996:16). It then proposes an alternative strategy of improving socialization to alleviate the problems associated with dysfunctional families.

It is in the course of listing the "[m]any approaches [that] have been tried with considerable success" that Blumstein and Cork mention the snitching policy. Based on communications with Police Chief Greenberg, Blumstein and Cork note that "Charleston has offered a $100 bounty for reports of illegal guns that can be confiscated" (1996:17). Other than classifying this policy as one that has "been tried with considerable success," they do not purport to establish that the snitching policy has been successful. Later they refer to the policy, and the other approaches listed, as "focused primarily on achieving short-term effects," and they propose for the long term a focus on socialization. Blumstein and Cork do not attempt to prove how a policy of snitching will change the social meaning of juvenile gun possession and reduce gun carrying.

The Donna Harrington-Lueker source is a two-page article, "Metal Detectors: Schools Turn to Devices Once Aimed Only at Airport Terrorists," published in the *American School Board Journal* in May 1992. In passing, the article reports that, according to public school security chief Peter Blauvelt of Prince George's County, Maryland, "most of the guns found this year [1992] in the Prince George's County Public Schools have been found as a result of [student] reports. Detroit's gun hot line gives students a similar chance; students can simply dial 871-HELP to report a weapon on school premises" (1992:27). This article does not discuss the policy of rewarding snitching, and does not purport to establish an interpretive theory of social meaning.

The final reference is to an article by Fox Butterfield in the *New York Times,* "Police Chief's Success in Charleston, S.C., Is What's Raising Eyebrows Now." Butterfield reports that Police Chief Greenberg—with whom Blumstein and Cork also communicated—stated that "[k]ids are the greatest snitches in the world" (Butterfield 1996) and suggested that the snitching policy reversed the psychology of carrying guns. Butterfield's lone interview with the Charleston police chief, however, is hardly evidence that "this tactic works."

My independent review of the literature has not revealed any other studies at the time of this writing specifically concerning the use or effectiveness of snitching policies to combat juvenile gun possession. At the more general level of juvenile informants and gun possession, the literature raises two potential concerns: first, about the safety of the informants, and second, about the possible effectiveness of rewarding snitching. According to one general study on the management of juvenile informants, conducted in England and Wales, of the seventy-five police officer informant handlers interviewed in that study, thirty-nine (or 56 percent) "believed that juveniles should not be used [as informants] for serious or major crime, or in circumstances in which they may come to harm" (Balsdon 1996:15). In a study of juvenile gun possession in New Mexico, based in part on a self-report questionnaire administered to 380 juvenile delinquents in confinement, the investigators report that only 16.9 percent of the respondents thought that having juveniles "control each other" might be effective in reducing juvenile gun possession (LaFree and Birkbeck 1998:51). Of course, neither of these two studies addresses the norm-focused hypothesis per se. But they do raise some additional concerns about juvenile snitching policies that need to be investigated.

## Methodological Concerns

It may be somewhat surprising, but the empirical evidence supporting the effectiveness of these policing initiatives is simply not there. The purported correlations are not established. What is perhaps even more troubling is that, even if the purported correlations were present, this evidence would not verify the social norm hypotheses. There is an even more fundamental problem with the *type of evidence* that proponents marshal in support of the order-maintenance approach to criminal justice. Even if, for instance, Skogan's data and statistical findings were reliable—which, clearly, they are not—the data *could not* establish the specific social norm–focused hypothesis that it is the social meaning of disorder that causes crime. Skogan's data include measures of neighborhood disorder and crime victimization obtained from surveys. These data cannot tell us what the *social meaning* of order or disorder is. They cannot tell us that disorder *means* that the residents do not care about their neighborhood, or that the residents do not try to exercise control over their neighborhood. At most, they could tell us that disorderly neighborhoods are neighborhoods where there is a lot of crime victimization. But, again, that gives us very little information about the *social meaning* of disorder. Moreover, the data cannot tell us whether a disorderly neighborhood can become an orderly neighborhood. And even if a neighborhood could become orderly, the data still could not tell us whether it was the *social meaning* of order, and not something else about order-maintenance policing (such as enhanced surveillance and search and seizure power), that would have an effect on the level of criminal activity. A social norm hypothesis that focuses on the social meaning of order cannot be tested by a single time frame regression of neighborhood disorder and crime. That is simply asking too much of the data.

The same is true of the data in the 1988 Sampson and Cohen study. It is worth emphasizing at the outset that Sampson and Cohen recognize this limitation of their data and expressly acknowledge that their study is not able to choose definitively between a social norm explanation and a more traditional deterrence theory. "It is true," the authors write, "that our analysis was not able to choose definitely between the two alternative scenarios" (1988:185). This is an important methodological point worth emphasizing: the data cannot verify the norm-focused hypothesis except in the most banal way.

Sampson and Cohen test the norm-focused hypothesis by conducting a statistical analysis of the relationship between the measure of police aggressiveness and robbery crime rates, controlling for other known or suspected determinants of crime (1988:171–172). They find that, "[i]ndependent of urban social structure, proactive policing of DUI and disorderly conduct has a direct inverse effect on robbery. The magnitude of the effect is clearly much less than that of divorce, but it is similar to that of region, income, and size. . . . [T]he effect of police aggressiveness on burglary is very weak" (1988:176). But the exclusive focus on the statistical relationship between the policing technique and the crime rate tells us nothing about social meaning. It does little to explicate the social meaning of order, or to support an interpretation of the role of changing social meaning.

And the same is true of the anecdotal evidence concerning the drop in crime in New York City, in Chicago, or in Charleston. Even if the data could demonstrate that the policing initiatives were accompanied by a decline in the crime rate *and* that no other factor—whether it be changing drug usage patterns, demographics, economic conditions, computerized police tracking, or incarceration rates—was responsible for the decline in crime, the correlation between the policing, order, and crime rates would not *establish* the specific norm-focused hypotheses. In the case of New York City, it would not confirm that the *social meaning* of order changed people's behaviors. As we saw, other explanations exist, including the enhanced surveillance that accompanies order-maintenance policing, the increased number of searches and seizures, the deterrent effect of increased police presence, or the increased certainty of arrest.

The important methodological point is that, once we have taken the "social meaning turn"—as I believe we must—quantitative correlations between enforcement and crime will no longer be sufficient. In order to study a norm-focused hypothesis, we need to rethink our methodology.

An Illustration: Juvenile Snitching Policies

An illustration may help here. Proponents of the Charleston policy argue that encouraging snitching will change the social meaning of gun possession and thereby lower the incentive to carry. This is a plausible account of social meaning, but it is by no means the only plausible account. Once we have taken the "social meaning turn," other competing interpretations arise. This is true for juvenile gun possession, but it is equally true for most other practices, including policing strategies and punishment more generally. Toni Massaro's brilliant work on the social meaning of shaming penalties, for example, is a good illustration of the multiple meanings that may attach to contemporary punitive practices (Massaro 1997 and 1999).

In the specific context of a policy of encouraging juvenile snitching, the question that arises is: How else might such a policy affect social meaning? Here are some rival hypotheses. Perhaps snitching will develop negative social meaning. Maybe snitches will be ostracized, or worse, physically harmed. Maybe snitching will be viewed as cowardly. Maybe snitching will eventually "signal fear and thus invite aggression" (Kahan and Meares 1998b:824). Perhaps juveniles will form into bands of non-snitches and become aggressive toward non–band members or other bands. Maybe, over time, juveniles will develop ways of determining to whom they can show their weapons and to whom they cannot. Maybe, with time, membership in a particular non-snitching band will replace open gun carrying as the vehicle that "confer[s] status on the carrier because it expresses confidence and a willingness to defy authority" (Kahan and Meares 1998b:824). Perhaps juveniles will recruit others into their non-snitching band or will require certain rites of admission to their group.

Several of these hypotheses may turn out to be correct at any one time, or sequentially. Perhaps there first will be a period in which gun possession declines as a result of the changed social meaning. But maybe that period will be followed by an increase in gun carrying as non-snitching bands emerge and snitches are physically harmed. The initial decline in gun possession may last only a few days, or until the first snitch is murdered, or until the parents of that first snitch sue the school district for implementing a policy of snitching without affording snitches any protection. Or perhaps the first period may bring about some order that will positively influence behavior away from gun possession more permanently.

Moreover, juvenile gun possession itself may carry altogether different meanings. Especially in the aftermath of the tragedy at Columbine High School in Littleton, Colorado, juvenile gun possession in school may now be perceived by many students as extremely threatening rather than a source of admiration. Some juveniles possibly regard gun possession in terms of self-reliance. Others may think of guns as purely a market commodity. Still others may regard firearms as an object of curiosity.

In a 1999 incident in a middle school in Tucson, Arizona, a sixth-grader brought a forty-caliber pistol and approximately thirty rounds of ammunition to school. He had apparently obtained the weapon from his older brother, who belonged to a gang. According to the police officer who investigated the case and interviewed over forty students, the juvenile's apparent intention was to sell the gun for cash. Two other students reportedly indicated that they were interested in buying the gun for approximately eighty dollars, because they lived in a high-crime neighborhood and felt they needed protection on their way home from school. The gun passed through several hands and lockers at school, was displayed and examined by several students in the boys' bathroom, and was apparently fired in the air at a bus stop. Ultimately, a student told the authorities. The gun and ammunition were seized, and several students were punished (Huber 1999).[7]

The point of this sad story is that the gun had *different* meanings for different children. For some, guns may symbolize independence and self-reliance. For others, it may connote defiance of authority. For still others, it may represent authority. Others may view guns purely as a curiosity or as a commodity. Many of these different and complex meanings may have contributed to the juvenile gun possession in this instance. Yet many of these different and complex meanings may not be amenable to change by means of a policy of encouraging snitching. The social meaning of *that* gun possession was multifaceted, complex, and highly contextual.

None of this is to suggest in any way that we should *not* engage in this kind of interpretive analysis. To the contrary, at the conceptual level, I support the effort to move criminal law policy analysis in the direction of social meaning. I agree that it is the social meaning of be-havior—and not the behavior *standing alone*—that matters when we try to design public policies. In this respect, I endorse the turn to norms and meaning that Banfield, Wilson, and the New Progressives initiated in criminal justice. The purpose of my intervention is not to return to more behavioral approaches, but rather, as I will discuss later, to build on the social meaning turn and to give that turn critical potential.

But for present purposes—for purposes of methodology—the key question that arises is a *question of proof*. How do you prove that an in-terpretation of social meaning is not just *plausible* but *correct*? What re-search design and methods of proof does the social meaning turn call for? One thing that is clear is that, even if reliable data did suggest that the snitching policy in Charleston was accompanied by decreased gun carrying, the correlation itself could not establish that the snitching policy changed the *social meaning* of gun carrying. Nor would it estab-lish that it was the *change in social meaning* and not some other feature of the snitching policy, such as the reward itself in classic cost-benefit terms, that had an effect on behavior. To establish the specific norm-focused hypothesis, more research would be necessary.

The same is true with regard to Chicago's anti-gang loitering ordi-nance. Even if there had been a statistical correlation between the enforcement of the ordinance and a drop in gang activity (holding constant other influences on crime rates), the statistical relationship would tell us little, if anything, about *changes in social meaning*. It would tell us practically nothing about the specific norm-focused hypothe-sis, other than that the hypothesis is not obviously false. It would give us practically no information about the social meaning of gang mem-bership, about the possibility that the social meaning can be changed, or about whether the social meaning has in fact changed under the or-dinance. Even if it were possible to control fully for the myriad other influences on crime, a statistical correlation still would not reveal whether it was the purported change in *social meaning*, and not some *other* phenomenon associated with anti-gang loitering ordinances (such as incapacitation or deterrence), that brought about the reduc-tion in gang activity.

Proponents of the Chicago ordinance call for "properly controlled studies" of the correlation between enforcement and crime, studies that "control for the myriad other influences on crime rates" (Kahan and Meares 1998b:822 and n.24). But that is just the tip of the iceberg. It serves merely as a preliminary check to determine whether the norm-focused hypothesis has any chance of being verified. If there is *no* correlation between enforcement and lower crime rates, then clearly the *norm component* of the norm-focused hypothesis is unlikely to be correct. If there is a correlation, then a lot more research would need to be done. We would need to conduct in-depth qualitative analyses that explore the structure of meaning in the relevant community, the possibility of change in social meaning, and the effect on behavior. The study of social meaning is a complex, delicate, and difficult task. Social meanings are fluid: they may be socially constructed, they may change, and they may be changed. In addition, they are not necessarily transparent: they may be buried in our consciousness and may require some digging. The study of social meaning calls for intensive participant observation, open-ended interviews and conversations with multiple informants, and in-depth exploration of particular communities. It also calls for longitudinal studies in order to investigate fully any change in social meaning over time. In addition, once the qualitative data have been carefully obtained, it may be possible to code the data—to translate the data into a measurement system—and run quantitative analyses on the relationships between the policing initiative and changes in social meaning, and between those changes in social meaning and their effect on behavior.

The study of social meaning calls for the integration of qualitative and quantitative methods, an integration which is being increasingly reflected in the social sciences today. From political science and sociology to program evaluation in psychology, there is a growing movement to overcome the traditional paradigm war, and to combine qualitative and quantitative approaches in order to increase the amount of information brought to bear on hypotheses (King, Keohane, and Verba 1994:229 and 1995:479–480; Seale 1998:2; Reichardt and Rallis 1994:10–11). Researchers are increasingly finding that different methodological approaches compliment one another, and that "all good research . . . is best understood . . . to derive from the same underlying logic of inference" (King, Keohane, and Verba 1994:4). This is certainly true in the field of criminal law policy analysis after the social meaning turn.

Rethinking the Methodology

As I suggested in Chapter 2, the order-maintenance approach rests on norm-driven explanations and is best understood as a constructivist or interpretive social theory. This has important implications for methods of proof. The very question of proof is rendered, though not impossible, certainly more complicated. In contrast to proof in the context of a more behavioralist hypothesis or a rational choice hypothesis, proving a social meaning traditionally involves offering a rich contextual analysis of multiple meanings and countermeanings that intersects with and deepens other compelling accounts of social meaning and that is based on in-depth knowledge acquired through intensive interviewing, participating, observing, and exploring by detached researchers, corroborated as much as possible by statistical analyses.

The constructivist nature of social norm hypotheses has specific implications for social-scientific methods and research design—implications that need to be addressed head-on. Clifford Geertz's writings are the natural place to start.[8] In the 1960s, Geertz led the interpretive turn in anthropology (Geertz 1995:114). The discipline of anthropology at the time was dominated by a notion of culture that had begun to lose its critical edge. Geertz narrowed the idea of culture and redefined it, in interpretive terms, as the structure of meaning within which we come to understand human actions, relations, emotions, thoughts, and desires. "The concept of culture I espouse," Geertz explained, "is essentially a semiotic one. Believing, with Max Weber, that man is an animal suspended in webs of significance he himself has spun, I take culture to be those webs, and the analysis of it to be therefore not an experimental science in search of law but an interpretive one in search of meaning" (1973:5). Geertz participated in the effort to redefine the ethnographic enterprise and to create what has come to be known as "symbolic anthropology." In his words, "[T]his redefinition consisted in placing the systematic study of meaning, the vehicles of meaning, and the understanding of meaning at the very center of research and analysis: to make of anthropology, or anyway cultural anthropology, a hermeneutical discipline" (1995:114).

Geertz's use of the term "culture" bears a strong resemblance to the use of the term "social meaning" by norm-focused scholars. Geertz's explanation, for instance, of the social meaning of the Balinese cockfight as a dramatization of status concerns, and of the multiple expressive dimensions involved in the kinship loyalties, hostility relationships, or cross-loyalties in the center bet of a Balinese cockfight (1972:18–23), could be a model for social norm explanations of the social meaning of, for example, juvenile gun carrying or disorderly behavior. Both situations locate human activity within a web of meaning that helps us make sense of the feelings, perceptions, emotions, and thoughts of the participants. Because of the strong kinship, Geertz's writings are a natural place to look for a discussion of the implications of the interpretive turn for social-scientific methods.

And, as Geertz eloquently demonstrated, those implications are profound. The interpretive turn entails a different sensitivity to methods of proof, to conceptions of knowledge, and to notions of objectivity. In anthropology, Geertz suggests, proof is a matter more of detailed and convincing case studies, of thick descriptions derived from intense participant observation, and of immersion in language, customs, and practices, than it is of using someone else's data and running regressions. Although Geertz concedes that "numbers normally carry the day," he suggests that "they remain somehow ancillary: necessary of course, but insufficient, not quite the point. The problem—rightness, warrant, objectivity, truth—lies elsewhere, rather less accessible to dexterities of method" (1995:18). Where it lies, according to Geertz, is in facilitating further understanding, further insight, further meaning. It lies in creating a structure of representation that helps make sense of events. "What recommends [certain interpretations], or disrecommends them if they are ill-constructed, is the further figures that issue from them: their capacity to lead on to extended accounts which, intersecting other accounts of other matters, widen their implications and deepen their hold" (1995:19). As Geertz explains:

> [W]e are all suspicious of casting the social sciences in the image of the natural sciences, and of general schemes which explain too much. We have sought, rather, to advance a conception of research centered on the analysis of the significance of social actions for those who carry

them out and of the beliefs and institutions that lend to those actions that significance. Human beings, gifted with language and living in history, are, for better or worse, possessed of intentions, visions, memories, hopes, and moods, as well as of passions and judgments, and these have more than a little to do with what they do and why they do it. An attempt to understand their social and cultural life in terms of forces, mechanisms, and drives alone, objectivized variables set in systems of closed causality, seems unlikely of success. (1995:127)

The interpretive turn also calls for a methodology that recognizes, among other things, the important role of the researcher in formulating and building structures of representation within which events have meaning. It calls for a self-conscious and critical assessment of the researcher's role in interpreting meaning. The perceived force or aptness of an interpretation may depend on the intellectual context within which the discipline exists, as well as the wider moral and cultural setting that frames the representation. The force of specific interpretations may change as a result of personal and professional experiences and political shifts in academia and beyond. In anthropology and other social sciences, for instance, the framework of meaning based on earlier ethnographic methods has been undermined by later writings, especially postcolonialist writings (1995:128–130). The changing political, professional, and disciplinary landscapes, as well as one's own professional and emotional development and engagement in observation, inevitably affect the perceived strength of proposed interpretations. This is not something to ignore but rather something to adjust to, to work through, to understand, and, most important, to value.

Geertz's writings are representative of how interpretive theory affects—or should affect—social science methodology: insofar as norm-focused scholarship is a moderate type of constructivist theory, it should go hand in hand with what Geertz calls a "post-positivist critique of empirical realism" (1995:167). And it is here that I sense a disconnect in the order-maintenance approach. Though interpretive *in theory*, the norm-focused writings *in practice* rely too often on numerical studies that correlate police enforcement with criminal conduct. These studies tell us little, if anything, about *social meaning*.

Concrete Implications

The implications of interpretive theory for methods of proof translate into concrete, practical suggestions for the study of social meaning. Social norm hypotheses focus on the intermediary role of social meaning in the relationship between policing practices and changes in behavior. The typical social norm explanation involves a hypothesis of the following type:

| Police technique [A] | → | Change in behavior [B] | → | Change in social meaning [C] | → | Change in criminal behavior [D] |

So, for instance, a policy of rewarding snitching [A] will produce some snitching [B] which will change the social meaning of gun possession [C] and thereby reduce gun carrying [D]. Anti-gang loitering ordinances [A] result in less hanging around [B] which may change the meaning of gang membership [C] and reduce gang activity [D]. Similarly, reverse drug stings [A] will result in the arrest of suburban buyers [B] which will change the social meaning of drug-enforcement policies [C] and result in more respect for the police in the inner city [D].

Moreover, the typical social norm explanation must exclude other hypotheses that do not necessarily focus on social meanings, of the following type:

| Police technique [A] | → | Change in behavior [Y] | → | Change in criminal behavior [D] |

So, for example, the police technique of order-maintenance policing [A] may result in a reduction in criminal activity in neighborhoods that are rendered more orderly [D]. Two competing hypotheses may be offered to explain the relationship between [A] and [D]. The first is a norm-focused hypothesis and it relies on a change in social meaning [C]: order-maintenance policing [A] produces a lot of order, and order has a different social meaning from disorder. The change of norms from disorder to order, therefore, entails a change in social meanings [C] which encourages law-abiding behavior and discourages disorderly conduct. This change results in decreased criminal activity [D]. The second hypothesis, a more behavioral hypothesis, focuses on a change in behavior [Y]. The police strategy [A] produces an increase in the number of police misdemeanor arrests and incarcerations [Y], resulting in the incapacitation of a greater number of would-be serious criminals; for example, when the police arrest a turnstile jumper, the police may have incapacitated a potential thief and thereby reduced the number of serious criminal acts. This second hypothesis is more behavioral in the sense that the intermediating factor [Y] can be measured by the number of misdemeanor arrests and incarcerations. There are, of course, numerous other hypotheses, but for purposes of this discussion, we can stop here.

This modeling makes clear an important theoretical implication: it is the *interpretive* element of the norm-focused hypothesis that yields predictive knowledge. Although the "social meaning turn" may not originally have been intended to be predictive (Geertz 1973:14), social meaning plays a predictive role in the order-maintenance approach to criminal justice. The purely behavioral relationship between [A] and [D] alone is not what allows social norm theorists to predict the effectiveness of other proposed policing strategies. It is the interpretive element of social meaning [C] that allows for generalization and prediction.

In this regard, the order-maintenance approach departs from more traditional views of the social sciences. Many scholars associate the social sciences with *explanation* in contrast to *interpretation,* which they associate with literary or postmodern or other interdisciplinary approaches such as feminism, critical race theory, or critical legal studies (see, e.g., Galanter and Edwards 1997:377, 384). Explanation is traditionally linked with causality and prediction, interpretation with description and critique. Marc Galanter and his co-author, Mark Edwards, for instance, suggest that "if there is a pivotal intellectual rivalry in the legal academy, it exists not among the economic and other social scientific versions of explanatory inquiry, but between explanatory and interpretive approaches to understanding law and its social context" (1997:384). By espousing both the "interpretive turn" as well as predictions based on norm-focused hypotheses, social norm scholars directly challenge this traditional understanding.

What is also clear from this analysis is the implication for methods of proof: if we focus exclusively on the quantitative relationship between order-maintenance policing [A] and the change in criminal activity [D], we will learn very little, if anything, about our two competing hypotheses. In other words, a time-series analysis of the drop in the crime rate in New York City will tell us little, if anything, about social meanings or about the social norm hypothesis. If we are able reliably to exclude independent variables other than [A]—for example, other known or suspected determinants of crime—we might conclude that neither hypothesis has been falsified. We might conclude that they both may be true. But we could say little more about those hypotheses.

Now, it may well be the case that some policy analysts are prepared to endorse order-maintenance policing purely because of the relationship between [A] and [D]—if, for instance, they are confident that no other factor was chiefly responsible for the decrease in crime and that the benefits of [D] outweighed the costs of [A]. Some policy analysts might argue that we should support the quality-of-life initiative for the reason that it has coincided with a decline in crime in New York City. Similarly, some policy analysts might argue that we should endorse juvenile snitching policies because they have coincided with reduced crime rates in Charleston, South Carolina; or that we should support anti-gang loitering ordinances because crime in Chicago has decreased since 1992. But surely a social norm policy analyst would not be content leaving matters at this rudimentary stage. The social norm explanation is more than mere untestable speculation about the relationship between [A] and [D]. It is intended to be predictive. It is intended to allow us to design *prospective* policing initiatives based on the norm pathway. The goal of social norm theory is to enrich policy analysis, explain the causal pathway, and offer prospective solutions. "Law and norms can interact in ways that either enhance the deterrent aims of the law or inhibit them," Kahan and Meares emphasize. "Devising effective law enforcement policies *requires taking this interaction into account*" (1998b:809, emphasis added). In order to enrich the discussion, the policy analyst must do more than conduct statistical analyses of the relationship between [A] and [D].

The policy analyst must instead study the social meaning of order [C], which calls for careful qualitative analysis. It calls for in-depth interviews of informants, participatory observation, and other investigatory or experimental techniques that probe the structure of meaning. It is unlikely that a survey will be fully adequate in unearthing social meaning. This is not to suggest, though, that there is no role for quantitative methods. Once the qualitative data have been obtained, it may well be possible to code the data, to translate the data into a measurement system that would allow the researcher to run quantitative studies on the relationships between [A] and [C] and between [C] and [D].

A further crucial task is to distinguish between the two competing hypotheses, and to choose whether the social norm factor [C] is a better explanation than the more behavioral factor [Y]. Sampson and Cohen investigate and try to distinguish between two such hypotheses. As noted earlier, they concede that, from their model, they are unable to distinguish which is correct. Ultimately, they support the social norm hypothesis for two reasons: first, because the hypothesis has a "strong theoretical framework" (Sampson and Cohen 1988:185); and second, because the deterrence hypothesis, which has been subjected to more testing, "has been seriously questioned on both empirical and theoretical grounds in previous research" (1988:183). The problem with this approach, however, is that the lack of serious validity problems regarding the social norm hypothesis may be a result of the fact that testing to date has been "sparse" (1988:166), and also that the type of testing represented in this study (testing the statistical relationship between [A] and [D]) is not particularly discriminating.

In contrast, it is possible that qualitative analyses and in-depth case studies may themselves lend support to the social norm hypothesis. Another approach, consistent with the first, is to multiply, to the extent possible, the observable implications of the two hypotheses in order to try to find ways in which the two hypotheses would lead to diverging results—ways in which the hypotheses implicate consequences at odds with one another—and then test which results obtain. That would be a better way of distinguishing between competing hypotheses.

This kind of work, however, has not yet been done in the context of norm-focused hypotheses. As a result, we have no reason to believe that, even if order-maintenance policies were found to be effective, they are operating through social norm and social meaning pathways. In sum, from a methodological perspective, the existing and available data tell us little if anything about the meaning and social influence of the norm of orderliness—about the core insight of order-maintenance policing.

# PART II

# Theoretical Critique

As I have shown to this point, the order-maintenance approach lacks an evidentiary foundation. Contrary to accepted wisdom, the broken windows theory has not been established. Wesley Skogan's data are so weak that it is probably best not to draw any conclusions from the data at all. Even if one were to do so—as Skogan does in *Disorder and Decline*—the conclusion would not support the broken windows theory. In Skogan's data, the most reliable crime victimization variable is burglary victimization, since it has the highest number of observations, is among the better-reported crimes, and is, by definition, *neighborhood specific*. When I replicate Skogan's analysis, however, burglary is inversely related to disorder, holding constant Skogan's measures of poverty, stability, and race, and it has a high p-value (0.875). (See Table 3.4.) This remains true when I correct for certain design decisions. (See Table 3.9.) The only crime victimization variable that is significantly related to disorder—robbery victimization—is based on a survey question that is not neighborhood specific, and the possible link vanishes when the Newark neighborhoods are excluded from the data, which suggests that they exert excessive influence on the robbery findings.

The more recent study of Robert Sampson and Stephen Raudenbush finds that when antecedent neighborhood characteristics such as poverty and social solidarity were taken into account, "the connection between disorder and crime vanished in 4 out of 5 tests" (1999:637). While Sampson and Raudenbush recognize that there may be some link between robbery and disorder, they conclude, given the consistent and strong relationship between disorder, collective efficacy, and structural disadvantage across all crime variables, that in all likelihood "public disorder and most predatory crimes share similar theoretical features and are consequently explained by the same constructs at the neighborhood level, in particular the concentration of disadvantage and lowered collective efficacy" (1999:637).

There is little evidence that Mayor Giuliani's quality-of-life initiative in New York City significantly contributed to the concurrent sharp decline in crime. In the first place, there are numerous other factors—including an increase of over six thousand police officers, shifting drug use patterns, computerized tracking systems, and other changes—that together contributed to the drop in crime. Second, and more important, whatever impact the quality-of-life initiative may have had on crime rates, it is in all likelihood due not to a broken windows effect but rather to the enhanced surveillance afforded by a policy of aggressive policing. There is likewise no good evidence—in fact, there are mostly inverse correlations—that enforcement of Chicago's anti-gang loitering ordinance has reduced gang-related criminal activity in Chicago. And there is no evidence whatsoever that juvenile snitching policies have been effective in Charleston in reducing illegal juvenile gun possession.

Perhaps even more damning, the focus on purported correlations between enforcement and crime rates is methodologically simplistic. Even if there were a positive correlation between disorder and crime, or between enforcement and crime, the correlation itself would tell us nothing about whether social norms or meaning played any role in reducing criminal activity. The correlation would, to be sure, make it unlikely that the hypothesis was patently false from the start—at least, if all other relevant factors were taken into account. But it would tell us nothing about the *social norm* component of order maintenance. It would tells us nothing about the social meaning of disorder, gang membership, or juvenile gun possession. In other words, it would not even begin to address the difficult task of interpreting social meaning.

As we turn to the theoretical realm, then, it is important to recognize that we are dealing with purely speculative ideas. This is, of course, hardly out of the ordinary. Many, perhaps most, theoretical accounts in policy debates are generally not validated scientifically. My purpose, again, has been not to hold "broken windows" to an unrealistically high social-scientific standard, but rather to clear the ground of significant misperceptions about the order-maintenance approach and to place the approach on a more accurate and realistic empirical footing.

At the theoretical level, the lack of empirical evidence, though startling at first, is not entirely surprising. The order-maintenance approach rests on certain dichotomies—between, for instance, order and disorder, or law abiders and the disorderly—that are somewhat unexamined. The squeegee man, the panhandler, the homeless person, the turnstile jumper, the unattached adult, the public drunk: these are, according to the new approach, the true culprits of serious crime. Wilson and Kelling refer to them as "disreputable or obstreperous or unpredictable people" (Wilson and Kelling 1982:30; see also Wilson 1968:39). They are the ones, Wilson and Kelling argue, who turn a stable neighborhood into "an inhospitable and frightening jungle" (1982:31–32). Wesley Skogan refers to them as "[u]nattached males, the homeless, and the aimless [who] live in boarded up buildings, seedy residential hotels and flophouses" (Skogan 1987:86). Dan Kahan rehearses the same categories. He writes:

> Disorder is . . . pregnant with meaning: Public drunkenness, prostitution, aggressive panhandling and similar behavior signal not only that members of the community are inclined to engage in disorderly conduct, but also that the community is unable or unwilling to enforce basic norms. . . . In this environment, *individuals who are otherwise inclined to engage in crime* are much more likely to do so.
>
> The meaning of disorder can also influence the behavior of *committed law-abiders* in a way that is likely to increase crime. If they can, *law-abiding citizens* are likely to leave a neighborhood that is pervaded by disorder. Their departure increases the concentration of *law breakers*, thereby multiplying their interactions with each other and accentuating their mutually reinforcing propensities to engage in crime. *Law-abiders* who stick it out, moreover, are more likely to avoid the streets, where their simple presence would otherwise be a deterrent to crime. . . . The *law-abiders'* fear of crime thus facilitates even more crime. (1997a:370–371, emphasis added)

These sharp categories—of law abiders and disorderly—divide the world into two distinct realms. But is the line really so clear? After all, who are the disorderly and what is disorder? What does disorder really communicate? And why are disorderly activities such as loitering, littering, and begging—once viewed simply as nuisances—now perceived as so harmful to society? How have the bums, winos, and hustlers—the "Ratsos" of the world—once just the losers of society, become so dangerous to our social fabric? It is to these more theoretical questions that I turn in Part II.

# CHAPTER 5

# On Disorderly, Disreputable, or Unpredictable People

The order-maintenance approach places great emphasis on the norm of orderliness. The approach privileges the law abider who cares for his home, his lawn, and his children, and the neighborhood merchant. It frowns on the unattached adult and the kids hanging out on corners. It privileges order, regularity, and predictability. It frowns on the disorderly, the obstreperous, and the unpredictable. And the line between the two is clear. It is second nature for many of us—especially those of us who grew up in a large city such as New York or Chicago. It is intuitive for most police officers. The line between order and disorder is natural and instinctive.

But how, one might ask, do some police officers deal with the disorderly people? "In the words of one officer," Wilson and Kelling report, "'We kick ass'" (1982:35). The police "rough up" young toughs and arrest on suspicion (1982:33). Elsewhere Kelling notes: "Another officer in Chicago described in similar terms how he dealt with gang members who would not follow his orders: 'I say please once, I say please twice, and then I knock them on their ass.' The officer meant it: although a courteous and generally congenial man, he had grown up in Chicago's public housing developments and was not prepared to stand by and watch gangs terrorize his family, friends, and neighbors" (Kelling and Coles 1996:166).

On close inspection, the desired order depends on a lot of disorder, irregularity, and brutality. "'We kick ass.' Project residents both know and approve of this," Wilson and Kelling contend. "None of this is easily reconciled with any conception of due process or fair treatment" (1982:35). But that is not a problem, perhaps because force is so vital to the order-maintenance function. That function, after all, harks back to the 1950s, when police officers assisted neighborhoods in asserting control over delinquency, "sometimes violently" (1982:33). It looks back to a time when "[y]oung toughs were roughed up, people were arrested 'on suspicion' or for vagrancy, and prostitutes and petty thieves were routed. 'Rights' were something enjoyed by decent folk, and perhaps also by the serious professional criminal, who avoided violence and could afford a lawyer" (1982:33).

The order-maintenance strategy, it turns out, depends on arresting people on meaningless charges. What makes the system work is the availability of broad criminal laws that allow the police to take people off the streets because they look suspicious. "Until quite recently in many states, and even today in some places," Wilson and Kelling note, "the police make arrests on such charges as 'suspicious person' or 'vagrancy' or 'public drunkenness'—charges with scarcely any legal meaning. These charges exist not because society wants judges to punish vagrants or drunks but because it wants an officer to have the legal tools to remove undesirable persons from a neighborhood when informal efforts to preserve order in the streets have failed" (1982:35). In these situations, the desire for order excuses the questionable legality of the arrests. Referring to a police officer on the Newark beat, Wilson and Kelling state: "Sometimes what [he] did could be described as 'enforcing the law,' but just as often it involved taking informal or extralegal steps. . . . Some of the things he did probably would not withstand a legal challenge" (1982:31). These are, after all, euphemisms for "illegal."

Wilson and Kelling refer to many rules, especially the "informal but widely understood rules" of police-civilian encounters (1982:30). They seem to privilege regularity. But in fact, *irregularity* is central to their analysis, because it is precisely the application of universal rules that most clearly undermines the order-maintenance function. The rigidity of rules, even rules that may be perfectly appropriate in individual cases, deprives police officers of needed flexibility. "[N]o universal standards are available to settle arguments over disorder," they contend. This explains why "a judge may not be any wiser or more effective than a police officer" in resolving street disputes. In fact, "[a] particular rule that seems to make sense in the individual case makes no sense when it is made a universal rule and applied to all cases" (1982:35). As Wilson explained in 1968:

> In any particular case, the patrolman may act improperly by abusing or exceeding his authority, making arrests or street stops on the basis of personal prejudice or ill-temper, or handling a situation differently from the way the administrator or mayor might handle it. But to say that in a given case the observer or the community could have prescribed a better course of action is not to say that a better course of action, applicable to all or most situations, could be prescribed generally and in advance. Put another way, the possibility of deciding in a particular instance that the police behaved wrongly does not mean that one can formulate a meaningful policy for how the police should behave in all cases. (1968:278)

In effect, regularity on the street depends on irregularity in police practice—mixed, of course, with some regularity in the choice of suspects. The need for irregularity, in turn, triggers a demand for police discretion and expertise. Instead of burdening the police with rules of engagement, Wilson and Kelling rely, for instance, on training and selection. "[H]ow do we ensure that age or skin color or national origin or harmless mannerisms will not also become the basis for distinguishing the undesirable from the desirable?" they ask. The response: "We can offer no wholly satisfactory answer to this important question. We are not confident that there *is* a satisfactory answer, except to hope that by their selection, training, and supervision, the police will be inculcated with a clear sense of the outer limit of their discretionary authority" (Wilson and Kelling 1982:35).

Surprisingly, disorder, brutality, and irregularity are inscribed in the "Broken Windows" essay. They are linked to order, rules, and regularity. And, ironically, they operate at cross-purposes. For if, as the essay suggests, there is such a clear line separating order from disorder, then why do the police need so much discretion? Wouldn't disorder be immediately apparent to anyone? To a review board? To an administrative panel? To a rule-making body? To a court? It turns out that there seems to be a lot of disorder in order, and also, importantly, some order in disorder, some regularity with regard to the usual targets of police discretion and excessive force. There is some order in who may be getting roughed up.

Who drew the line between order and disorder in the first place? And how do we define disorder? Why is it, exactly, that *loitering* is disorderly? Or *littering?* In some neighborhoods, residents sit on the steps of their houses and chat. They gather. They socialize. They hang out. They are idle. They are unattached. They light a cigarette and, after smoking it, throw the butt on the ground or in the gutter. Kids make chalk markings on the street, play ball, kick empty Coke cans, tussle, chase after and scream at one another. They buy an ice cream from the truck and throw the wrapper on the ground. A homeless man rummages through the garbage bin looking for cans to recycle and asks for money as customers exit the grocery store. A passerby gives him some change. The passerby has seen him before. He has been a regular at that corner for some time now. What makes some of these acts disorderly and others not? And where is the line between absent-mindedness, laziness, bad manners, and disorder?

How many of us have done these things? Tossed a cigarette on the sidewalk, beat a fare, drunk a beer on the street, or even urinated in a public place? How many of us have slipped a bus pass to a friend or jumped a turnstile when we were in a hurry to get home and all our spending money was gone? How many of us have defied authority, hung out, broken the rules—particularly when we were adolescents or young adults? How many of us got away with these acts—or just got a slap on the wrist and a warning—because we were cute, inoffensive, maybe white, maybe middle class, or just plain lucky? And why should we distinguish so sharply between street disorder and other disorder? Paying a housekeeper under the table is a crime. So is avoiding sales tax by paying cash or giving a false out-of-state residence, underestimating taxes, or taking office supplies home. Tax evasion, insider trading, insurance or loan misrepresentation, noncompliance with environmental or waste disposal regulations and police brutality—these are all disorderly acts, and yet they figure nowhere in the theory of order-maintenance policing. Who gets to define disorder for purposes of order maintenance and on what basis? How come the focus of disorder is on youthful street crimes, the types of crimes committed predominantly by males aged fifteen to twenty-nine, and not on more mature white-collar crimes, the types of crimes committed predominantly by older white males? How come the focus of disorder is not on police misconduct?

The truth is, it is often hard to distinguish between the law abider and the disorderly. This is illustrated well, for instance, in both Wilson and Kelling's "Broken Windows" article and Kahan's writings. They both discuss and rely heavily on a particular social science experiment conducted in 1969 by Philip Zimbardo, a Stanford University psychologist. Zimbardo arranged to have an abandoned automobile parked in a public space to see whether it would be vandalized. He conducted the study twice, parking the automobile once on the campus of Stanford University and once in the Bronx in New York City. In the Bronx, the car was promptly vandalized. At Stanford, the abandoned car remained intact for a week. After a week, Zimbardo smashed the windshield, whereupon passersby then began to vandalize the car. Yet the vandals in Zimbardo's study did not fit the bill of the typical disorderly person. Wilson and Kelling describe the Bronx suspects as follows:

> The car in the Bronx was attacked by "vandals" within ten minutes of its "abandonment." The first to arrive were a family—father, mother, and young son—who removed the radiator and battery. Within twenty-four hours, virtually everything of value had been removed. Then random destruction began—windows were smashed, parts torn off, upholstery ripped. Children began to use the car as a playground. Most of the adult "vandals" were well-dressed, apparently clean-cut whites. (Wilson and Kelling 1982:31)

Curiously, these vandals do not fit well in the category of "disreputable or obstreperous or unpredictable people" (Wilson and Kelling 1982:30). They do not seem to be drunks, addicts, rowdy teenagers, or unattached adults. Dan Kahan describes the vandals as "clean-cut passersby, many of whom gratuitously inflicted damage upon [the car]" (Kahan 1997a:356 n.27). Similarly, Wilson and Kelling describe the experiment at Stanford University: "The car in Palo Alto sat untouched for more than a week. Then Zimbardo smashed part of it with a sledgehammer. Soon, passersby were joining in. Within a few hours, the car had been turned upside down and utterly destroyed. Again, the 'vandals' appeared to be primarily respectable whites" (Wilson and Kelling 1982:31). Kahan writes:

Zimbardo placed the car, hood up, on the campus of Stanford University, where it remained in pristine condition for over a week. Zimbardo then smashed the windshield with a sledgehammer. At that point, passersby spontaneously joined in the carnage, gleefully visiting further destruction upon the car and (over time) stripping it of valuable parts. The sight of others openly pillaging the car, Zimbardo concluded, had released passersby from their inhibitions against vandalism and theft. (1997a:356)

In what category do we place these "vandals"? Wilson and Kelling characterize them as "people out for fun or plunder," and even "people who ordinarily would not dream of doing such things and who probably consider themselves law-abiding" (Wilson and Kelling 1982:31). Are they "individuals who are inclined to commit crime"? Or are they respectable "law abiders"? The point is, of course, that these may be the wrong questions. The proper question may be, why use these categories in the first place?—particularly since the category of the disorderly is so unstable. It triggers an aggressive response to the disorderly—reflected in the idea of "cracking down" on disorderly people—even in the absence of any empirical evidence.

What exactly does disorder mean? What does it communicate? Proponents of the broken windows theory assume that it means a neighborhood has lost control and doesn't care about crime. But surely there are other plausible meanings. It could signal artistic ferment, a youth hangout, rebellion, or an alternative lifestyle. It could communicate frenzied commercial activity, a frantic pace of life, or a bullish stock market. It could signal theatrical performance or loose sexual mores. Or it might just signal poverty, unemployment, and despair.

Similarly, the meaning of order is not so transparent. An orderly neighborhood could well signal that the community is organized and vigilant. It could also mean that it is a commercial sex strip and that the owners and operators want johns to feel safe and welcome. Or it could signal a strong Mafia presence. Or maybe a lot of wealth. Or maybe a strong police presence. Or maybe police brutality. There may not be such a clean line between law abiders and order on the one hand and the disorderly on the other. As Sampson and Raudenbush report,

> in an interesting twist, [Mary] Pattillo found that the leader of a major
> black gang [in Chicago] was a long-time resident who engaged in mul-

tiple acts of social control (e.g. threats, monitoring) to keep the neighborhood free of street crime and signs of disorder (e.g., graffiti, vandalism, prostitution). Patillo writes that both sides—the residents and the
gang leaders—"spurn disorder, actively combat graffiti, and show dis-
dain for activities that may invite negative attention, such as loitering or
public fighting." . . . The phenomenon of informal efforts to socially
control local crime and disorder has long been reported in white work-
ing-class neighborhoods dominated by the mob. (1999:611)

Similarly, commercial sex neighborhoods are often very orderly (see
Chapter 3; Sampson and Raudenbush 1999:611 n.6).

On close examination, the meaning of order and disorder is not as
stable or as fixed as social norm theorists suggest. The order that
seems at first so natural, so apparent, and so obvious may be at one
and the same time disorderly, and the disorder does not allow itself to
be minimized, compartmentalized, or explained away. When we begin
to investigate the order, it turns out that matters are more complicated. There is a striking passage in Michel Foucault's *The Order of
Things* that describes this experience:

> The fundamental codes of a culture . . . establish for every man, from
> the very first, the empirical orders with which he will be dealing and
> within which he will be at home. At the other extremity of thought,
> there are the scientific theories or the philosophical interpretations
> which explain why order exists in general, what universal law it obeys,
> what principle can account for it, and why this particular order has
> been established and not some other. But between these two regions
> . . . lies a domain which, even though its role is mainly an intermediary
> one, is nonetheless fundamental. . . . It is here that a culture, impercep-
> tibly deviating from the empirical orders prescribed for it by its pri-
> mary codes, instituting an initial separation from them, causes them to
> lose their original transparency, relinquishes its immediate and invisi-
> ble powers, frees itself sufficiently to discover that these orders are per-
> haps not the only possible ones or the best ones; . . . that there exists,
> below the level of its spontaneous orders, things that are in themselves
> capable of being ordered, that belong to a certain unspoken order; the
> fact, in short, that order *exists*. (1970:xx; 1966:11–12)[1]

The meaning of order in social norm writings seems to be unmediated
in this fundamental way. It resembles "the fundamental codes of a cul-

ture"—a code that has not yet been questioned, that has not yet lost its "original transparency." But the meaning of order may not be so clear.

The order-maintenance approach does not explore the extent to which the social meaning of order and disorder itself may be constructed, may change, and may be changed. Norm-focused scholars treat the social meaning of order and disorder as *natural, fixed, or necessary*. This is surprising, because the central insight of the norm-focused approach is precisely that social meaning may be constructed and may change, but that when the meaning is not contested, it can become fixed or natural. As Lawrence Lessig explains:

> [W]hen these understandings or expectations become uncontested and invisible, social meanings derived from them appear natural, or necessary. The more they appear natural, or necessary, or uncontested, or invisible, the more powerful or unavoidable or natural social meanings drawn from them appear to be. The converse is also true: the more contested or contingent, the less powerful meanings appear to be. Social meanings carry with them, or transmit, the force, or contestability, of the presuppositions that constitute them. They come with the pedigree, presumed or argued for, of their foundation. (1995:960–961)

The order-maintenance approach fully appreciates Lessig's argument. Most of the proposed police strategies—youth curfews, anti-gang loitering ordinances, juvenile snitching policies—depend for their effectiveness on contesting and changing the social meaning of practices and institutions such as gang membership or gun possession. Yet, with regard to the most central practice of all, namely order and disorder, the social norm literature is uncritical. It does not question their social meaning, and offers no explanation why their meaning should have a different ontological status from that of all other social meaning.

The category of "the disorderly" and the meaning of "disorder" are not so clear after all. Our intuitions about who constitutes the disorderly may be more troubling than they seem at first blush. This should be obvious, yet it is so hard to remember. And it is hard to remember precisely because the categories have become so natural to so many of us. They have become second nature.

Broken windows embraces an unmediated aesthetic of order, cleanliness, and sobriety. But it also embraces irregularity, illegality, and brutality. Perhaps this is no accident. To borrow a phrase from Wilson and Kelling, "disorder and crime are usually inextricably linked, in a kind of developmental sequence" (1982:31). The authors were referring, of course, to disorder in the streets, not disorder in the police station house. Yet the disorder that the authors seek to repress may return to haunt them.

## Tracing the Problem Back to Social Theory

It is somewhat jarring to uncover what appears to be a straightforward policy of aggressive misdemeanor arrests masquerading as a neighborhood beautification program or as an innocent phenomenon of social influence. It is especially jarring given that broken windows proponents want to find alternatives to the traditional devices of arrest and incarceration. Where did the new approach go off track? The difficulty can be traced back to the categories of "honest persons" and "the disorderly." Under the broken windows theory, these categories are vested with a certain naturalness, or fixity, or organicity. It is as if the world were naturally divided into law abiders and lawbreakers—as if these divisions were organic to society. In this sense, the categories appear to be borrowed from a traditional sociological approach, and it is there, I suggest, that we need to return in order to work our way out of the difficulty.

On close examination, the categories in the broken windows theory—somewhat paradoxically, yet not entirely surprisingly—resemble certain categories in the work of Emile Durkheim. It is not surprising because social norm scholars claim Durkheim as an intellectual predecessor, especially in relation to punishment and social construction (Kahan 1996:594–596; Lessig 1995:949 n.19). But it is somewhat paradoxical because Durkheim is one of the first to have recognized the social basis of human consciousness—the fact that conceptual categories are deeply linked to social origin and that knowledge is socially constructed.

Durkheim discussed the social basis of human consciousness in *The Elementary Forms of Religious Life*, and positioned his theory as a synthetic resolution of the traditional debate between apriorists and empiricists (Durkheim 1995:18). Durkheim took from the apriorists a conception of human categories but infused that notion with social history: he described the categories as collective representations that derive from the religious, moral, political, and economic institutions and histories of society. These collective representations, he wrote, are "the product of an immense cooperation that extends not only through space but also through time; to make them," he emphasized, "a multitude of different minds have associated, intermixed, and combined their ideas and feelings; long generations have accumulated their experience and knowledge" (1995:15).

From this one might have expected to gain some critical leverage on collective representations—some critical leverage that might have allowed, for instance, questioning of the categories of law abiders and lawbreakers. But, in Durkheim's view, these collective representations were, in a complex way, necessary. They were not, he argued, simple habits that we could slip off with no effort—though they were also neither permanent nor unchanging. They were not purely artificial constructs—though they also were not entirely naturally given (1995:17). For Durkheim, these collective representations were "works of art, in a sense, but an art that imitates nature ever more perfectly" (1995:17 n.22). And they worked together to form a coherent understanding of the world. This coherence was shared, Durkheim argued, by the members of a society. "To live," he emphasized, "[society] requires not only a minimum moral consensus but also a minimum logical consensus that it cannot do without either. Thus, in order to prevent dissidence, society weighs on its members with all its authority" (1995:16).

Order maintenance, I would argue, shares this Durkheimian understanding of social categories as imitating nature. It shares, more specifically, the categories of law abiders and lawbreakers, as well as the emphasis on order over disorder. Durkheim's discussion of criminal sanctions, especially his legitimation theory, rests on this distinction between honest and disorderly persons. Similarly, Durkheim's discussion of anomie and, more generally, of the role of law in society, also reflects a similar privileging of order over disorder. This, I argue, may be the source of the problem in the order-maintenance approach.

## Durkheim's Discussion of Criminal Sanctions

Durkheim's theory of legitimation received its most lucid treatment in his 1893 work, *On the Division of Labor in Society*. Durkheim explored there the issue of social solidarity—that is, the issue of the moral cohesiveness of society. He argued that, in modernity, repressive criminal sanctions played a decreasing role in the production of social solidarity. In their place, legal regulations in the private law context—restitutionary principles in contract, property, and commercial law—increased, resulting in the prospect of a healthier, in fact more robust, social solidarity.

Although criminal sanctions contributed less to the formation of social cohesion in modern times, the moral dimension of punishment nevertheless remained central to Durkheim's analysis. It was, in fact, this moral dimension that he identified as the function of criminal punishment. According to Durkheim, criminal sanctions in modern society served to legitimate social norms and reinforce solidarity within the community. Writing against the tradition of utilitarian theories of punishment, he argued that criminal punishments played a very small role in deterring crimes and an equally minimal role in rehabilitating offenders. It was, instead, legitimation of society that criminal sanctions achieved. (See generally Lukes and Scull 1983:1–27; Garland 1990:23–46.) Durkheim explained:

> [The role of punishment] is not the one commonly perceived. It does not serve, or serves only very incidentally, to correct the guilty person or to scare off any possible imitators. . . . Its real function is to maintain inviolate the cohesion of society by sustaining the common consciousness in all its vigour. If that consciousness were thwarted so categorically, it would necessarily lose some of its power, were an emotional reaction from the community not forthcoming to make good that loss. Thus there would result a relaxation in the bonds of social solidarity. . . . This is why it is right to maintain that *the criminal* should suffer in proportion to his crime, and why theories that deny to punishment any expiatory character appear, in the minds of many, to subvert the social order. . . . Thus, without being paradoxical, we may state that punishment is above all intended to have its effect upon *honest people.* (1984:62–63)

The broken windows characters are all there: the honest persons and the criminals. They play an integral role in Durkheim's analysis. For Durkheim—as well as for order-maintenance proponents—the criminal sanction exerts social influence on the honest person and on the disorderly *in different ways*. When control is exerted, honest persons bond, develop richer social solidarity, a thicker social fabric; criminals, by contrast, are sent on their way. These are, after all, the very characters that reappear in the broken windows theory, and they follow the very same pathways.

## Durkheim's Discussion of Legal Regulation

There is also a striking parallel between Durkheim's emphasis on legal regulation and the broken windows emphasis on order. For Durkheim, the social cohesion of modern society was at its optimal level when there was proper and sufficient legal regulation of commercial transactions on the basis of restitutionary principles. In contrast to societies that achieved healthy social solidarity by means of legal regulation, societies that became pathological suffered either from insufficient legal regulation (a state of anomie) or from the wrong kind of legal regulation (a state of forced division of labor). The categories of healthy social solidarity versus pathological anomic conditions bear a sharp resemblance to the privileging of order over disorder in the order-maintenance approach to criminal justice.

It is important to understand, as a preliminary matter, that the role of law in Durkheim's writings was itself paradoxical. At the methodological level, Durkheim treated law merely as an evidentiary fact, entirely derivative of the social phenomenon of the division of labor. Law was merely an effect, a consequence of social phenomena. This is, after all, the core of Durkheim's methodological insight: to use positive law as the *measure* with which to evaluate his dual hypotheses that, first, the function of the division of labor is to produce social solidarity, and second, that the organic solidarity produced by the division of labor in modern societies is more robust than the mechanical solidarity produced by collective consciousness in ancient societies. Durkheim states this explicitly in the first chapter of the *Division of Labor,* which is dedicated to method (Durkheim 1984:24). He there refers to positive law as an "external" datum which "symbolizes" the phenomenon of social solidarity. Law is the "perceptible effects" of social solidarity. It is "nothing more than this very organisation [the organization of social life] in its most stable and precise form" (1984:24–25). To use Durkheim's words, at the methodological level, law symbolizes, reproduces, mirrors, corresponds to, and provides an external interpretation of the moral phenomenon of social solidarity (1984:24–25, 27–28).

Durkheim was careful to differentiate the concept of effect from that of function or result. As he explained, he set out to investigate the *function* of the division of labor:

> We cannot use "aim" or "purpose," and speak of the goal of the division of labour, because that would suppose that the division of labour exists *for the sake of results* that we shall determine. To use "results" or "effects" cannot satisfy us either, because no idea of correspondence is evoked. On the other hand, the term "role" or "function" has the great advantage of implying that idea, but in no way prejudges the question of knowing how that correspondence has been established, or whether it arises from some intended and preconceived adaptation or from some adjustment after the event. (1984:11)

Durkheim realized this project—to investigate the *function* of the division of labor—by treating law within the category of *effects*. He denied positive law any autonomy: if there were any autonomous development of the law, it would not so perfectly mirror social organization. In this sense, law approximated a superstructure with no autonomy and no reciprocal effect on the change in the social environment. Durkheim concluded: "[O]ur method is clearly traced out for us. Since law *reproduces* the main forms of social solidarity, we have *only* to classify the different types of law in order to be able to investigate which types of social solidarity correspond to them" (1984:28, emphasis added). And so Durkheim's principal texts on punishment—*On the Division of Labor in Society* and his article in *L'Année Sociologique* (1899–1900) titled "Deux lois de l'évolution pénale"—told a story about the declining role of repressive law in modern society.

This is in sharp contrast, however, to Durkheim's substantive argument about the modern regulation of society through private law principals. At the substantive level, law, regularity, and order reigned in Durkheim's enterprise. And not just any law but an "iron law . . . against which it would be absurd to revolt" (1984:122). The primacy of legal regulation is clearly reflected in his diagnosis of the pathological condition which he calls "the anomic division of labor." Anomie—from the Greek *anomia*, "without law"—represents for Durkheim the primary pathology of modern society. It may take the form of the complete lack of regulation resulting in economic crises and bankruptcies. Or it may take the form of inappropriate regulation, as in the case of the forced division of labor and the resulting class war. But in all events, it is the lack of regulation that "does not allow the functions to perform regularly and harmoniously" (1984:303).

Under normal circumstances, Durkheim argued, human exchanges produce "a body of rules" (1984:304): "[T]he division of labour gives rise to rules ensuring peaceful and regular co-operation between the functions that have been divided up" (1984:338). The lack of such rules—anomie—is pathological, and arises only in "exceptional and abnormal circumstances" (1984:307). Thus, for Durkheim, the division of labor takes on a heavily regulated nature. His is an idea of social organization based on the paradigm of rule making and obedience—what we might call today the rule of law. Law played an equally important role in Durkheim's essay—as evidenced by the very title, "Deux lois de l'évolution pénale." The project of that essay was precisely to establish and explain certain "laws" about law, "two laws that appear to dominate the evolution of the punitive system" (Durkheim 1901:65). These two "laws" were, first, that the intensity of punishment increases in lower societies, as well as in authoritarian societies; and second, that deprivation of liberty alone tends to become the normal type of punishment (1901:65 and 78).

There is, consequently, a strong similarity between Durkheim and order maintenance—beyond merely the shared categories of honest persons and the disorderly. Durkheim privileged regulation and minimized repressive sanctions. Similarly, the order-maintenance approach presents itself as an "alternative to the severe punishments that dominate contemporary criminal law" (Kahan 1997b:2478). Rather than punish severely to deter, broken windows policing seeks to enforce, in part, order or rules of civilian conduct that are geared toward producing a more harmonious social environment with strong moral bonds. In sum, order maintenance endorses a similar form of social solidarity based on ordered relations.

## The Problem of Subject Creation

The problem with the categories of honest and disorderly persons is that they may not be as natural or organic as Durkheim or broken windows assume. The categories themselves may be the product of the very processes of punishment that legitimate society. In other words, the practices of punishment that we choose may participate in creating the categories of law abider and disorderly. But if, in fact, the processes of punishment not only create social solidarity among honest people but also simultaneously create the very category of honest people, then the legitimating effect on society is fabricated or artificial. It is not that punishment legitimates social cohesion or society, but that punishment shapes society—and different techniques of punishment would shape society differently.

The same is true of the social solidarity produced by extensive legal regulation. Under Durkheim's theory, ordered legal regulations serve and uphold the natural division of labor, which in turn produces social solidarity. But what if the legal regulations, instead of merely upholding the social division of labor, actually divide society into the different social strata and create the division of labor that marks modern society? Certainly the division of labor would be less "organic," to use Durkheim's terminology. It would be less natural and healthy, and would instead resemble far more the "mechanical," imposed social solidarity achieved by premodern systems of repressive criminal sanctions.

Similar questions arise in the context of order-maintenance policing. Under the broken windows theory, order maintenance influences the behavior of individuals who are inclined to engage in crime and of committed law abiders. It reduces law abiders' fear of crime and thereby encourages them to engage in conduct that discourages crime—such as walking the streets at night. At the same time, it dissuades the disorderly from engaging in crime by communicating that offenses will be punished. But what if order-maintenance policing, instead of merely influencing the behavior of these categories of individuals, actually helps shape or create these categories? What if the order itself—the order privileged by order-maintenance policing—does not simply uphold the community norms that result in greater moral cohesion and lower crime rates, but instead creates those community norms?

Michel Foucault asked precisely these questions of Durkheim's work. In fact, in the very first pages of his genealogy of the prison, *Discipline and Punish,* Foucault specifically defined his project in opposition to Durkheim:

This book is intended as a correlative history of the modern soul and of a new power to judge; a genealogy of the present scientifico-legal complex from which the power to punish derives its bases, justifications and rules, from which it extends its effects and by which it masks its ex-orbitant singularity.

But from what point can such a history of the modern soul on trial be written? . . . By studying only the general social forms, *as Durkheim did* . . . , one runs the risk of positing as the principle of greater le-niency in punishment processes of individualization that are rather one of the effects of the new tactics of power, among which are to be included the new penal mechanisms. (1979:23, emphasis added; 1975:27–28)

Foucault appropriates Durkheim's celebrated concepts the better to distance himself from Durkheim's method. Foucault's reference point is Durkheim. And so, immediately after the preceding passage, Foucault writes—and I italicize the words that refer to Durkheim:

This study obeys four general rules:

1. Do not concentrate the study of the punitive mechanisms on their *"repressive"* effects alone, on their "punishment" aspects alone, but situate them in a whole series of their possible positive effects, even if these seem marginal at first sight. As a conse-quence, regard punishment as a *complex social function.*
2. Analyze punitive methods not simply as consequences of legisla-tion or *as indicators of social structures,* but as techniques possessing their own specificity in the more general field of other ways of ex-ercising power. Regard punishment as a political tactic.
3. . . . . [M]ake the technology of power the very principle both of the *humanization of the penal system* and of the knowledge of man.
4. Try to discover whether this entry of the *soul* on to the scene of penal justice, and with it the insertion in legal practice of a whole corpus of "scientific" knowledge, is not the effect of a transforma-tion of the way in which the body itself is invested by power rela-tions. (1979:23–24; 1975:28)

Whereas Durkheim treats punishment as evidence of the function of other social phenomena, such as the social division of labor, Foucault instead sets out to explore discipline as the object itself of a

Durkheimian functional analysis. By explicitly citing only Durkheim and by appropriating Durkheim's concepts, such as the "repressive" and the "social function," Foucault readily acknowledges Durkheim's preeminent place in the tradition. But when Foucault instructs, as the first tenet of his method, "regard punishment as a complex social function," he is essentially claiming to turn Durkheim's enterprise on its head: Durkheim realized his project—to investigate the *function* of the division of labor—by treating law and punishment within the category of *effects*. Foucault flips this and treats, as his chief object of study, the *function* of punishment. The principal deficiency of Durkheim's work, according to Foucault, is his failure to take account of the enabling effects of punishment on the subject. This critique may apply with equal force to the order-maintenance approach to criminal justice.[2]

## Foucault and the Category of the Disorderly

Foucault's discussion of the role of the delinquent in the modern carceral society illuminates, by analogy, the role of the disorderly in the broken windows theory. The delinquent and the disorderly have much in common, and it is, for this reason, crucial to rehearse Foucault's analysis. But the categories are also different in important ways. Whereas delinquency correlates with treatment, psychotherapy, and correction, the category of the disorderly is more closely associated with a militaristic method of rectification. The broken windows theory by no means advocates the more rehabilitative or psychotherapeutic remedies that characterize certain of the institutions described in *Discipline and Punish*. The broken windows theory borrows instead from the classical method of deterrence through excessive punishment, as well as the drill sergeant model of discipline. For this reason, the category of the disorderly offers an opportunity to refine Foucault's diagnosis of the modern carceral society.

Foucault's description of the modern carceral society draws on a number of different mechanisms of disciplinary practice—for instance, discipline in the hospital, army, workplace, school, court, or home—and his discussion benefits from grouping these strategies together and highlighting their kinship. Nevertheless, the consolidation may detract from a more nuanced discussion of the different modalities of discipline that characterize modern penalty—the differences precisely between discipline in the hospital and discipline in the workshop. By selecting from those different approaches within the larger rubric of discipline, we can begin to differentiate between ways of disciplining, between techniques of punishment. This may allow us to evaluate the quality-of-life initiative.

First, however, let me turn to the details of Foucault's analysis. In *Discipline and Punish*, Foucault explores three very different ways in which punishment has created the subject—how punishment has fundamentally altered the subject's self-understanding, habits, emotions, and desires. The three different modalities correspond to three different stages in the history of punishment: first, the brutal, torturous corporal punishments of the seventeenth and early eighteenth centuries; second, the representational and theatrical aspirations of the eighteenth-century reformers; and third, the disciplinary mechanisms of spatial, temporal, and bodily control that capture the modern carceral system. Foucault suggests that these three modalities are not entirely distinct. Certain techniques from earlier historical periods are incorporated into later modalities. Foucault also suggests that the three mechanisms share important features. Each operates on the body of the convicted: the body is the intermediary between society and the subject (Foucault 1979:25; 1975:30). Each relates, idiosyncratically, to truth formation: that is, each helps constitute the truth. "The truth-power relation," Foucault suggests, "remains at the heart of all mechanisms of punishment" (1979:55; 1975:59). And each seeks to induce obedience among subjects (1979:129; 1975:132)—but through very different operations on the body.

The severe, brutal techniques of dismembering, quartering, or branding convicts that characterize the seventeenth and early eighteenth centuries—what Foucault refers to as *les supplices*—inscribed the sovereign's power on the body of the condemned. The mark of punishment on the body of the convict served to confirm the truth of the crime and to rectify sovereign power (1979:47; 1975:50). It signified to the people that the convicted subject, who was often led by torture to confession, had committed the crime, and it expressed the consequence of that crime. As Foucault explains, "It was the task of the guilty man to bear openly his condemnation and the truth of the crime that he had committed. His body, displayed, exhibited in procession, tortured, served as the public support of a procedure that had hitherto remained in the shade; in him, on him, the sentence had to be legible for all" (1979:43; 1975:47). It also served to reconstitute the sovereign's power. The dissymmetry between the criminal act and the torturous punishment reflected the gross imbalance of power between the subject and the sovereign, and served as a spectacle of that very imbalance and excess. Punishment functioned as an example that demonstrated both the crime's existence and also the sovereign's ability to master it. In terms of prevention, it operated through terror.

In contrast, the eighteenth-century reformers dreamed of another modality of punishment—one that, ultimately, would not be realized except through its faint reflections in the modern carceral system. Drawing first on themes of the eighteenth-century Enlightenment period—themes of equality, humanity, lenience, autonomy, and universality—and, second, on utilitarian principles of prevention and correction, the reformers imagined a system of coded penalties that would speak directly to the general public. Punishment was to be effectuated through countless different symbolic or "picturesque" sanctions scattered throughout all walks of life (1979:113; 1975:115). Each penalty was to represent to the observer, in a more muted way than the classical model, the lesson to be learned. The idea was that of a "punitive city":

> At the crossroads, in the gardens, at the side of roads being repaired or bridges built, in workshops open to all, in the depths of mines that may be visited, will be hundreds of tiny theatres of punishment. . . . It will be a visible punishment, a punishment that tells all, that explains, justifies itself, convicts: placards, different-coloured caps bearing inscriptions, posters, symbols, texts read or printed, tirelessly repeat the code. (1979:113; 1975:115)

This humanized spectacle was to serve primarily as a constant morality play, intended to teach a lesson to children and adults about the consequences of vice. As Foucault explains, "Around each of these moral 'representations,' schoolchildren will gather with their masters and adults will learn what lessons to teach their offspring" (1979:113; 1975:115). By reaching into all facets of everyday life, the reformist ideal sought to extend the reach of the example of punishment throughout the social body in a more egalitarian, effective, constant, yet economic manner. This project depended on publicity as a way to deeply reinforce the immediate association of crime and punishment—to "reactivat[e] the signifying system of the code" (1979:128; 1975:131).

The modern carceral system operates by training the body with an arsenal of coercive techniques. These techniques include the strict control of time and space; the ranking of individuals and activities; the forced repetition of exercises; the examination and its accompanying comparisons, hierarchies, and classifications; and the forced internalization of control through panoptic mechanisms of surveillance. Unlike the reformers' emphasis on signs, the modality of modern punishment focuses on exercises such as "time-tables, compulsory movements, regular activities, solitary meditation, work in common, silence, application, respect, good habits" (Foucault 1979:128; 1975:131–132). These exercises alter the subject's behaviors and habits, but also operate on the subject's desires and self-understanding. They correspond to the emergence of the subject as an object of knowledge. It is here, in the words of Foucault, "in these 'ignoble' archives," that can be found "the birth of the sciences of man" (1979:191; 1975:193).

Discipline is a multifaceted phenomenon composed of several different subsidiary clusters of techniques, corresponding to at least six primary social structures: the family, the school, the military, the workshop, the hospital, and the court. Foucault illustrates this point by means of a detailed discussion of Mettray, a juvenile center opened in 1840 that housed not only juvenile delinquents but also juveniles acquitted for mental health reasons and boarders. Mettray was a combination of prison, mental institution, and boarding school—what Foucault called "the carceral archipelago" or "the first training college in pure discipline" (1979:297, 295; 1975:302). Foucault characterizes Mettray as the crowning moment of the carceral system: "the date of completion of the carceral system" (1979:293; 1975:300). "Why Mettray?" Foucault asks. "Because it is the disciplinary form at its most extreme, the model in which are concentrated all the coercive technologies of behavior" (1979:293; 1975:300).

Mettray combined several disciplinary clusters, replicating the authority of the big brother, the inspections of the military superior, the supervision of the factory foreman, the examination of the school instructor, and the punishment meted out by the judge. The authorities at Mettray combined all these features. "They were in a sense technicians of behavior: engineers of conduct, orthopaedists of individuality" (1979:294; 1975:301). Mettray is the picture-perfect illustration of the carceral system. And it is important to note for our purposes here that the juridical model formed a part of the disciplinary model—that it was incorporated as one element of the larger carceral system and not entirely discarded.

Modern carceral techniques are premised on the idea that subjects need to be trained in order to be improved, that they need to be "normalized"—to be made more like the norm that society aspires to—rather than selected, with preexisting habits and behaviors, from a fixed pool of individualities. By improving the subject, the techniques serve not just the negative function of preventing crime, but the positive function of increasing utility and social wealth as well. This is the "functional inversion of the disciplines": "At first, they were expected to neutralize dangers, to fix useless or disturbed populations, to avoid the inconveniences of over-large assemblies; now they were being asked to play a positive role, for they were becoming able to do so, to increase the possible utility of individuals" (1979:210; 1975:211). These techniques reflect a fundamental shift in the object of judgment. Whereas in the classical period a crime was judged, in the modern period something else is being judged: "the passions, instincts, anomalies, infirmities, maladjustments, effects of environment or heredity" (1979:17; 1975:23). The judge no longer passes judgment on the criminal act, but on the soul of the convicted criminal and on his delinquency. These techniques are all embodied in the prison, the institution that colonized punishment during the late eighteenth and nineteenth centuries.

What differs, then, in the three modalities of punishment—the monarchical law, the reformers' dreams, and the carceral society—is not the theoretic basis of the right to punish, or the leniency of the punishment, or even its effectiveness on the subject. It is, instead, the way in which the punishment operates on the body and shapes the subject: "The difference is to be found in the procedure of access to the individual, the way in which the punishing power gets control over him, the instruments that it uses in order to achieve this transformation; it is in the technology of the penalty, not in its theoretical foundation; in the relation that it establishes with the body and with the soul, and not in the way that it is inserted within the legal system" (1979:127; 1975:130). The three modalities differ as techniques, as arts of punishment. In their trilogy they comprised "the sovereign and his force, the social body and the administrative apparatus; mark, sign, trace; ceremony, representation, exercise; the vanquished enemy, the juridical subject in the process of requalification, the individual subjected to immediate coercion; the tortured body, the soul with its manipulated representations, the body subjected to training" (1979:131; 1975:134).

It is within this framework that we can begin to assess order-maintenance policing. The policy of aggressive misdemeanor arrests bears a close resemblance to the juridical model in a number of respects. First, it bears the mark of sovereign excess. The idea of subjecting someone who has been, for instance, drinking in a public space to several hours in a cramped police van, to a strip search, to overnight detention, and to a criminal record bears the trappings of that imbalance between the subject and the sovereign that marked the more brutal punishments of the seventeenth-century. The theory of punishment mirrors the early seventeenth century reliance on dissymmetry. Second, it has the trappings of the juridical—rather than normalizing—judgment: an all or nothing, guilty or innocent dichotomy. Discipline and normalization operate by creating a spectrum of comparison along which individuals can be classified and compared. In contrast, the classical juridical model was binary. As Foucault explains, the essential function of classical juridical penalty

> is to refer, not to a set of observable phenomena, but to a corpus of laws and texts that must be remembered; [it] operates not by differentiating individuals, but by specifying acts according to a number of general categories; not by hierarchizing, but quite simply by bringing into play the binary opposition of the permitted and the forbidden; not by homogenizing, but by operating the division, acquired once and for all, of condemnation. (1979:183; 1975:185)

Broken windows policing is, in this sense, the quintessential penal mechanism at the core of the disciplinary process. It is the juridical element in the panoply of disciplinary techniques, the juridical model embedded in a cluster of discipline. Foucault writes, "At the heart of all disciplinary systems functions a small penal mechanism" (1979:177; 1975:180). Order-maintenance policing is precisely that mechanism.

At the same time, however, order maintenance feeds into the disciplinary project by producing a subject to normalize: the disorderly. By normalizing along the axis of disorder, the quality-of-life initiative, for example, breaks down and blends together the line between disorder and crime. Disorder becomes a degree of crime: breaking a window, littering, jumping a turnstile become grades along a spectrum that leads to homicide. The analogy, from Foucault, is to the penitentiary technique:

> This vast mechanism established a slow, continuous, imperceptible gradation that made it possible to pass naturally from disorder to offence and back from a transgression of the law to a slight departure from a rule, an average, a demand, a norm. . . . You will end up in the convict-ship, the slightest indiscipline seems to say; and the harshest of prisons says to the prisoners condemned to life: I shall note the slightest irregularity in your conduct. (1979:198–199; 1975:306)

Just like the category of the delinquent, the category of the disorderly breaks down the lines between minor infraction, minor disorder, and major offense. Moreover, as we saw earlier, the quality-of-life initiative also feeds into the disciplinary project of surveillance.

To say, however, that broken windows policing is part of the disciplinary project is to say too little; *everything* is today, since we live, according to Foucault, in a disciplinary society. Until such time as another paradigm presents itself, what we have to do today is compare the different genres of discipline. It is here that we can refine Foucault's analysis, for there are many things that order maintenance is not. It is not modeled on the rehabilitative ideal central to many disciplinary projects, especially that of the mental hospital or welfare and social work institutions. It does not feed into the psychotherapeutic. It does not coddle the disorderly. It does not aim to reform the disorderly so much as it does to punish them and to exclude them, in the sense of getting them off the street. Insofar as the strategy does seek to influence their behavior, it does not employ the traditional rehabilitative methods. Nor does broken windows policing incorporate the concept of examination—the calling card of school discipline. These are different subtypes of disciplinary techniques.

Order-maintenance policing seems to draw more heavily on both the juridical model and the military form of discipline: the juridical insofar as it utilizes punishment that may seem somewhat excessive; the military in the sense that it is normalized along an axis of disorder with a type of military observation, inspection, and exercise. Military discipline is captured in the ideal model of the military camp, where, Foucault writes, "all power would be exercised solely through exact observation" (1979:171; 1975:173). The military space is designed "to act on those it shelters, to provide a hold on their conduct, to carry the effects of power right to them, to make it possible to know them, to alter them" (1979:172; 1975:174).

Under this analysis, the weakness of broken windows policing is that it normalizes in a militaristic way along an axis of disorder even though there is inadequate empirical support. The disorderly may be the wrong target—or at least, there is not sufficient evidence to suggest that they are the right target. As we saw earlier, the social-scientific data suggest that poverty, stability, collective efficacy, and race—rather than disorder—may account for the discrepancies in neighborhood crime levels. This hypothesis needs to be further operationalized and verified. If it is true, however, then our normalizing disciplinary practices should be reoriented along the axes of income, employment, cohesion, mutual trust, and stability—and the issue of race should be directly addressed. If true, our policing and enforcement strategies should perhaps focus on workshop discipline rather than on the juridical or military models—regardless of the fact that workshop discipline is a target of Foucault's critique.

Foucault's important contribution here is to shed light on how the techniques of punishment associated with order maintenance create the category of the disorderly. The approach focuses on the presence of the disorderly rather than on the criminal act. It judges the disorderly not simply by giving the individual a criminal record, and not simply by convicting the person, but by turning the individual into someone who needs to be policed and surveyed, relocated and controlled. It facilitates a policy of surveillance, control, and exclusion of the disorderly. The category of the disorderly is the product of broken windows policing, and it promotes a policy of aggressive arrest and detention.

## Foucault and Legal Regulation

Foucault's writings also offer an alternative interpretation of the role of legal order—an antithesis to the second argument in Durkheim's work. Whereas, for Durkheim, ordered legal regulation produces healthy moral cohesion (through the intermediary of the division of labor), for Foucault it is the disciplines that enforce moral cohesion under the cover of legal order. As a result, Foucault's writings on law are critical to an appraisal of the order-maintenance approach.

A number of scholars suggest that Foucault lacks a theory of law. Duncan Kennedy, in his essay "The Stakes of Law, or Hale and Foucault!" criticizes Foucault for not taking law seriously enough. He argues that Foucault has an antiquated, prerealist view of juridical power, "a typically European but utterly misconceived picture of the legal system as a domain governed by rules (as opposed to standards), by individualist (as opposed to altruist) definitions of legal rights, and by deductive (as opposed to 'policy-oriented') reasoning" (1993:118 note). According to Kennedy, "law and legal discourse play superstructural and mystificatory roles in Foucault's disciplinary society analogous to their roles in Marx's political economy" (1993:122). Similarly, Alan Hunt and Gary Wickham, in *Foucault and Law*, charge that "Foucault does not have a theory of law" and that he "tends to expel law from any major role in modern forms of government" (1994:viii, 22). Hugh Baxter agrees: "A straightforward reading of Foucault's writings on power suggests, as Hunt and Wickham observe, that Foucault tends to 'expel law from any significant role' in modern society." He continues, "Foucault's conception of law as sovereign command is too crude a tool for understanding modern law" (1996:464).

Law, however, is by no means an untheorized concept for Foucault. To the contrary, law is at the heart of Foucault's project. In Foucault's stated purpose—"a genealogy of the present scientifico-*legal* complex from which the power to punish derives its bases, justifications and rules" (Foucault 1979:23; 1975:27, emphasis added)—law and knowledge play equally important roles.[3] The fact is, Foucault develops in his work a complex, multifaced relation between law and discipline.

In Foucault's writings, law is most often associated with notions of sovereignty and the social contract tradition. When Foucault discusses "juridical power," he is referring to the prerevolutionary understanding of sovereign rights, as opposed to the forms of disciplinary power that have evolved since the eighteenth century, namely, surveillance, examination, *emploi de temps, cloture, repartitions,* and, of course, panopticism. Modernity, understood as our modern experience of the carceral society, is the product of the interplay between juridical power and disciplinary power. On the one hand, the new forms of discipline contain juridical elements; they model, in part, legality and have a place for juridical judgment. In addition, they are often taken over by the state, the police, and other legal institutions. On the other hand, these new disciplinary powers are made possible because they are masked by juridical power. Underneath that mask, juridical and disciplinary power clash, and it is precisely that conflict that gives rise, according to Foucault, to a new form of power/law: the norm.

It is possible to discern, then, in this complex relation between law and discipline four significant moments: (1) juridical power as it existed before the French Revolution; (2) the elements of law contained in the new forms of disciplinary power; (3) the clash between disciplinary and juridical power; and (4) the new form of law that emerges from the confrontation. In the following, I treat each of these moments separately.

*Juridical Power before the French Revolution*
"Juridical power" is a term of art for Foucault. It corresponds to the model of sovereignty and sovereign rights developed during the Renaissance period. It signifies a type of reasoning based on notions of sovereignty, rights, and consent that excludes any real appreciation of modern forms of power and knowledge. Foucault has in mind Hobbes's theory of sovereign rights, Locke's theory of sovereign limits, and subsequent theories of sovereignty. So in his writings and lectures, Foucault refers to the social contract tradition and the liberal conception of political power as "juridical" (Foucault 1980:88). He also refers to the theories of sovereignty and sovereign right of the sixteenth through the eighteenth centuries as "juridical" (1980:103).

Foucault conceives of "juridical power" principally as it developed out of monarchical institutions. "It seems to me," Foucault writes, "that in Western societies since Medieval times it has been royal power that has provided the essential focus around which legal thought has been elaborated. It is in response to the demands of royal power, for its profit and to serve as its instrument or justification, that the juridical edifice of our own society has been developed. Right in the West is the King's right" (1980:94).

This is the concept of juridical power that infuses the brutal physical punishments and tortures described in the first part of *Discipline and Punish*. *Les supplices* give voice to, reflect, and restore juridical power: "The tortured body is first inscribed in the legal ceremonial that must produce, open for all to see, the truth of the crime" (1979:35; 1975:39). Foucault associates *les supplices* with the kind of antiquated law he attributes to classical political theory. He writes: "The public execution, then, has a juridico-political function. It is a ceremonial by which a momentarily injured sovereignty is reconstituted. It restores that sovereignty by manifesting it at its most spectacular. The public execution . . . belongs to a whole series of great rituals in which power is eclipsed and restored" (1979:48; 1975:52). The brutality of torturous executions is meant to restore the rights that were assailed by the criminal act. It serves both to produce the truth and, simultaneously, to restore juridical power. Thus, Foucault concludes, "[i]f torture was so strongly embedded in legal practice, it was because it revealed truth and showed the operation of power" (1979:55; 1975:59).

*Elements of Law in the New Forms of Disciplinary Power*
Foucault draws a sharp distinction between juridical power and the new forms of disciplinary power that evolved in the eighteenth century. While the premodern forms of punishment served to restore juridical power and are sharply differentiated from the new forms of disciplinary power, the latter nevertheless contain elements of juridical power. Mettray provides a perfect example. Mettray reflects all five models of the disciplinary institution: the family, the army, the factory, the school, and the justice system. For our purposes, I will focus on the last, the "judicial model." This is a model of punishment that is woven in tightly with other forms of discipline, with surveillance and sequestration. It is a mutated form of punishment that plays off the idea of justice but combines many other elements. Describing this judicial model, Foucault writes:

> [E]ach day "justice" was meted out in the parlour: "The least act of disobedience is punished and the best way of avoiding serious offences is to punish the most minor offences very severely: at Mettray, a useless word is punishable"; the principal punishment inflicted was confinement to one's cell; for "isolation is the best means of acting on the moral nature of children; it is there above all that the voice of religion,

even if it has never spoken to their hearts, recovers all its emotional power" . . . The entire parapenal institution, which is created in order not to be a prison, culminates in the cell, on the walls of which are written in black letters: "God sees you." (1979:294; 1975:301)

What is important here is that the judicial model is one of five models of disciplinary power, all wrapped together in the institution of Mettray; also, that the judicial model feeds into the other disciplinary techniques, including here divine surveillance—the ultimate panopticon.

At the same time, the traditional arteries of juridical power— namely, the state and the police—borrow and appropriate the new forms of disciplinary power. There is, as Foucault calls it, *l'étatisation*[4] of the mechanisms of discipline. So, for instance, the function of social discipline in France is taken over, very soon, by the police. "The organization of the police apparatus in the eighteenth century sanctioned a generalization of the disciplines that became co-extensive with the state itself" (1979:215; 1975:217). Foucault describes the police function—a state, legalistic function—in terms of disciplinary power:

> And, in order to be exercised, this power had to be given the instrument of permanent, exhaustive, omnipresent surveillance, capable of making all visible, as long as it could itself remain invisible. It had to be like a faceless gaze that transformed the whole social body into a field of perception: thousands of eyes posted everywhere. . . . And this unceasing observation had to be accumulated in a series of reports and registers. . . . And, unlike the methods of judicial or administrative writing, what was registered in this way were forms of behavior, attitudes, possibilities, suspicions—a permanent account of individuals' behavior. (1979:214; 1975:215–216)

And it is precisely these police controls, with all their reports and classifications, that give rise to delinquency (1979:280–281; 1975:286). As Foucault explains: "In short, the carceral archipelago assures, in the depths of the social body, the formation of delinquency on the basis of subtle illegalities, the overlapping of the latter by the former and the establishment of a specified criminality" (1979:301; 1975:308). The state appropriations of disciplinary power play, in Foucault's work, a critical role in the production of the carceral society. Foucault writes:

"The carceral . . . communicates a type of power that the law validates and that justice uses *as its favourite weapon*" (1979:302; 1975:309, emphasis added).

In addition to direct appropriations, there is also a feedback effect from disciplinary power to the justice system. Foucault explains: "During the 150 or 200 years that Europe has been setting up its new penal systems, the judges have gradually, by means of a process that goes back very far indeed, taken to judging something other than crimes, namely, the 'soul' of the criminal" (1979:19; 1975:24). The structural transformation of punishment, according to Foucault, has brought about a change in the object that the justice system judges, as well as changes in the character of judicial decision making. "A whole set of assessing, diagnostic, prognostic, normative judgments concerning the criminal have become lodged in the framework of penal judgment" (1979:19; 1975:24).

In sum, juridical and disciplinary power, though different, borrow from each other. As Foucault suggests: "The regulations of the disciplinary establishment may reproduce the law, the punishments imitate the verdicts and penalties, the surveillance repeat the police model" (1979:302; 1975:309).

### The Clash between Disciplinary and Juridical Power

According to Foucault, it is the interplay between disciplinary and juridical power that gives rise to the modern carceral system. Discipline is a form of counter-law, of dissymmetry and inequality, that operates underneath the discourse of juridical power to make possible the stated or facial claims of equality and rights characteristic of the French Revolution. Just as disciplinary power shaped the workers to make possible the industrial revolution (1979:220–221; 1975:222), discipline shapes normal individuals, non-delinquents, in order to allow the rights talk to which we are so accustomed today.

Foucault describes the interplay between juridical and disciplinary power as follows:

[T]he theory of sovereignty, and the organisation of a legal code centered on it, have allowed a system of right to be superimposed upon the mechanisms of discipline in such a way as to conceal its actual procedures, the element of domination inherent in its techniques, and to guarantee to everyone, by virtue of the sovereignty of the State, the exercise of his proper sovereign rights. The juridical systems—and this applies both to their codification and to their theorisation—have enabled sovereignty to be democratised through the constitution of a public right articulated upon collective sovereignty, while at the same time this democratisation of sovereignty was fundamentally determined by and grounded in mechanisms of disciplinary coercion. (1980:105; see also 1975:223–224)

Modern society, for Foucault, is defined, then, by this conjunction of legal discourse (rights talk) and disciplinary coercion. The carceral system is constructed within a space constituted by both: "[T]he powers of modern society are exercised through, on the basis of, and by virtue of, this very heterogeneity between a public right of sovereignty and a polymorphous disciplinary mechanism" (Foucault 1980:106).

Foucault is expressing, in these dense passages, several thoughts. First, the notion that disciplinary power shapes modern individuals in such a way that we are comfortable with the ideals of equality and universality—comfortable in the sense that we accept and believe in these ideals. This resembles what Foucault suggests about the industrial revolution, namely, that it was the disciplines that shaped peasants into factory workers. Second, the idea that the disciplines make possible the very claims of universality and equality. The disciplines bridge the gap between the ideal of legal norms and the reality of modern life. They make possible the claim to equal and fair treatment for all by creating categories (such as delinquents or the insane) that are not entitled to benefit from the legal norms themselves. They marginalize or exclude certain people or groups and thereby make it possible for the rest of us to believe in, espouse, and promote the legal ideals that we do. Third, the idea that legal norms are a cover for the disciplinary processes. The coercive and unequal nature of the disciplines are masked by the legal norms that we espouse, such as human rights, civil rights, freedom, and equality.

Regarding this last point, what Foucault has in mind, at a more concrete level, is that the democratization of rights discourse, resulting in claims of equality, humanity, and universality, is the discourse that empowered the concepts of measured and equal punishment. Equality permeates the idea of one carceral punishment for all, with different lengths of time measured according to the delinquency of the individual. Humanity permeates the idea of incarceration: "[T]he penalty must be nothing more than the deprivation of liberty" (1979:248; 1975:251). And universality justifies and legitimizes the power to punish. Juridical discourse, then, serves as a cover that allows disciplinary power to grow.

It would be wrong, however, to characterize the relationship between the disciplines and law as merely "superstructural." In fact, Foucault himself acknowledges the temptation and rejects it. "In appearance, the disciplines constitute nothing more than an infra-law," Foucault observes. "The disciplines should be regarded as a sort of counter-law. They have the precise role of introducing insuperable asymmetries and excluding reciprocities" (1979:222; 1975:224).

Law and counter-law: claims of equality, humanity, and universality that clash with micro-processes of inequality, dissymmetry, and singularity. Rather than base and superstructure, the analogue in Marxian terms would be the conflict between modes of production and social relations. It is the conflict between rights talk and disciplinary power that gives rise to the prison and to the carceral system that permeates modern society. The clash is the point where the prison must be situated. It is the point where Mettray is established. It is the point where delinquency is crafted. In Foucault's words, it is the point where the law inverts itself "and passes outside itself, and where the counter-law becomes the effective and institutionalized content of the juridical forms" (1979:224; 1975:225). What does this mean? Though somewhat obscure, it can only mean a new kind of law.

*The New Form of Law that Emerges from the Confrontation*
The new law that emerges is normalization, a process that simultaneously creates and excludes the delinquent and justifies the power to punish. Foucault explains:

> With this new economy of power, the carceral system, which is its basic instrument, permitted the emergence of a new form of "law": a mixture of legality and nature, prescription and constitution, the norm. This had a whole series of effects: the internal dislocation of the judi-

cial power or at least of its functioning; an increasing difficulty in judging, as if one were ashamed to pass sentence; a furious desire on the
part of judges to judge, assess, diagnose, recognize the normal and abnormal and claim the honour of curing or rehabilitating. . . . The
judges of normality are present everywhere. We are in the society of
the teacher-judge, the doctor-judge, the educator-judge, the "social-
worker"-judge . . . The carceral network, in its compact or disseminated
forms, with its systems of insertion, distribution, surveillance, observation, has been the greatest support, in modern society, of the normalizing power. (1979:304; 1975:310–311)

The clash between juridical and disciplinary power gives rise to the
tendency toward normalization—toward the spectrum from normal to
abnormal (Foucault 1980:106). This *pouvoir normalisateur* defines, categorizes, and excludes the delinquent, surveys all aspects of modern
existence, and gives rise to the human sciences whose object is the individual. This *pouvoir normalisateur* is neither wholly disciplinary nor
entirely juridical. It is a mixture. It contains both elements. And it is
important for Foucault that both juridical and disciplinary power be
part of the new law. Thus, Foucault writes:

I believe that the process which has really rendered the discourse of the
human sciences possible is the juxtaposition, the encounter between
two lines of approach, two mechanisms, two absolutely heterogeneous
types of discourse: on the one hand there is the re-organisation of right
that invests sovereignty, and on the other, the mechanics of the coercive forces whose exercise takes a disciplinary form. And I believe that
in our own times power is exercised simultaneously through this right
and these techniques and that these techniques and these discourses,
to which the disciplines give rise invade the area of right so that the
procedures of normalisation come to be ever more constantly engaged
in the colonisation of those of law. I believe that all this can explain
the global functioning of what I would call a *society of normalisation*.
(1980:107)

The resulting carceral system—the normalizing society—is what justifies the power to punish. It makes punishment seem natural, necessary, preordained.

This may well explain why the category of the disorderly and the meaning of disorder appear so natural to us today. And it may explain why we so easily brush off the fact that so many of the disorderly are being stopped, frisked, arrested, and detained. Foucault's writings have important implications for the order-maintenance approach to criminal justice.

# CHAPTER 6

# The Implications of
# Subject Creation

Let's return for a moment to January 22, 1840, the official opening of Mettray, the juvenile prison *qua* home, school, military com-
pound, courthouse, and factory described in chilling detail by Michel
Foucault in *Discipline and Punish*. Consider for a moment the policy at
Mettray, as originally reported by Ducpétiaux in 1852: "The least act
of disobedience is punished and the best way of avoiding serious offences is to punish the most minor offences very severely" (Foucault
1979:294; 1975:301). Reconsider the strategy of the early penitentiary,
as described by Foucault: "This vast mechanism established a slow, con-
tinuous, imperceptible gradation that made it possible to pass naturally from disorder to offence and back from a transgression of the law
to a slight departure from a rule, an average, a demand, a norm"
(1979:298; 1975:306). It is eerie how much this resembles the order-
maintenance approach to criminal justice—an approach that seeks to
avoid more serious crime by cracking down on minor disorder and
reconfiguring inducements. Order maintenance, it turns out, may not
be so new after all. The focus on order and orderliness in the "Broken
Windows" essay may trace back to Edward Banfield, but these writings themselves trace back to much earlier disciplinary practices of order maintenance. Foucault's writings—especially the notion of subject
creation—have important implications for the order-maintenance approach.

The notion of subject creation that I invoke here comprises two separate phenomena. The first has to do with how the practices and institutions that surround us affect us as contemporary subjects and re-

searchers. They shape, in part, the way we think, desire, and judge others. The second has to do with the way in which practices and institutions define and categorize people—how they create the category of the disorderly. The first involves the way in which, for example, order-maintenance policing shapes how we perceive and judge a dirty, homeless street person or how we think about propensities and human nature more generally. The second involves the way in which order-maintenance policing categorizes who qualifies as disorderly—for instance, the homeless person but not the brutal police officer. I call these two effects subject creation, and suggest that they can be documented, investigated, and criticized. They are the product of historical, political, cultural, and social factors.

I should emphasize that by subject creation I do not simply mean superficial effects or influence on short-term behavior and perceptions. I am not referring to how a public announcement in a subway may influence whether we give a quarter to a homeless panhandler. I am instead addressing a more profound claim about the constitutive categories through which we see the world around us, the categories that shape the very way we perceive and understand order and disorder. These categories represent the lens through which we interpret social practices and argue for public policies. They include, for instance, the very notion of thick propensities and of human nature. They include the very idea of social meaning—in which I firmly believe, not surprisingly, since these categories are so ingrained. In this chapter I develop this notion of subject creation and explore its implications for the order-maintenance approach.

## Shaping the Category of the Disorderly

The first significant implication is that the category of the disorderly may not be pre-political, but may itself be constructed in part through lengthy processes of policing and punitive practices. This first point addresses the very heart of order maintenance, the central categories that organize the analysis: in Banfield's work, the distinction between lower-class individuals, who are present-oriented, and upper-class individuals, who are future-oriented; or between southern Italians, who are amoral familists, and Americans, who are generally community-oriented and associational; in Wilson's work, the distinction between the obstreperous people, who are defiant of authority and prone to commit crimes, and the respectable, law-abiding people, who follow the law, mow their lawns, and paint their fences; in the writings of the New Progressives, the distinction between the disorderly people, who are prone to commit crimes, and the committed law abiders; or between the inner-city teens, who believe that a majority of their peers admire gang membership, and suburban teens, who predominantly do not. These categories, I suggest, are not as natural as they appear, but are instead shaped by policing and punitive practices. The norm of order-liness, as well as the policing techniques of order-maintenance crack-downs, shapes both the category of the disorderly and our perception, thinking, and judgments about disorderly persons.

Foucault's writings shed light on how punishment and policing practices may shape these categories. The techniques of punishment associated with, for instance, New York City's quality-of-life initiative fo-cus on the presence of the disorderly rather than on the criminal act. They judge the disorderly not simply by giving the individual a crimi-nal record, and not simply by convicting the person, but by turning the individual into someone who needs to be policed, relocated, and controlled. It is in this sense that Foucault writes, regarding the analo-gous delinquent:

> It is said that the prison fabricated delinquents; it is true that it brings back, almost inevitably, before the courts those who have been sent there. But it also fabricates them in the sense that it has introduced into the operation of the law and the offence, . . . the non-corporal re-ality of the delinquency that links them together and, for a century and a half, has caught them in the same trap. (1979:255; 1975:258)

To say that the quality-of-life initiative shapes the disorderly subject is not to say that it promotes more disorderly conduct by labeling the individual as disorderly—whether or not that is true.[1] It is, instead, to suggest that the theory of deterrence and punishment focuses on the disorderly person rather than the criminal act, and thereby facilitates a policy of control, relocation, and exclusion of the disorderly; and that the category of the disorderly is the product, in part, of the quality-of-life initiative itself.

What is crucial, then, is how these categories of order and the disor-derly are shaped by the policing techniques that we as a society en-dorse, witness, experience, and inflict. Policing strategies shape these categories and the contemporary subject as well. The long-standing emphasis on the norm of orderliness in broken-windows policing—an emphasis on order that traces back much further in time—shapes the category of the disorderly to include the inebriate, the homeless, the street person, the loiterer. It helps turn these people into individuals to be watched, relocated, excluded. It turns them into subjects that need to be controlled. At the same time, it shapes us as contemporary subjects of society. It shapes the way we judge a dirty, smelly person pushing a shopping cart down the street. It helps form our perceptions of risks, of assistance, of exchange.

In other words, in addition to changing short-term perception and behavior in the manner described by social norm theorists, these policing techniques may also shape the contemporary subject fundamentally and mold the way we think about, judge, and relate to others. We may judge the person who is out of order—who is dirty or apparently loitering—as dangerous, as a source of transgression, in need of being controlled or banished. Rather than judging the act of loitering, we may attribute to the person who is loitering certain propensities—certain tastes, attitudes, and values. We may begin to discern a certain ethos, or "characteristic usages, ideas, standards, and codes by which a group is differentiated and individualized in character from other groups" (Banfield 1958:10 n.3). We may begin to know certain things about, and impute social meaning to, certain types of people.

The same is true of the other proposed policing policies. They too shape who we are. Mass building searches in the inner city are going to affect our conception of privacy, of authority, of political power, and of citizenship. Youth curfew laws are going to have an impact on the cultural and intellectual lives of our children. Anti-loitering ordinances will have an effect on street life. Curfews and anti-loitering ordinances will result in police records and contribute to legal or extralegal disenfranchisement. Policing techniques shape us. I am not thinking simply about the fact that the police may want to extend a practice such as mass building searches outside the inner city—which certainly may happen. I am thinking about the fact that the very occurrence of these police practices affects all of us.

### Facilitating the Proposed Public Policies

In addition, the conception of thicker propensities at the heart of the order-maintenance approach may itself facilitate, through a feedback mechanism, the proposed police initiatives. Foucault describes how the category of the delinquent in the modern carceral system facilitates a rehabilitative approach to punishment by making correction and normalization seem natural. In a similar vein, the meaning that we give to the norm of orderliness, understood in terms of preventing serious crime, may itself facilitate policies such as youth curfews, order-maintenance crackdowns, and anti-gang loitering ordinances. Once order is defined in terms of murder and robbery, there is little else to do but crack down on the disorderly. Who in their right mind, after all, would side with people who break windows, hang out with gang members, aggressively accost passersby, or vandalize other people's property? Who in their right mind would condone urinating in the streets or carrying guns in schools? The persons who are arrested are disorderly: they have committed crimes. They are the type of people who will commit more crimes or promote criminal activity. They *should* be punished.

In discussing the modern carceral society, Foucault writes that "perhaps the most important effect of the carceral system and of its extension well beyond legal imprisonment is that it succeeds in making the power to punish natural and legitimate, in lowering at least the threshold of tolerance to penalty. It tends to efface what may be exorbitant in the exercise of punishment" (1979:301; 1975:308). This may explain why we so easily adopt a policy of aggressive arrests and incarceration—even those among us, like the New Progressives, who favor social norm approaches and seek alternatives to incarceration. We have so internalized the norm of orderliness that even those who seek alternative policies fall back on a quality-of-life approach that relies extensively on law enforcement, on stops and frisks, arrests, and incarceration. Order-maintenance policies seem so natural because, after all, the people being arrested *are* disorderly. Criminals today continue to be a class of people that many feel entitled to hate and exclude (Honig 1993:126–161; Gaubatz 1995). As Richard Posner has stated: "I do not consider it immoral to hate criminals, philanderers, braggarts, or even beggars (who in today's America are mainly a species of con man)" (Posner 1998b:4).

These categories of the criminal, braggart, and beggar seem natural, at least at first blush. The petty vandal, the aggressive street hustler, the idle loiterer—these figures seem to belong naturally in the category of the disorderly. It is a matter of simple intuition. Yet when we start to scratch the surface, these categories become more murky. There are many forms of disorder. Street life is only one. Tax evasion, "Nannygates," political corruption: these forms of disorder—disorder that we experience as much as we do street life—are somehow different. They are not central to the broken windows hypothesis. They are not part of the crime problem. Why? Precisely because the category of the street disorderly has become second nature; it has become natural, necessary, and unquestioned. It makes order-maintenance policing seem so right—despite the fact that there is scarcely any empirical evidence supporting the broken windows theory.

An incident in New York City in 1999 illustrates this complex relationship between policing techniques, perceptions of disorder, and the category of the disorderly. On November 16, 1999, a young woman who had recently moved to New York City from Texas was brutally assaulted and critically injured in broad daylight in midtown Manhattan. An unknown assailant smashed a six-pound paving stone into the back of her head as she waited to cross at the corner of Forty-second Street and Madison Avenue. Witnesses at the scene described the assailant as a black man with close-cropped hair and a white beard, about five foot four, in his forties, wearing a dark jacket and blue jeans. Little else was known about the assailant, and it seemed that the crime would not easily be resolved. Suspicion soon focused on a homeless man who had often been seen in the neighborhood where the attack took place and who was believed to be mentally ill (Newman 1999:B5; Blair 1999:B5).

Just days after the attack, Mayor Giuliani vowed to step up efforts to get the homeless off the streets. In a radio address four days after the assault he stated: "The streets are not for sleeping. Streets do not exist in civilized cities for sleeping. Bedrooms are for sleeping" ("City Plan: Get Homeless off Streets" 1999:A21). Giuliani then had the police implement a new policy toward the homeless: police officers were to approach homeless people and ask them to go to a shelter or to the hospital. If the homeless refused help, they were to be arrested for disorderly conduct. Between November 20 and early December, the police arrested 88 homeless people on misdemeanors, 10 on felonies, and 66 on ordinance violations, issued 114 summonses to homeless people for offenses such as public drinking, and transported 380 homeless people to shelters and 67 to hospitals. By December 21, the homeless sweeps in New York City had resulted in the arrests of 269 homeless people, with an additional 776 taken to shelters (Bernstein 1999:53; Polner 1999:A4; Topousis 1999:18).

A suspect was arrested on November 30 and charged with attempted murder. The evidence against him consisted of two jailhouse informers and an eyewitness who picked him out of a lineup after having identified a different man in an initial photo array. A jury ultimately convicted the suspect of assault after deadlocking twice in three days of deliberation (Finkelstein 2000). It was initially unclear whether the suspect was or was not homeless. When a reporter suggested to Giuliani that the suspect may not have been homeless, the mayor took offense. "The man didn't have an address," Giuliani responded. "He was living at the Port Authority bus depot and panhandling. He fits every description of homelessness. The fact is, he was homeless" (Bernstein 1999:53).

What facilitated the crackdown on the homeless was precisely the category of the disorderly and the way in which order-maintenance policing changes how we perceive and judge people such as the homeless. It is the meaning of the disorderly—understood in terms of causing serious crime such as robbery and assault—that made it easier, to some degree, to implement homeless sweeps. That meaning helped make it natural to arrest hundreds of homeless people.

## Masking the Disorder

In his legal theory, Foucault suggested that the interplay between discipline and law is at the heart of the modern carceral system and that legal processes are often a cover for disciplinary practices. In a similar vein, the proposed policing initiatives may mask aggressive disciplinary practices. In New York City, for example, order maintenance has been achieved, in large part, by means of a proactive policy of stops, frisks, and misdemeanor arrests that has been accompanied by a significant increase in complaints of police misconduct. The law enforcement policy of stops and arrests—the cover of law—may facilitate irregular disciplinary practices.

The "Broken Windows" essay, as we saw, betrayed itself. In place of a struggle between order and disorder, the essay revealed two competing sources of power, two competing forces of social control. The "police view," according to Wilson and Kelling, is that "the cops and the gangs are the two rival sources of power in the area, and that the gangs are not going to win" (1982:35). This bears a striking resemblance to former police commissioner Bratton's statement that "criminals are our competition" (Beiser 1995:39). Bob Herbert of the *New York Times* reports a chilling exchange between a police officer from the Bronx and a commission investigating police misconduct:

> "Did you beat people up who you arrested?"
> "No. We'd just beat people in general. If they're on the street, hanging around drug locations. It was a show of force."
> "Why were these beatings done?"
> "To show who was in charge. We were in charge, the police." (Herbert 1997:13)

With the exception of the public outcry and protest that occur in the aftermath of highly publicized incidents of police brutality and use of deadly force—such as the brutal torture of Abner Louima by police officers in Brooklyn's Seventieth Precinct station house on August 9, 1997, the multiple-shooting death of Amadou Diallo by four Street Crime Unit officers on February 4, 1999, or the shooting death of Patrick Dorismond by undercover police officers pretending to be drug dealers in the early morning of March 16, 2000 (Human Rights Watch 1998:286–289; Spitzer 1999:5; Barstow 2000:A1)—there has been very little recognition that complaints of police misconduct have increased significantly under broken windows policing. The fact is, however, that the quality-of-life initiative was immediately accompanied by a sharp increase in charges of misconduct.

In New York City, complaints increased sharply beginning in 1993. The Civilian Complaint Review Board is the mayoral agency in New York City that receives charges of misconduct against police officers, including allegations of the use of excessive or unnecessary force, abuse of authority, discourtesy, or the use of offensive language (CCRB 2000:iii). For 1993, the year Giuliani was elected mayor, the CCRB received 5,597 allegations of police misconduct contained in 3,580 complaints.[2] During the first three years that the quality-of-life initiative was implemented, allegations of police misconduct rose steadily by 68 percent to 9,390 for 1996, and the number of complaints rose by 55 percent to 5,550. Allegations and complaints generally declined in the following three years. Nevertheless, in 1999 allegations were still up 25 percent from 1993 levels, and complaints were up 37 percent. The trend in allegations and complaints received by the CCRB is reflected in Table 6.1 (Jackson 1998; CCRB 2000:21).

The rise in complaints received by the CCRB during the implementation of the quality-of-life initiative tracks other indices of police misconduct. According to the *New York Times*, New York City received, from 1994 to 1996, 8,316 court claims of abuse by police officers, in comparison with 5,983 during the three previous years (Purdy 1997). In addition, the *Times* reports, "from 1994 to 1996, the city paid about $70 million as settlements or judgments in claims alleging improper police actions—compared with about $48 million in the three previous years" (Purdy 1997). Another commentator reports that legal filings against the police of civil rights claims for abusive conduct rose 75 percent during the period 1994–1998 (Greene 1999:175–176).

Amnesty International, in a June 1996 report titled "Police Brutality and Excessive Force in the New York City Police Department," also noted that complaints of police brutality in New York City "have been rising steadily for some years" (Amnesty 1996:14). According to Amnesty's statistics, "the number of people bringing claims for police misconduct against the City of New York has increased substantially in recent years, from 977 in 1987 to more than 2,000 in 1994." Furthermore, "[t]he amount paid out by the city each year in settlements or judgments awarded to plaintiffs in police abuse cases has also risen," from around $13.5 million in 1992 to more than $24 million in 1994 (Amnesty 1996:14).

Amnesty also found racial disparities among complainants, reporting that "the large majority of the victims of police abuses are racial minorities, particularly African-Americans and people of Latin American or Asian descent. Racial disparities appear to be especially marked in

Table 6.1 CCRB complaints and allegations of police misconduct, 1993–1999

|             | 1993  | 1994  | 1995  | 1996  | 1997  | 1998  | 1999  |
|-------------|-------|-------|-------|-------|-------|-------|-------|
| Complaints  | 3,580 | 4,877 | 5,618 | 5,550 | 4,768 | 4,930 | 4,903 |
| Allegations | 5,597 | 8,060 | 9,356 | 9,390 | 7,933 | 8,105 | 6,991 |

cases involving deaths in custody or questionable shootings" (Amnesty 1996:14). The CCRB confirms the disparity, noting that, for the period 1995–1999, whites averaged 21.2 percent and African-Americans 50.2 percent of all complaints in which the race of the complainant was known, despite the fact that the white population of New York City is around 43 percent and the African-American population around 25 percent (CCRB 2000:24).[3]

Police officials suggest that the increase in complaints of police misconduct may be due to the increase in the number of police officers in the NYPD. Bratton, for instance, minimizes the significance of the numbers, suggesting that "complaints always rise after there is a large influx of new police officers" (Bratton 1997). Elsewhere, he suggests that the numbers increased because there were more police-civilian contacts. "We were taking back the streets, and it wasn't easy work," Bratton remarks. "In the course of enforcing laws that had not been enforced for twenty-five years, we were being more proactive, we were engaging more people, and often they didn't like it" (1998:291).

Perhaps these explanations are correct. There are reasons to be somewhat skeptical, however. The CCRB reported to Amnesty delegates that "most of the complaints arose from encounters with patrol officers that did not involve arrests or persons receiving summonses" (Amnesty 1996:346). Moreover, the CCRB also reported that "most complainants had no prior complaint history, thus discounting suggestions that many of those lodging complaints were 'chronic' complainers" (Amnesty 1996:346). In addition, although the increase in police officers may account, in some part, for the rise in complaints of police brutality, the complaints seem to have increased at a greater pace—at least through 1999. Table 6.2 reflects the number of allegations and complaints received by the CCRB in relation to the number of police officers on the NYPD force.[4]

**Table 6.2**  Ratio of CCRB complaints and allegations to police force, 1993–1999

|                     | 1993   | 1994   | 1995   | 1996   | 1997   | 1998   | 1999   |
|---------------------|--------|--------|--------|--------|--------|--------|--------|
| NYPD police officers | 29,327 | 30,135 | 37,450 | 37,090 | 37,219 | 39,149 | 39,642 |
| Complaints/officer  | .122   | .162   | .150   | .150   | .128   | .126   | .124   |
| Allegations/officer | .191   | .267   | .250   | .253   | .213   | .207   | .176   |

The ratio of allegations and complaints per officer rose sharply during the first few years of the quality-of-life initiative, but tapered off after that. While the ratio of allegations to police officer was lower in 1999 than it was in 1993—recall, however, that the CCRB questions the reliability of the allegation figures (CCRB 2000:21)—the ratio of complaints to police officer was still slightly higher in 1999 than it was prior to the quality-of-life initiative. And it certainly increased sharply, even in proportion to the increase in the police force, during the first years of the strategy of aggressive arrests. What is particularly noticeable is the sharp increase in the ratio of complaints and allegations during the first year of implementation. Even though the number of police officers increased by only 808 (2.75 percent) between October 31, 1993, and October 31, 1994, the ratio of complaints to officers increased by almost 33 percent.

With regard to the ratio of allegations and complaints to the number of arrests, the evidence is somewhat similar, as shown in Table 6.3.[5] Again, the rate of increase in complaints and allegations outpaced the rate of increase in arrests, resulting in a sharp increase in the ratio in the first few years of the initiative. Although the ratio tapered off after 1996, it did not return to its level of the years before the quality-of-life initiative.

I am not arguing, nor have I attempted to establish, that there is a causal link between the quality-of-life initiative and the increase in complaints of police misconduct. Nor have I argued that there is an empirical link between order-maintenance policing and police brutality. The possible explanations for the increases and reductions in the number of complaints are far too complex to lend themselves to such a simple analysis. These shifts are highly contextual and difficult to interpret. The publicity surrounding the police torture of Abner

Table 6.3 Ratio of CCRB complaints and allegations to total adult arrests (per 100 arrests), 1993–1999

|  | 1993 | 1994 | 1995 | 1996 | 1997 | 1998 | 1999 |
|---|---|---|---|---|---|---|---|
| Total arrests | 255,084 | 307,797 | 316,700 | 314,367 | 335,265 | 345,325 | 314,20 |
| Complaints/100 arrests | 1.40 | 1.58 | 1.77 | 1.77 | 1.42 | 1.43 | 1.56 |
| Allegations/100 arrests | 2.19 | 2.62 | 2.95 | 2.99 | 2.37 | 2.35 | 2.22 |

Louima, on the one hand, may have increased some citizens' awareness of police brutality and of the CCRB, leading to more complaints, as Police Commissioner Howard Safir suggested ("Complaints against Police Rise" 1998:A25). On the other hand, that type of incident might have discouraged others from even filing a police complaint.

My point is simply that the raw number of complaints of police misconduct, as well as the ratios of complaints to officers and complaints to arrests, increased significantly with the change in law enforcement in New York City. This suggests that the legal changes *may* have covered up disorderly disciplinary practices—that discipline increased under cover of law. Moreover, in New York City the issue of increased complaints of police brutality seems to have been overshadowed—at least prior to the Louima, Diallo, and Dorismond tragedies—by the rhetoric of order and cleanliness surrounding the quality-of-life initiative. Why is it, after all, that the issue of police brutality and the causes of brutality are not on the research agenda of the order-maintenance approach to criminal justice? Why is it that police disorder within order-maintenance policing is minimized in the "Broken Windows" essay? Why is it not included in the category of disorder?

Equally important, order-maintenance policing may incorporate and reinforce notions of black criminality. Dorothy Roberts of Northwestern University has explored the racial meaning of order-maintenance policing and has shown how the categories of order and disorder—of law abiders and the disorderly—are also shaped by pernicious racial stereotypes about criminality. The way that we define "visibly lawless people," Roberts explains, "adopts America's longstanding association between blackness and criminality" (Roberts 1999:805). Roberts catalogues the numerous ways in which blackness is associated with crime. Psychological studies, for instance, have revealed a disproportionate rate of error in eyewitness identification when the witness is white and the suspect African-American (1999:805–806). In addition, many police officers consider race in their decision to investigate, and defend racial profiling. This results in disproportionate arrests of African-American men and women for traffic and drug offenses (1999:806–809). Heightened arrests become, in turn, self-fulfilling prophecies: when the authority to arrest is exercised along racial lines, it likely increases the racial imbalance in convictions for other crimes (1999:818). In sum, Roberts writes:

One of the main tests in American culture for distinguishing law-abiding from lawless people is their race. Many, if not most, Americans believe that Black people are "prone to violence" and make race-based assessments of the danger posed by strangers they encounter. One of the most telling reflections of the association of Blacks with crime is the biased reporting of crime by white victims and eyewitnesses. The myth of Black criminality is part of a belief system deeply embedded in American culture that is premised on the superiority of whites and inferiority of Blacks. Stereotypes that originated in slavery are perpetuated today by the media and reinforced by the huge numbers of Blacks under criminal justice supervision. As Jody Armour puts it, "it is unrealistic to dispute the depressing conclusion that, for many Americans, crime has a black face." (1999:805)

Law enforcement policies that target minor disorderly conduct only aggravate the black face of crime. The fact is that misdemeanor arrests have a disparate impact on minorities. The demographic breakdown of misdemeanor arrests reflects that a disproportionate number of minorities are arrested for misdemeanors—disproportionate in relation to the percentage of minorities in the population, though not necessarily in relation to the racial breakdown of persons committing misdemeanor offenses. The point is not that the police are necessarily disproportionately targeting black versus white misdemeanants. It is practically impossible to gauge misdemeanors reliably by race. The point is that more blacks are arrested for misdemeanors than whites given their proportion in the overall population. The decision to arrest misdemeanants—rather than not arrest them—is a policy that has a disparate impact on minorities.

In cities throughout the United States, a large percentage of persons arrested for misdemeanors are black. This is reflected in Table 6.4, which compiles the racial breakdown for arrests in cities in 1995.[6] The table reveals how misdemeanor arrests disproportionately affect blacks. It is particularly striking in the case of arrests for vagrancy and on suspicion, where 46.4 and 58.7 percent, respectively, of persons arrested are black. It is also striking in most other categories, given that the 1990 Census reported that African-Americans make up only about 13 percent of the population of metropolitan areas (U.S. Department of Commerce 1990:7, table 5). As a result, a policing strategy that *tar-*

*gets* misdemeanors is likely to have a disproportionate effect on minorities. Such a strategy may also have a disproportionate impact on the homeless, who, almost by definition, violate misdemeanor laws against loitering and public drinking (Barnes 1998).

Moreover, the policy of aggressive stops and frisks also may target minorities. In New York City the preliminary evidence suggests that it actually does. In 1999 New York State Attorney General Eliot Spitzer, with the assistance of Columbia University's Center for Violence Research and Prevention, conducted an empirical analysis of 174,919 stop-and-frisk UF-250 forms—the forms that NYPD officers are required to fill out in a variety of stop encounters.[7] The forms analyzed involved stops that had occurred during the period January 1, 1998, through March 31, 1999.

In an initial series of analyses, covering the raw number of stops and frisks by race, Spitzer found, first, that the number of stops was higher for minorities—African-Americans and Hispanics—than whites relative to their respective proportion of the population. Whereas whites, who represent 43.3 percent of the population in New York City, accounted for 12.9 percent of all stops, blacks, who represent 25.6 percent of the population, and Hispanics, who represent 23.7 percent, accounted for 50.6 percent and 33.0 percent, respectively, of all stops (1999:94–95). Second, Spitzer found that there were more stops in precincts where blacks and Hispanics constitute the majority of the population, and less in majority white precincts. So, for instance, al-

Table 6.4 Demographic breakdown of misdemeanor arrests for large cities in 1995

|  | Percent white | Percent black |
|---|---|---|
| Population (132,911,000) | 83.0 | 12.6 |
| Misdemeanor arrests: |  |  |
|   Disorderly conduct | 61.2 | 36.9 |
|   Drug abuse | 58.7 | 40.3 |
|   Drunkenness | 79.4 | 17.7 |
|   Prostitution | 59.9 | 37.7 |
|   Suspicion | 40.9 | 58.7 |
|   Vagrancy | 50.9 | 46.4 |
|   Vandalism | 71.0 | 26.3 |

though about half of the city's seventy-five precincts have a white majority, of the ten precincts that experienced the highest rate of stops and frisks per resident, only three were majority white precincts, and of those three, two were business districts and therefore do not accurately reflect daytime racial population for purposes of policing (1999:96). Third, Spitzer found that the rate at which stops and frisks turned into arrests—in other words, the number of stops and frisks that turned up evidence of criminal behavior—differed by race. For every stop that would lead to an arrest, the NYPD stopped 9.5 blacks, 8.8 Hispanics, and 7.9 whites (1999:111). The rate of stops to arrest for stops conducted by the Street Crime Unit is even more disproportionate: 16.3 for blacks, 14.5 for Hispanics, and 9.6 for whites (1999:111–112, table I.B.1).

In a second series of tests, Spitzer reanalyzed the raw numbers, this time taking account of the crime rates and the population composition in different precincts. Since crime rates are generally higher in minority communities, Spitzer used regression analysis to hold constant those varying crime rates. To measure precinct crime rates, Spitzer used 1997 arrest data provided by the New York State Division of Criminal Justice Services for four crime categories (violent crimes, weapons crimes, property crimes, and drug crimes). After controlling for crime and population composition, Spitzer found significant disparities here, too, across all precincts and crime categories. He found that "in aggregate across all crime categories and precincts citywide, blacks were 'stopped' 23% more often (in comparison to the crime rate) than whites. Hispanics were 'stopped' 39% more often than whites" (1999:123). Spitzer concludes from the data that "even when crime data is taken into account, minorities are still 'stopped' at a higher rate than would be predicted by both demographics and crime rates" (1999:89).

Commissioner Safir preliminarily attacked Spitzer's conclusions, emphasizing the fact that, within racial categories, stops and frisks citywide are conducted in proportion to the composition of arrests and reflect the proportion by race of suspect descriptions. In a response to another report concluding that the NYPD engages in racial profiling—the Draft Report of the U.S. Commission on Civil Rights—Safir argued strenuously that "the ethnic breakdown of those stopped-and-frisked in the city as a whole *corresponds closely* with the ethnic breakdown of *those committing crimes in the city*." Safir suggested that Spitzer's report is fundamentally flawed for failing to analyze the stops and frisks in terms of the "demographics of crime suspects *as reported by victims.*" According to Safir, blacks constitute 62.4 percent of violent crime suspects as identified by victims, but only 52.3 percent of persons stopped and 57.7 percent of persons arrested for violent crime. Hispanics represent 26.8 percent of identified suspects, 32.9 percent of persons stopped, and 29 percent of persons arrested for violent crime (NYPD Response 2000:13). Safir has argued that Spitzer's report is seriously flawed, and, according to Jeffrey Fagan, director of Columbia University's Center for Violence Research and Prevention, retained Price Waterhouse to review the findings. A more detailed response was likely to be forthcoming.

Nevertheless, at least preliminarily, Spitzer seemed to have had the better of the argument. As an initial matter, the data reveal that fewer than a third (29.9 percent) of stops took place because the police officer believed that a person matched the description of a suspect. Therefore, the race of the suspect described by the victim was not a factor in more than two-thirds of stops (Spitzer 1999:122 n.30). More important, the statistical comparison between stops, victim descriptions, and arrests "does not compare the treatment of different races, but only considers each race in isolation" (1999:123). It is necessary instead, Spitzer argued, to compare the ratio of the absolute number of stops to the absolute number of arrests for a given racial group, and to compare the difference between those ratios for the different racial groups. When that is done, the analysis reveals that the ratio of stops to arrests is 1.54 for blacks, 1.72 for Hispanics, and 1.24 for whites. The result is that the black stop/arrest ratio is 23 percent higher, and the Hispanic ratio is 39 percent higher, than the white ratio (1999:123 n.31). Given the evidence so far, the policy of aggressive stops and frisks in New York City does seem to have had a racially discriminatory impact.

### Normalizing the Disorderly

In addition, the categories of the disorderly, the wicked, and the present-oriented are often portrayed as abnormal—as being in need of normalization, relocation, control, and surveillance. Edward Banfield, in fact, used the term "normal" to refer to future-oriented individuals in contrast to the lower class. There is a striking passage in *The Unheavenly City Revisited* where Banfield declares that "[i]n the chapters that follow, the term *normal* will be used to refer to class culture that is not lower class." Banfield explained that "[t]he implication that lower-class culture is pathological seems fully warranted both because of the relatively high incidence of mental illness in the lower class and also because human nature seems loath to accept a style of life that is so radically present-oriented." Feeling somewhat self-conscious, perhaps, he added that "[t]his is not the main reason for using the word *normal*, however, rather, it is that *some* word is needed to designate the sector of the class-cultural continuum that is not lower class, and no other word seems preferable on the whole" (1974:63).

Treating the disorderly as abnormal makes it a lot easier for law abiders to accept and condone possibly unfair treatment or excessive force. The fact is that, even apart from police misconduct and racial discrimination, misdemeanor arrests themselves are a serious, often traumatic ordeal. "Handcuffed, fingerprinted and often strip-searched, defendants spend as much as a day in jail before seeing a judge, who generally considers that punishment enough" (Purdy 1997).[8] According to the *New York Times,* "some people were held in cells for more than 60 hours waiting to see a judge for crimes like fare-beating, sleeping on park benches and drinking beer in public" (Cooper 1996). Transportation to the precinct, if by van, could take up to four or more hours. In addition, arrests create a criminal record that may haunt people on future job and school applications.

In order to enhance surveillance, Bratton changed the procedures for arrest, making them more onerous. Desk appearance tickets became less common, and the arrest process shifted to detaining, in jail, persons accused even of minor misdemeanor offenses for purposes of checking their identity and determining whether any outstanding warrants existed (Cooper 1996; Purdy 1997; Bratton 1998:155). In 1998 the NYPD went even further and began implementing a new policy of detaining anyone arrested for even a minor misdemeanor offense "until a computerized fingerprint check verifies the person's identity" (Kocieniewski and Cooper 1998). A valid form of identification—such as a driver's license—would no longer suffice. This process apparently could "take . . . up to eight hours in many cases" (Kocieniewski and Cooper 1998).

The *New York Times* published a short self-help manual for dealing with arrest and offered the following tips: "While being handcuffed, cross one hand over the other. It's more comfortable"; "If you are worried about being assaulted while in custody, sit near the front of the cell where guards can see you" (Cooper 1996). These are discomfiting reminders of what it means to be arrested. The ordeal of arrest can be a harrowing experience. A sample of cases reported in the papers illustrates this well. Chris C. was in the wrong place at the wrong time. Looking for a friend's name on the mailbox in the lobby of an apartment building in the East Village, Chris fell into the hands of officers hunting for drug activity. Accused of trespass, Chris was arrested, handcuffed, taken to jail, strip-searched, and held for nineteen hours. His case was dismissed two months later (Purdy 1997). Nancy T. was pulled over and arrested in Chinatown for driving without her license and talking back to a police officer ("failure to comply with an order"). She was handcuffed, taken to the station house, strip-searched, and locked up until early the next morning (Sontag and Barry 1997). Max M., a twenty-one-year-old college student, "was accused of drinking a beer on the street on the Upper West Side and spent a day in jail" (Purdy 1997).

Attorney General Spitzer recounts several personal narratives he heard during his investigation of the NYPD's stop-and-frisk initiative. One involved a fifty-four-year-old African-American woman who resides in Brooklyn. She was walking home from work one evening in March 1999 at about 10:30 P.M. when she noticed a white male in what was a predominantly black neighborhood. Apprehensive, she quickened her pace. She was almost home when the man apparently approached her from behind and grabbed her around the neck. "I screamed," she reports. "I thought I was being attacked so I screamed. . . . The man told me to be quiet because he was a police officer, but I really didn't know whether to believe him because he did not show me any identification. . . . The next thing I knew, the man was forcing me to walk down the street, back towards the direction he came from." She was taken to a car, where another man got out. They put her hands on the hood, first frisked her, and then conducted a full search of her person. Ultimately, they told her that she was free to go (Spitzer 1999:78–79).

Spitzer recounts another story of a fifty-year-old man, born in the

Virgin Islands and a resident of the Bronx, who was pulled over by a police officer. The man, employed as a teacher by the New York City Board of Education, was dressed in a suit and tie, and was driving his Mercedes-Benz to pick up medication for his daughter during his lunch break. After twenty minutes had gone by, the man leaned out his car window and said that he needed to return to his school. According to him, "the police officer then got out of his vehicle, visibly agitated. He came to my car window, and told me to get out of the car. . . . [T]hen he frisked me, saying that I had no right to question a police officer." He was cuffed, taken to the precinct, and refused permission to call his school. He was released at about 3:30 P.M. When he asked for proof that he had been stopped—to explain his absence from work—he was issued a desk appearance ticket for disorderly conduct and resisting arrest (Spitzer 1999:81).

Spitzer also describes the perspective of a principal of a Catholic high school for boys in Upper Manhattan, who conducts special classes on how to deal with the police. He tries to discourage his students from arguing with the police, to keep their hands visible and stay calm (Spitzer 1999:83). To be sure, these are just news stories and narratives, mere anecdotes reported secondhand. But they do force us to see what we so badly want to ignore. Misdemeanor stops and searches and arrests affect real people, not just statistics. The order-maintenance approach does not pay sufficient attention to these effects. It does not examine how the category of the disorderly allows us to treat people as deviant and outside the realm of our legal ideals, or how it allows us to implement a policy of aggressive arrests without really noticing.

The reading of Foucault that I propose—especially his legal theory—may help explain how. The explanation turns, in large part, on the treatment of the disorderly as abnormal. In this sense, the explanation draws equally from other contemporary strands of political and social theory. In her essay "Punishment, Treatment, Empowerment," for instance, Iris Marion Young describes how drug treatment programs shape the drug-addicted pregnant mother. According to Young, public policies aimed at punishing drug-addicted pregnant women serve to construct these women as delinquent and to marginalize them further from the full benefits of social membership. In her words, "[P]unishment seems only to have the function of marking the women as deviant, publicly reaffirming their exclusion from the class of upstanding citizens" (1997:80–81). Similarly, Judith Butler argues, in her article "Contingent Foundations," that the laws of sex discrimination and rape effectively construct and regulate women's subject position. Butler suggests that, by defining the specific qualifications that must be met in order for a woman to be able to claim sexual harassment or rape, the law excludes certain women from the category of the oppressed. "Subjects are constituted through exclusion," Butler emphasizes, "through the creation of a domain of deauthorized subjects, presubjects, figures of abjection, populations erased from view" (1995:47). In the same way, the normalization of the disorderly serves to construct such persons as outsiders and legitimate unfair treatment—treatment that most of us recognize "would not withstand a legal challenge" (Wilson and Kelling 1982:31).

### Overshadowing Other Costs of Order Maintenance

Finally, these processes of categorization, facilitation, and normalization may overshadow numerous other costs associated with the proposed policing initiatives. The meaning of orderliness—understood in terms of preventing serious crimes—may blind us to some significant disadvantages of order-maintenance policing. It is easy to look back from today's standpoint and count the number of people who protested NYPD abuses in the wake of the Louima, Diallo, and Dorismond incidents—and to describe how those incidents polarized New Yorkers (Spitzer 1999:5). But the fact is that, before these high-profile tragedies, and while complaints of police brutality were sharply rising, very few were raising any questions about police misconduct.

Order maintenance may facilitate an uncomfortable delegation of the power to define community standards. Clyde Haberman of the *New York Times* has asked, slightly facetiously, "a humble question" about the quality-of-life initiative: "Whose life is it, anyway, that we're talking about?" (Haberman 1998). Referring to the campaign against squeegee men, Haberman remarked to himself: "Wait a minute, dummy, you don't own a car. No squeegee man ever ruined *your* day. And you know what? The same is true for most New Yorkers, since the city's Transportation Department says that 56 percent of them do not have access to a car, let alone even occasional contact with curbside window washers" (1998).

Haberman's musings must be taken in perspective. The quality-of-life initiative has also targeted the subway system and other pedestrian venues. But his humble question is still an important one. How do we define minor disorder? Clearly, we are not talking about arresting those who pay their housekeeper in cash to benefit knowingly from IRS underreporting. The quality-of-life initiative focuses instead on the type of minor offenses—loitering, fare beating, and panhandling—that affect the poorer members of society, a group that, tragically, includes a disproportionate number of minorities. By handing over the informal power to define deviance to police officers and a few community members, we may be making possible the repression of political, cultural, or sexual outsiders in a way that is antithetical to our conceptions of democratic theory.

In addition, arrests and prosecutions are very expensive. A typical prosecution for prostitution—one of the offenses targeted by the quality-of-life initiative—costs upwards of $2,000 (Rhode 1995). That is a lot of money for a single transaction. Finally, a policy of arrest may have unintended consequences. Someone arrested for turnstile jumping may be fired from his job for missing work; and strained police-civilian relations can create friction between the community and the police force that may be detrimental to solving crimes.

## From Social Meaning to Subject Creation

In sum, the order-maintenance approach converges on a richer notion of propensities but fails to explore sufficiently how that conception is constructed, over lengthy periods of time, by the practices and institutions that surround us. While the approach concentrates on the construction of social meaning, it fails to pay enough attention to the way that social meaning may construct the subject and to how our understanding of the subject fosters certain disciplinary strategies. The focus on social meaning is an important contribution to criminal justice. But it is crucial to investigate, beyond the impact of social meaning on behavior, the effect of police practices on the subject.

# PART III

# Rhetorical Critique

We are left with a disarming theory, a theory that has great rhetorical power but little empirical substance and troubling theoretical implications, a type of aesthetic policing that focuses on the disorderly. The order-maintenance approach appropriates the aesthetic of order and sobriety, and, at the same time, empowers the police as the only rival to the criminals. By commandeering these categories, the theory leaves most of its interlocutors speechless. Very few contest the policing strategy—even though the broken windows theory, especially as implemented in New York City, leads to a false choice. No reasonable person would choose the gangs, the criminals, or the disorderly. No one would advocate disorder, littering, or panhandling. No one would seriously come out in favor of breaking windows—even if, as the "Broken Windows" essay playfully suggests, "[i]t has always been fun" (Wilson and Kelling 1982:31).

Why is it, then, that broken windows policing has been received with so much enthusiasm across the spectrum of political ideology? Why is it that many liberal New Yorkers—at least during periods when there are no major police scandals such as the Amadou Diallo and Patrick Dorismond affairs—have embraced Mayor Giuliani's quality-of-life initiative? If the order-maintenance approach is in fact built on categories that are not critically examined, how has it become such a leading voice in criminal law policy analysis?

These are fascinating questions. The emergence and popularity of order maintenance in this country is a deeply intriguing topic. A full

181

answer would need to address large-scale political, social, and historical factors, such as macro-geopolitical change (for example, the fall of the Berlin Wall and the collapse of the Soviet Union), national and international social movements (such as civil rights movements, anti–Vietnam War protest, and liberation struggles), as well as long-term demographic changes and, perhaps, the recent period of American economic prosperity. Massive social, cultural, and political upheavals during the second half of the twentieth century may account for the swing in public opinion and political ideology in this country. What these changes seem to have brought about, at the political level, is a retreat from leftist reformist idealism—represented by social welfare programs, rehabilitative treatment approaches, and anti-poverty measures—and its replacement with an ethic of individual responsibility and accountability, correspondingly represented by welfare-to-work programs, more retributive approaches to punishment, and decreased government intervention and programs.

Many scholars and social critics have observed and documented these larger trends, and several have related them to dramatic changes in techniques of governing over the course of the last two centuries (Burchell, Gordon, and Miller 1991:102–103; Rose and Miller 1992; Hunt and Wickham 1994; Beckett 1997). Some argue that these changes reflect what Katherine Beckett describes as "the effort to replace social welfare with social control as the principle of state policy" (Beckett 1997:106). Disappointed with the failure of various anti-poverty initiatives, these theorists argue, American liberals have abandoned the 1960s agenda of social programs and turned instead to law enforcement measures as the principal way to control the poor and uneducated. This turn to social control ends up highlighting the harms associated with crime, urban decay, single motherhood, and the disintegration of social solidarity, and it underscores the need to reestablish and maintain order.

There is, certainly, good evidence to support these explanations. Our recent national investment in law enforcement in contrast to welfare programs is remarkable. As Beckett observes: "[B]etween 1976 and 1989, the percentage of state budgets allocated to education and welfare programs declined dramatically—the former by 12% and the latter by 41%. . . . Meanwhile, state and federal 'correctional' expenditures grew by 95% and 114% (respectively) between 1976 and 1989 and continue to increase dramatically" (1997:106). Moreover, as discussed earlier, incarceration rates have skyrocketed in this country since the 1970s.

What I would like to suggest here is another contributing factor that has received much less, if any, attention in the criminal justice context. What has also contributed to the popularity of the order-maintenance approach is the fact that its proponents deploy what is perhaps the most effective rhetorical maneuver today, namely, the turn to harm. The approach reflects a fascinating rhetorical shift in law and politics. What it has succeeded in doing is to transform *offensive* conduct into *harmful* conduct. It used to be the case, in the 1950s and 1960s, that loitering, panhandling, public urination, public drinking, and prostitution were, in some sense, moral and aesthetic offenses. They were unseemly acts that violated our shared code of civility. Yet they were tolerated by progressives because the dominant principle of punishment in liberal political theory—the harm principle—allowed the prohibition of *harmful acts,* not immoral or unseemly ones. Today, however, these same acts are viewed as *positively harmful.* They are seen as the cause of serious crime. This reflects a significant shift in rhetoric that occurred during the last few decades of the twentieth century— what I call, drawing on writings in legal semiotics, the ideological shift and collapse of the harm principle (Balkin 1991:1833; Balkin 1993; Duncan Kennedy 1989, 1997:133–156).

By focusing on rhetoric and justification, I do not intend to displace the other explanations that have been offered to account for the birth of the punitive state. Instead, I intend to supplement them. My point is that rhetorical shifts in the policing debate have contributed to some degree to the popularity of broken windows policing. In other words, the justifications that have been offered to support order maintenance, and the rhetoric of the policing debate, are not autonomous or inconsequential but rather have real implications for concrete practices—practices such as stops and frisks, arrests, and punishment.

By focusing on rhetoric, I also intend to highlight a final flaw in the order-maintenance argument. As I demonstrate in Chapter 7, the turn to harm has inadvertently undermined the force of harm arguments. It has collapsed the harm principle. The proliferation of harm arguments in late modernity has weakened any single claim of harm. In the context of order maintenance, the fact that a broken window may cause harm is no longer determinative. Whatever harms that disorder may cause, these injuries must now be weighed against other potential harms, especially those associated with order-maintenance policing. In other words, the argument that disorder causes crime—even if it were true—does not end but is rather the beginning of the policing debate.

# CHAPTER 7

# The Turn to Harm
# as Justification

The rise and triumph of the liberal harm principle in the 1960s and 1970s gave way, in the 1980s and 1990s, to a proliferation of harm arguments. Armed with social science studies, with empirical data, and with anecdotal evidence, the proponents of regulation and prohibition turned to the harm principle as the main justification for the enforcement of legal intervention. This shift in justification is evident in a wide range of political debates, including debates over pornography, homosexuality, illicit drug use, and alcohol consumption. It is also evident in debate over quality-of-life offenses.

The broken windows theory, in fact, is a perfect illustration of this turn to harm and of the power of that rhetorical move. Before order maintenance, the disorderly were merely the "losers" of society. They were hoboes, bums, winos—a nuisance to many, but not threatening or dangerous. Similarly, practices like loitering and panhandling were, again for many, mere inconveniences. Today, however, the disorderly are considered the agents of crime and neighborhood decline. Loitering, panhandling, and prostitution supposedly attract serious criminal activity. Sheer disorder has become the harm that justifies criminal punishment. And the principal justification is no longer offense nor immorality but harm—the harm that these misdemeanor offenses cause. "[I]f a climate of disorder and lack of mutual respect is allowed to take root," Mayor Giuliani argued, "incidence of other, more serious antisocial behavior will increase. . . . [M]urder and graffiti are two vastly different crimes. *But they are part of the same continuum"* (1998, emphasis added).

By appropriating harm, the order-maintenance approach has disarmed the traditional liberal response. It has produced a significant disequilibrium in the rhetorical structure of the policing debate. And this may account in part for the power of the broken-windows approach. It may explain why so many New Yorkers support order maintenance. In this chapter, I explore this turn to harm. I trace it to a fascinating development in the larger debate over the legal enforcement of morality. It is a development in three movements, involving, first, the triumph of the harm principle; second, the proliferation of harm arguments; and, third, the collapse of the harm principle. For present purposes, it makes sense to begin with John Stuart Mill.[1]

## The Rise of the Harm Principle

Mill set forth the liberal harm principle in its most concise form in his essay *On Liberty*. Mill succinctly stated the principle there in a now famous passage in the opening pages:

> The object of this essay is to assert one very simple principle, as entitled to govern absolutely the dealings of society with the individual in the way of compulsion and control. . . . That principle is that the sole end for which mankind are warranted, individually or collectively, in interfering with the liberty of action of any of their number is self-protection. That the only purpose for which power can be rightfully exercised over any member of a civilized community, against his will, is to prevent harm to others. (1978:9)

Though simple at first blush, the harm principle actually was far more complicated than it looked, and, over the course of *On Liberty*, it took on many nuances. Mill gave the principle different formulations in his essay, and his argument became more complex with each restatement (Donner 1991:189). In Mill's short essay, the harm principle metamorphosed from a simple inquiry into harm, to a more complex analysis of interests (self-regarding and other-regarding interests), and eventually to a quasi-legal determination of rights. In his final restatement of the harm principle, Mill ultimately defined the concept of harm on the basis of recognized or legal rights (1978:73).

As Mill explained, the notion of rights embodied in this final restatement rested on a modified utilitarian calculus grounded in the permanent interests of man as a progressive being (1978:10). Mill's emphasis, ultimately, was on the notion of human self-development (Berger 1984:229–230; Buchanan 1989:862; Hittinger 1990:51–52; Donner 1991:188–197).

About a century later, in the mid-1950s, debate over the harm principle reignited. In England the debate was sparked by the recommendation of the Committee on Homosexual Offences and Prostitution (the "Wolfenden Report") that private homosexual acts between consenting adults no longer be criminalized. In the United States the debate was rekindled by the Supreme Court's struggle over the definition and treatment of obscenity and the drafting of the Model Penal Code (Dworkin 1966:986–987; Grey 1983:4). In both countries the debate was fueled by the perception among liberal theorists that legal moralist principles were experiencing a rejuvenation and were threatening to encroach on liberalism.

More than anyone else, Patrick Devlin catalyzed this perceived threat. In his Maccabaean Lecture, delivered to the British Academy in 1959, Lord Devlin argued that purportedly immoral activities, such as homosexuality and prostitution, should remain criminal offenses (Devlin 1977). Lord Devlin published his lecture and other essays under the title *The Enforcement of Morals,* and soon became associated with the principle of legal moralism—the principle that moral offenses should be regulated *because* they are immoral. H. L. A. Hart responded to Devlin in a series of lectures delivered at Stanford University in 1962, and the debate over the harm principle was reignited (Hart 1963).

There thus emerged, in the Hart-Devlin exchange of the early 1960s, a pairing of two familiar arguments: the harm principle and legal moralism. All the participants at the time recognized, naturally, that this structure represented a recurrence of a very similar pairing of arguments that had set the contours of the debate a hundred years earlier (see, e.g., Schwartz 1963:670 n.1). The Hart-Devlin debate replicated, in many ways, the debate between Mill and another famous British jurist, James Fitzjames Stephen. In 1873, in a book titled *Liberty, Equality, Fraternity,* Lord Stephen had published a scathing attack on Mill's essay and strenuously advocated legal moralism. Stephen described his argument as "absolutely inconsistent with and contradictory to Mr. Mill's" (1973:162). Stephen's argument, like Mill's, was best captured in a now famous passage: "[T]here are acts of wickedness so gross and outrageous that, self-protection apart, they must be prevented as far as possible at any cost to the offender, and punished, if they occur, with exemplary severity" (1973:162).

Hart immediately underscored the similar structure of the emerging debate. "Though a century divides these two legal writers," he observed, referring to Lords Stephen and Devlin, "the similarity in the general tone and sometimes in the detail of their arguments is very great" (Hart 1963:16). In his defense, Devlin responded that at the time he delivered the Maccabaean Lecture he "did not then know that the same ground had already been covered by Mr. Justice Stephen" (1977:vii). Nevertheless, Devlin conceded that there was "great similarity between [Lord Stephen's] view and mine on the principles that should affect the use of the criminal law for the enforcement of morals" (1977:vii). Devlin also noted the similarity between Hart and Mill (1977:105).

Though the paired structure of arguments was similar, it was not exactly the same. In contrast to Stephen's straightforward legal moralist argument, Lord Devlin's argument in *The Enforcement of Morality* was ambiguous and susceptible to competing interpretations. His argument played on the ambivalence in the notion of harm—at times courting the idea of social harm, at other times aligning more closely with the legal moralism of his predecessor. As a result, the conservative position began to fragment, and there developed at least two interpretations of Devlin's argument: the first relied on public harm, the second on legal moralism. Hart and Joel Feinberg labeled these two versions, respectively, the moderate thesis and the extreme thesis (Hart 1963:48; Feinberg 1975:289–293).

Under the moderate interpretation, Devlin appeared to be arguing that morality should be enforced in order to protect society from the danger of disintegration—an argument that relied on harm. Feinberg, for instance, suggested that Devlin's moderate thesis was "really an application of the public harm principle" (1975:289). Jeffrie Murphy similarly read Devlin as advancing a public harm argument (1995:76). Robert George and Kent Greenawalt also interpreted Devlin as making a public harm argument (George 1990:19; Greenawalt 1995:722).

On this moderate view, the only difference between Hart and Devlin was that Hart focused on harm to the individual, whereas Devlin focused on harm to society as a whole. And there was ample textual support for this interpretation. In fact, it was precisely on this ground that Devlin criticized the Wolfenden Report (Devlin 1977:22).

One obvious flaw with the moderate interpretation was that Devlin never defined the causal mechanism of social harm. Although he repeatedly referred to "social disintegration," he failed to articulate the pathway of harm. But an even greater problem was that Devlin ignored completely the empirical dimension of the public harm claim. "[N]o evidence is produced," Hart exclaimed. "No reputable historian has maintained this thesis, and there is indeed much evidence against it. As a proposition of fact it is entitled to no more respect than the Emperor Justinian's statement that homosexuality was the cause of earthquakes" (1963:50). Three years later, Ronald Dworkin sounded the same refrain: "[Lord Devlin] manages this conclusion without offering evidence that homosexuality presents any danger at all to society's existence" (1966:992; see also Sartorius 1972:893; Murphy 1995:77; Gerald Dworkin 1999:931).

The empirical gap in Devlin's harm argument was terribly damaging, and, as a result, a second, more extreme reading of Devlin emerged. Under the second interpretation, referred to as the extreme thesis, Devlin argued that morality should be enforced for the sake of morality *tout court:* morality for morality's sake. If Devlin's claim (that private acts of immorality present a danger to society) was not intended to be an empirical claim, Hart suggested, then Devlin equated morality with society. "On this view the enforcement of morality is not justified by its valuable consequences in securing society from dissolution or decay," Hart argued. "It is justified simply as identical with or required for the preservation of the society's morality" (1963:55). Under the more extreme reading, Devlin's argument was much closer to the earlier statement of legal moralism in Lord Stephen's book *Liberty, Equality, Fraternity* (see Devlin 1977:25).

The ambiguity in Devlin's writings fractured the conservative position. It was unclear whether Devlin was advancing a prediction of actual social harm or a traditional argument about legal moralism. In response, Hart and other liberal theorists returned to Mill's essay *On Liberty* and to the original, simple statement of the harm principle.

The Return to Mill's Harm Principle

In *Law, Liberty, and Morality,* a set of lectures delivered in response to Lord Devlin in 1962, H. L. A. Hart rehearsed Mill's harm principle but carefully pared the argument down to its original, simple, and succinct statement. Right after posing the central question of his lectures— "Ought immorality as such to be a crime?"—Hart immediately cited Mill in support of his position. "To this question," Hart responded, "John Stuart Mill gave an emphatic negative answer in his essay *On Liberty* one hundred years ago, and *the famous sentence in which he frames this answer expresses the central doctrine of his essay*" (1963:4, emphasis added). Hart endorsed the simple harm argument and declared that "on the narrower issue relevant to the enforcement of morality Mill seems to me to be right" (1963:5).[2]

Similarly, in an early essay titled "Moral Enforcement and the Harm Principle"—an essay which sketched the terrain of his later four-volume treatise *The Moral Limits of the Criminal Law*—Joel Feinberg rehearsed Mill's harm principle. He, too, pared the principle down to its original simple formulation. Feinberg emphasized the importance of distinguishing between direct and indirect harm, but went no further, at the time, in developing the harm argument (Feinberg 1975:284). He endorsed the argument and wrote that the distinction, "as Mill intended it to be understood, does seem at least roughly serviceable, and unlikely to invite massive social interference in private affairs" (1975:286).[3]

In 1984 Feinberg published the first volume of *The Moral Limits of the Criminal Law,* titled *Harm to Others.* He explored there the contours of the harm principle and developed fifteen supplementary criteria, or what he called "mediating maxims," to assist in the application of the harm principle (1984:214–217; 243–245). Throughout the four-volume treatise, Feinberg maintained that the harm argument, as refined by the mediating maxims, was one of only two considerations (the other being the offense principle) that were always a good reason for prohibiting purportedly immoral activity.

Gradually, over the course of the 1960s, 1970s, and 1980s, Mill's famous sentence began to dominate the legal philosophic debate over the enforcement of morality. Harm became *the* critical principle used to police the line between law and morality within Anglo-American philosophy of law. Most prominent theorists who participated in the debate either relied on the harm principle or made favorable reference to the argument. Ronald Dworkin engaged the Hart-Devlin debate in an article first published in the *Yale Law Journal* in 1966 titled "Lord Devlin and the Enforcement of Morals." Although Dworkin focused on the implications for democratic theory—arguing that legislators must ultimately decide whether the community has expressed a reasoned moral position about purportedly immoral activities—Dworkin presented the harm principle as a leading response in the debate (1966:996; see also, e.g., Henkin 1963:413).

Over time, the harm principle essentially prevailed in the debate over the legal enforcement of morality. From one end of the spectrum to the other, there arose a consensus that Hart had carried the day. At the liberal end of the spectrum, Ronald Dworkin reported that Devlin's argument "was widely attacked" and that his thesis was, ultimately, "very implausible" (1989:487). On the other end of the spectrum, Robert George would report that "many . . . perhaps even most [commentators] think that Hart carried the day" (1990:30). Jeffrie Murphy—who is a skeptic of the harm principle—captured well the prevailing consensus. "I believed, along with most of the people with whom I talked about legal philosophy," Murphy wrote, "that legal moralism had been properly killed off, that liberalism had once again been vindicated against the forces of superstition and oppression, and that legal philosophy could now move on to new and more important topics" (1995:74–75).

This is not to suggest that the controversy simply disappeared from philosophic circles. Under one reading, the Hart-Devlin debate metamorphosed and resurfaced as the liberal-communitarian debate, a much larger debate about liberalism and its ability to accommodate the need for community (see, e.g., Sandel 1989). There have also been attempts to rehabilitate Devlin's position (Murphy 1995:76–78), and at least one attempt to radicalize Devlin's argument (George 1990:30–37; 1993). Devlin still has supporters. In fact, in 1999 Gerald Dworkin published a provocative essay titled "Devlin Was Right," in which he sides with Devlin "in believing that there is no principled line following the contours of the distinction between immoral and harmful conduct such that only grounds referring to the latter may be invoked to justify criminalization" (1999:928). Nevertheless, even Dworkin seems willing to concede that he is swimming against the liberal tide, and acknowledges that he is practically alone in defending Lord Devlin (1999:927–928). In essence, over time, a consensus emerged that the liberal harm principle had prevailed in the legal philosophic debate over the enforcement of morality.

## The Influence on Legal Rhetoric

As the harm principle began to dominate the debate in law and philosophy, the principle also began to colonize criminal law scholarship and legal rhetoric. Most of the leading criminal law scholars either adopted the harm principle or incorporated it in their writings. Herbert Packer, in *The Limits of the Criminal Sanction*, included the harm principle in his list of limiting criteria that justified the criminal sanction. Although Packer did not focus primarily on the harm principle— focusing instead on the effectiveness and social consequences of policing certain activities—he did incorporate it into his work and argued that "[t]he harm to others formula seems to me to have . . . uses that justify its inclusion in a list of limiting criteria for invocation of the criminal sanction" (1968:267; 296). The harm principle featured prominently in criminal law treatises and casebooks. One of the most popular casebooks, Monrad Paulsen and Sanford Kadish's first edition of *Criminal Law and Its Processes,* published in 1962, started off on page one with the debate over Devlin's Maccabaean Lecture. It extracted a lengthy portion of the lecture, as well as Hart's preliminary response published in the *Listener* in 1959 (Paulsen and Kadish 1962:1–17). Paul Robinson, in his popular treatise *Criminal Law,* refers first and foremost to societal harm in discussing the definition of criminal conduct (Robinson 1997:131).

The simple harm principle also permeated the rhetoric of the criminal law itself. This was reflected most clearly in the drafting of the Model Penal Code by the American Law Institute, which was begun in 1952 and completed in 1962.[4] Herbert Wechsler, the chief reporter and intellectual father of the Model Penal Code, strongly endorsed harm as the guiding principle of criminal liability. As early as 1955 Wechsler wrote: "All would agree, I think, that there is no defensible foundation for declaring conduct criminal unless it injures or threatens to injure an important human interest" (1955:527). In his scholarly writings, Wechsler consistently emphasized the harm principle: conduct "is not deemed to be a proper subject of a penal prohibition" unless it "unjustifiably and inexcusably inflicts or threatens substantial harm." This was, Wechsler emphasized, "a declaration designed to be given weight in the interpretation of the [Model Penal] Code" (1968:1432).

The language of the Model Penal Code reflected this emphasis on the harm principle. In the preliminary article, section 1.02, the drafters addressed the purposes of criminal law and stated, as the very first principle, the objective "to forbid and prevent conduct that unjustifiably and inexcusably inflicts or threatens substantial harm to individual or public interests" (MPCC 1985:1.02[1][a]). In the explanatory note attached to the final draft, the drafters referred to this harm principle as the "major goal" of the provisions governing the definition of crimes—in contrast to the other four stated purposes which are referred to as "subsidiary themes" (MPCOD 1985: note 14). The comment to the preliminary article refers to the harm principle as "the dominant preventive purpose of the penal law" (MPCOD 1985:16). It emphasizes that the harm principle "reflect[s] inherent and important limitations on the just and prudent use of penal sanctions as a measure of control" (MPCOD 1985:17). Substantially similar provisions regarding the harm principle were enacted in Alabama, Alaska, Delaware, Florida, Georgia, Nebraska, New Jersey, New York, Oregon, Pennsylvania, Tennessee, Texas, and Washington, among other states.[5]

The harm principle was also reflected in the definition of crimes, especially moral offenses and public decency crimes. "The Model Penal Code does not attempt to enforce private morality," the drafters explained. "Thus, none of the provisions contained in Article 251 purports to regulate sexual behavior generally" (MPCOD 1985:196). With regard to each moral offense, the drafters specifically discussed harm. In the case of prostitution, the drafters retained the criminal sanction specifically because of the potential harm in the spread of syphilis and gonorrhea (MPCOD 1985:458). In the case of consensual homosexual activity, the drafters rejected criminal responsibility on the ground of lack of harm (MPCOD 1985:369). With regard to obscenity, the drafters paid special attention to the relationship between obscene materials and overt misbehavior (MPCOD 1985:482). Even the proposed definition of public drunkenness incorporated the harm (and offense) principles. In the Model Penal Code, the offense of public intoxication "differs from prior law principally in requiring that the person be under the influence of alcohol or other drug 'to the degree that he may endanger himself or other persons or property, or annoy persons in his vicinity'" (MPCOD 1985:190).

From philosophy of law to substantive criminal law, the harm principle permeated the debate during the 1960s and 1970s. As evidenced by the writings of Hart and Feinberg in the legal philosophic debate, and of Wechsler and the drafters of the Model Penal Code in the substantive criminal law debate, the harm principle became the dominant discursive principle used to draw the line between law and morality. The decision to embrace Mill's original simple statement of the harm principle was a powerful rhetorical move. Devlin's writings had fragmented the conservative position by conflating harm and morality, and had significantly ambiguated the conception of harm at the heart of the debate. The liberal response reclaimed the conception of harm. It simplified and pared it back down to the mere idea of "harm." It bracketed out the competing normative dimensions of harm. It offered a bright-line rule, a rule that was simple to apply. And a rule, I argue, that was *simply applied.*

### The Proliferation of Harm Arguments

The rise of the harm principle gave way, in the 1980s and 1990s, to a proliferation of harm arguments. In a wide array of debates, ranging from pornography to homosexuality and fornication, to drug use and alcohol consumption, harm arguments were deployed—in the idiom of the harm principle—to justify legal intervention and prohibition. Whether the rhetorical shift was motivated by moral conviction or by sincere adherence to the harm principle, the result was the same: the harm principle underwent an ideological shift from its progressive origins.

### Pornography and Harm

In the mid-1980s Joel Feinberg discussed the feminist critique of pornography and suggested that the proper liberal position would be to leave open the possibility of regulating pornography if empirical evidence of harm developed. Feinberg intimated that further empirical research regarding some types of pornography—specifically hard-core pornography—might demonstrate harm. "In that case," Feinberg wrote, "a liberal should have no hesitation in using the criminal law to prevent the harm" (1985:157). Feinberg cautioned, however, that "in the meantime, the *appropriate liberal response* should be a kind of uneasy skepticism about the harmful effects of pornography on third-party victims, conjoined with increasingly energetic use of 'further speech or expression' against the cult of macho, 'effectively to combat the harm'" (1985:157, emphasis added; see also Feinberg 1988:xv).

Things changed over time. The "appropriate liberal response" to pornography at the turn of century, I would suggest, is the free speech argument, not the harm principle. Proponents of the regulation and prohibition of pornography have skillfully employed the harm argument in support of their own position, and thereby undercut the earlier progressive response.

Catharine MacKinnon, perhaps more than anyone else, has focused the debate on the harm to women caused by pornography. MacKinnon's work has emphasized at least three types of harm emanating from pornography. First, pornography inflicts harm on the women who are used to make the pornographic material. "It is for pornography," MacKinnon explains, "and not by the ideas in it that women are hurt and penetrated, tied and gagged, undressed and genitally spread and sprayed with lacquer and water so sex pictures can be made" (1993:15). Second, MacKinnon has argued, pornography harms the women who are assaulted by consumers of pornography. Men who consume pornography may be led—and in some cases are led—to commit crimes of sexual violence against women. "It is not the ideas in pornography that assault women," MacKinnon writes. "[M]en do, men who are made, changed, and impelled by it" (1993:15). Third, pornography supports and promotes a general climate of discrimination against women. It becomes a part of the identity of women and of women's sexuality. "As the industry expands," MacKinnon explains, "this becomes more and more the generic experience of sex, the woman in pornography becoming more and more the lived archetype for women's sexuality in men's, hence women's, experience" (1993:15). Pornography, in sum, causes multiple harms to women by shaping and distorting the modern subject.

MacKinnon's arguments have infiltrated American legal and political rhetoric. Though many resist MacKinnon's argument, or the full implications of her argument, there is no question that pornography is associated with harm in a way that it was not in the 1960s. At least in part because of MacKinnon's argument, several municipalities have begun to enforce regulations aimed at decreasing the amount of pornography. The city council of Indianapolis, for instance, implemented MacKinnon's model ordinance (*Hudnut* 1985). And in New York City, Mayor Rudolph Giuliani forcefully implemented a zoning ordinance, passed in 1995, aimed at closing down commercial sex establishments such as strip clubs, sex shops, and adult book and video stores. Giuliani justified the crackdown by citing the harm that commercial sex poses to ordinary citizens and to neighborhoods—not just in terms of increased crime against women, but also in terms of reduced property values, tourism, and commerce.

MacKinnon's focus on harm also has influenced the responses of her main opponents—Judge Frank Easterbrook, who struck down the Indianapolis ordinance in *American Booksellers Association, Inc. v. Hudnut*, and Judith Butler, whose 1997 book *Excitable Speech: A Politics of the Performative* takes issue with MacKinnon's approach.

Though Easterbrook, writing for the Seventh Circuit, struck down MacKinnon's ordinance on First Amendment grounds, he nevertheless acknowledged the harm that pornography may cause women. Easterbrook wrote in *Hudnut:*

> [W]e accept the premises of this legislation. Depictions of subordination tend to perpetuate subordination. The subordinate status of women in turn leads to affront and lower pay at work, insult and injury at home, battery and rape on the streets. In the language of the legislature, "[p]ornography is central in creating and maintaining sex as a basis of discrimination. Pornography is a systematic practice of exploitation and subordination based on sex which differentially harms women. The bigotry and contempt it produces, with the acts of aggression it fosters, harm women's opportunities for equality and rights [of all kinds]."[6]

Ironically, it is precisely the harm associated with pornography that, according to Easterbrook, "simply demonstrates the power of pornography as speech" (*Hudnut* 1985:329). It is the harm of pornography that triggers First Amendment protection. Easterbrook struck down the ordinance not because pornography causes no harm, but rather because the harm is evidence of the power of speech and of the importance of protecting free speech: "If the fact that speech plays a role in a process of conditioning were enough to permit governmental regulation, that would be the end of freedom of speech" (*Hudnut* 1985:330).

In the academy, Judith Butler has argued against MacKinnon's proposal to regulate pornography. Butler is concerned that regulation may give too much power to the state. The potential risk, according to Butler, is that the state will then deploy its regulatory power against the interests of minority groups. Butler warns that "such strategies tend to enhance state regulation over the issues in question, potentially empowering the state to invoke such precedents against the very social movements that pushed for their acceptance as legal doctrine" (1997:24). In the place of state regulation, Butler advocates nonjuridical, nonregulatory forms of resistance, such as everyday forms of opposition and organized group resistance. The paradigm of resistance, for Butler, is the way in which the term of abuse "queer" was reappropriated by gay men and lesbians and given new meaning through a process of resignification (1997:14).

What is important here is that throughout Butler's discussion the concept of harm plays a central role. Her argument attempts to refine MacKinnon's discussion of harm in order to insert a gap between pornography and its harm that would allow time and space for nonjuridical intervention. Butler's argument draws heavily on J. L. Austin's early distinction in *How to Do Things with Words* between illocutionary and perlocutionary speech acts.[7] Butler argues that MacKinnon wrongly ascribes both perlocutionary and illocutionary attributes to pornography. The perlocutionary aspect corresponds to the incitement to rape, the illocutionary to the demeaning of women and the shaping of women's identity. Butler explains, "In MacKinnon's recent work, *Only Words*, pornography . . . is understood not only to 'act on' women in injurious ways (a perlocutionary claim), but to constitute, through representation, the class of women as an inferior class (an illocutionary claim)" (1997:20–21). She suggests that the illocutionary character is a new development, and argues that it has negative political implications. The problem, according to Butler, is that if pornography is indeed illocutionary, there is no room for resistance. The very possibility of resistance, especially nonjuridical resistance, depends on there being some time and space between the speech act and the injury (1997:14). Butler argues that pornography should not be interpreted as having an illocutionary effect in order, precisely, to allow for linguistic struggle. Butler's argument underscores the perlocutionary aspect of the harm to women. Harm drives Butler's conception of individual agency and creates the need for a political struggle at the individual level against harmful speech. Butler's response both acknowledges harm and seeks to refine the harm argument.

In the specific context of the pornography debate, then, MacKinnon's use of the harm argument has produced an ideological shift in the harm principle. In contrast to an earlier period when the harm principle was employed by progressives to justify limits on the regulation of pornography, the principle is no longer an effective response to proposals to regulate. To the contrary, the proponents of legal regulation have essentially taken over the harm principle: harm has become the principal argument for state intervention, as illustrated and, in this particular case, at least temporarily implemented in Indianapolis and New York City. Easterbrook and Butler's responses to MacKinnon reflect how destabilizing this ideological shift has been. These contemporary responses essentially discard the liberal harm principle in favor of free speech and strategic arguments about political effectiveness. Most tellingly, these contemporary responses *incorporate harm* into their own arguments to bolster their position. The result is an entirely different structure in the debate over the legal enforcement of morality: a structure of competing harm claims with no internal mechanism to resolve them.

## Homosexual Conduct and Harm

The case of homosexual conduct is particularly interesting because here, it seemed, legal moralism was still strong. In 1986 the United States Supreme Court adopted legal moralism for purposes of rational basis review under the Fourteenth Amendment to the United States Constitution. In *Bowers v. Hardwick,* Justice White, writing for the Court, specifically held that moral sentiments provide a rational basis for enforcing Georgia's criminal ban on homosexual sodomy (*Bowers*

1986:196). In other words, morality alone justified limiting the liberty of homosexuals. Here it appeared, there was no real need for the proponents of regulation to turn to harm arguments to justify regulation or prohibition.[8]

The tragic advent of the AIDS epidemic, however, changed things. The threat of AIDS became the harm that justified increased regulation—so much so, in fact, that today, harm arguments appear to play at least an equal role with legal moralist arguments in the debate over the regulation of homosexual conduct. This is not to suggest that prior to the AIDS epidemic harm played no role in regulating homosexuality. It certainly did, as evidenced by the "homosexual advance" provocation defense to murder (Mison 1992; Dressler 1995), and child custody disputes involving a homosexual parent (Eskridge 1999:200; Trainor 1999:591). Nor is this to suggest that AIDS has played a role only in the regulation of homosexuality. HIV-infected persons have been convicted of a variety of crimes for exposing others to the virus, in sexual and non-sexual, heterosexual and homosexual, and civilian and military contexts (Schechter 1988; Sullivan and Field 1988; Note 1989). The point, rather, is that the AIDS epidemic has also been used as a harm to justify regulation in the debate over homosexual conduct.

This became immediately apparent in the debate over the closing of gay bathhouses at the outbreak of the AIDS epidemic. The issue of closing the bathhouses—and thereby regulating homosexual activity—first arose in San Francisco in 1984. With approximately 475 men in San Francisco diagnosed with AIDS, the director of public health announced that the city would prohibit sexual contacts in gay bathhouses and close down any establishment that did not comply with the new prohibition ("The Bathhouse War" 1984). Six months later the public health director ordered the closure of fourteen gay bathhouses and clubs. The bathhouses were allowed to reopen in November 1985 under strict court-ordered guidelines regulating sexual contacts (Barabak 1985).

What is important, for present purposes, is that the justification offered by the proponents of regulation was harm, not morality: the potential threat of the spread of AIDS. The director of public health accused the establishments of "fostering disease and death" by allowing high-risk sexual contacts ("Sex Clubs Must Close" 1984). In other words, the city officials relied on harm arguments rather than legal moralism, *even though* legal moralism may have been sufficient as a legal matter.

The same thing happened in New York City, beginning in October 1985. Around that time the Republican mayoral candidate, Diane McGrath, and the New York State AIDS Advisory Council recommended that gay bathhouses be closed in order to stop the spread of AIDS (Calderone 1985; Friedman 1985). The AIDS advisory panel proposed regulations that would have required gay bathhouses to get rid of bathtubs and other communal areas for sexual activity, ensure proper lighting, make condoms available, and post AIDS information (Saul 1985:4). Governor Mario Cuomo endorsed the regulations and threatened to close down any bathhouses that did not comply. Cuomo emphasized that the regulations were aimed at curbing the spread of AIDS: "We know certain sexual behavior can be fatal," Cuomo said at a press conference. "We must eliminate public establishments which profit from activities that foster this deadly disease" (Saul 1985:4).

Immediately following Cuomo's endorsement, the New York State Public Health Council ruled that local health authorities could close down gay bathhouses—asserting that "an AIDS emergency is at hand" (Schwartz 1985). The council declared that bathhouses were a public nuisance because high-risk sexual activities took place there. Dr. David Axelrod, New York State health commissioner, explained the emergency procedure, stating, "Every day we wait there are additional people who are being exposed" (Schwartz 1985). New York City health officials began implementing the regulations in November and December 1985, enjoining the closure of a gay bar and a bathhouse under the emergency regulations ("N.Y. AIDS Law Padlocks First Gay Bar" 1985:A16). They closed another bathhouse in the spring of 1986 ("Second Bathhouse Closed over AIDS" 1986). By November 1986, one year after the emergency regulations, two bathhouses had been closed and three had shut on their own, reducing the number of gay bathhouses in New York City by half (Henican 1986:7). Ultimately, gay bathhouses were allowed to reopen in 1990, provided that they not maintain "private rooms which are not continuously open to visual inspection" (*City of New York v. New St. Mark's Baths* 1990:642).

Similar efforts at regulating gay bathhouses occurred in other major cities, including Los Angeles. Other cities relied on zoning ordinances to close down gay clubs (Boxall 1997:B1). At the federal level, the House of Representatives passed a measure in October 1985 allowing the surgeon general to close down public bathhouses ("House Passes Tough Bill to Fight AIDS" 1985). And the House of Delegates of the American Medical Association also endorsed in 1986 efforts to close down gay bathhouses ("AMA Wants Smoking Banned in Planes, Hospitals, Schools" 1996).

The controversy over the closing of gay bathhouses demonstrates well how the AIDS epidemic became a symbol of harm and was used to justify restrictions on homosexual conduct. It was—and still is—a powerful rhetorical device in the debate over the regulation of homosexual conduct. As a result, in many cases today, the harm associated with the potential spread of AIDS has replaced legal moralism as the legal justification for restrictive legislation.

## Drug Use and Harm

The structure of the debate over the criminalization of the use of psychoactive drugs has also changed significantly since the 1960s. The early progressive argument that the use of marijuana was a "victimless crime" was countered in the late 1970s and 1980s by a campaign against drug use that emphasized the harms to society, and justified an all-out war on drugs. The proponents of legal enforcement—in this case modeled on military enforcement—forcefully deployed the harm argument. Here, again, the harm principle experienced an ideological shift from its progressive origins.

The progressive position in the 1960s and early 1970s was characterized by the argument that marijuana use was essentially a "victimless" crime. In his 1968 book *The Limits of the Criminal Sanction*, Herbert Packer emphasized the "fact" that "the available scientific evidence strongly suggests that marijuana is less injurious than alcohol and may even be less injurious than ordinary cigarettes" (1968:338). Packer refuted, one by one, the various claims of harm—including the claims that marijuana use stimulates aggression, causes antisocial behavior, and leads to the use of stronger narcotics. "[T]here is a total lack of solid evidence connecting its use with the commission of other crimes in a causative way," Packer argued (1968:338). John Kaplan, in his 1970 book *Marijuana: The New Prohibition,* similarly offered a point-by-point rebuttal of practically every possible harm argument associated with the use of marijuana. Ted Schneyer suggested that Kaplan's "treatment of these issues is unassailable and, on the basis of existing evidence, Kaplan's conclusion seems warranted—marijuana use can be considered no more harmful to users and other members of society than the use of alcohol" (Schneyer 1971:200). Schneyer remarked that Kaplan's arguments "are applicable . . . to policymaking in the general area of 'victimless' crime" (1971:201). Joel Feinberg placed the case of the use of psychoactive drugs under the rubric of "legal paternalism"—the principle that justifies criminal sanctions where an activity causes possible harm to the actor but no harm to others (Feinberg 1984:12–13).

All that has changed. Conservative harm arguments and the war on drugs have disarmed the traditional progressive position. As a result, the opponents of drug prohibition—a loosely grouped coalition critical of anti-drug enforcement policies—have abandoned the harm principle and instead argue about "harm reduction." The term "harm reduction" was crafted in the early 1990s as an alternative to "legalization." In fact, as late as 1988, the most vocal advocate of "harm reduction," Ethan Nadelmann, still made the argument for "legalization" rather than "harm reduction" (Nadelmann 1988:3–17).

Nadelmann, the director of the Lindesmith Center (a drug policy reform center established in New York City) and a leading spokesperson for the reform coalition, explains the "harm reduction" argument: we must "[a]ccept that drug use is here to stay and that we have no choice but to learn to live with drugs so that *they cause the least possible harm.*" Rather than continue the war on drugs, Nadelmann argues, "[t]he more sensible and realistic approach today would be one based on the principles of 'harm reduction.' It's a policy that seeks to reduce the negative consequences of both drug use and drug prohibition, acknowledging that both are likely to persist for the foreseeable future" (1999a).

In fact, the "harm reduction" movement has cleverly turned the table on their opponents, focusing instead on the harms caused by the policies prohibiting drug use. "[M]any, perhaps most, 'drug problems' in the Americas are the results not of drug use per se but of our prohibitionist policies," Nadelmann claims (1999a). He emphasizes: "[Milton] Friedman, [Thomas] Szasz and I agree on many points, among them that U.S. drug prohibition, like alcohol Prohibition decades ago, *generates extraordinary harms*" (1999b).

The counterargument from proponents of the enforcement of anti-drug laws has been to argue *even greater harm.* Barry McCaffrey, director in 1999 of the Office of National Drug Control Policy, better known as the "Drug Czar," responded to the "harm reduction" argument: "The plain fact is that drug abuse wrecks lives" (McCaffrey 1999a). "[E]ach year drug use contributes to 50,000 deaths and costs our society $110 billion in social costs" (McCaffrey testimony 1999). McCaffrey's response, in a nutshell, is that "[a]ddictive drugs were criminalized because they are harmful; they are not harmful because they were criminalized" (McCaffrey 1999b). In an editorial, McCaffrey argued that "[t]he so-called harm-reduction approach to drugs confuses people with terminology. All drug policies claim to reduce harm. No reasonable person advocates a position consciously designed to be harmful. The real question is which policies actually decrease harm and increase good. The approach advocated by people who say they favor 'harm reduction' would in fact harm Americans" (1999b). As a result, both sides to the debate are making harm arguments, and the debate itself centers on which harms are worse. In that debate, the harm principle, again, is silent.

## Alcohol Consumption and Harm

The traditional liberal position on alcohol consumption was always murky, in large part because of John Stuart Mill's writing on temperance. Relying on the harm and offense principles, Mill justified a wide and complex regulatory scheme directed at discouraging the use of alcohol. In addition to the prohibition on consuming excessive amounts of alcohol that could rightly be imposed on persons with prior convictions for drunken violence and on soldiers or policemen on duty, as well as the prohibition on public intoxication, Mill also approved of taxing the sale of alcohol and regulating the sale and consumption of liquor (Mill 1978:80; 96–100). Mill also favored the regulation of alcohol-serving establishments, though he opposed limiting the number of "beer and spirit houses" (1978:100).

The 1960s progressive position on drinking was equally murky. If anything, it rested on the offense principle. Drinking alcohol fit well

204 · RHETORICAL CRITIQUE

within the framework of Hart's analysis of prostitution: the public manifestations should be prohibited in order to avoid any affront to public decency—"in order to protect the ordinary citizen, who is an unwilling witness of it in the streets, from something offensive" (Hart 1963:45). The justification for regulation was based on public offense, which explains why the matter of drinking generally fell under the rubric of "public decency." In his later work, Joel Feinberg acknowledged one potential harm associated with drinking—specifically the risk of vehicular homicide and accidents—but nevertheless stressed the interests of the majority of innocent or harmless drinkers in being allowed to continue to drink (1984:197).

The contemporary debate seems less fragmented, again, because the proponents of regulation and prohibition have turned to the harm argument. Recent social and political movements in Chicago and New York City have zoomed in on the specific causal relationship between liquor and harm. In Chicago, the new temperance movement has targeted liquor stores, bars, and lounges because of the *harm* they are causing neighborhoods. The movement justifies closing businesses in order to revitalize neighborhoods, to cut down on crime, and to increase property values and commerce. And the temperance movement has met with success. Fourteen neighborhoods in Chicago voted to shut down their liquor stores, bars, and lounges in 1996, another fourteen neighborhoods passed dry votes in 1998, and about seven specific liquor establishments were voted shut in 1998 and 1999 (Annin 1998; Siegel 1998; Gibson 1999; "Vote Dry Referenda" 1999).

Reverend Al Meeks, a Baptist minister and leader of the temperance movement, emphasized that these closures were *economic* measures, and *not* moralistic measures. "We're trying to redevelop our community," he explained. "This is not a return to Prohibition, we're not saying that people can't drink. We're not even saying that people can't buy alcohol. . . . We're simply saying that on a commercial strip we need to have some immediate redevelopment" ("Vote Dry Referenda" 1999). Chicago Mayor Richard Daley made the same point. "This is a quality of life issue," Daley suggested, "not an attempt to impose prohibition" ("Booze and Ballots" 1998).

The target is slightly different in New York City, but the focus is also on harm. Mayor Giuliani's policing initiative targeted public drunks because of the *harm* they cause neighborhoods. The justification is the broken windows argument, and the claim that small disorder causes serious crime. On the basis of this justification, the New York Police Department cracked down on "the squeegee pests; people urinating in public; *people drinking in public;* [and] illegal peddling" (Bratton 1996:789).

The more intense focus on harm by the proponents of legal regulation and prohibition has transformed the structure of the debate. It has undermined whatever remained of the harm principle in the context of alcohol consumption—already a thin fragment of a principle in the 1960s owing to Mill's ambiguous writings on temperance. It has focused the debate on the different kinds of harm associated with liquor, ranging from the harms to commerce and community, to increased serious crime. And it has forced the participants in the debate to weigh harms, to value harms, and to compare harms. On these issues the harm principle itself offers no guidance.

## The Broken Windows Theory and Harm

It is within this context that we can better understand the rhetoric of the broken windows theory, for the theory represents yet another illustration of the turn to harm. The rhetorical shift is most clearly demonstrated if we focus on specific quality-of-life offenses. I will discuss prostitution first, and then turn to disorderly conduct more generally.

Prostitution had always presented a hard case for progressives. It implicated all three safe harbors in the harm principle: consent, privacy, and supposedly self-regarding conduct. The private act of consensual heterosexual fornication was, after all, the paradigm activity protected by the harm principle. What, then, distinguished a private act of consensual heterosexual prostitution?

Mill framed the question as follows: "Fornication, for example, must be tolerated, and so must gambling; but should a person be free to be a pimp, or to keep a gambling house?" (1978:98). Mill never really answered the question. "The case is one of those which lie on the exact boundary line between two principles," Mill suggested, "and it is not at once apparent to which of the two it properly belongs" (1978:98). Mill rehearsed strong arguments on both sides of the question. On the one hand, consistency militated in favor of toleration. On the other hand, pimps stimulate fornication for their own profit, and society may elect to discourage conduct that it regards as "bad" (1978:98). In the end, Mill refused to take a position regarding the pimp. "I will not venture to decide whether [the arguments] are sufficient to justify the moral anomaly of punishing the accessory when the principal is (and must be) allowed to go free; of fining or imprisoning the procurer, but not the fornicator" (1978:99). With regard to the fornicator, though, Mill clearly believed that no liability should attach to his conduct.

In *Law, Liberty, and Morality*, H. L. A. Hart also straddled the fence. As we saw earlier, Hart's lectures were a response to Lord Devlin, and Devlin had argued that all aspects of prostitution should be prohibited. Devlin had argued the flip side of Mill's consistency thesis: if the law can prohibit brothel keeping because it is exploitative, then surely the law could also regulate prostitution. "All sexual immorality involves the exploitation of human weaknesses," Devlin argued. "The prostitute exploits the lust of her customers and the customer the moral weakness of the prostitute" (1977:12). In contrast to Devlin, but like Mill, Hart refused to resolve the issue explicitly. Instead, he reported on the English Street Offences Act of 1959 and endorsed its underlying rationale. Under the act, prostitution was not made illegal, but solicitation in a street or public place was. According to Hart, this approach respected the important distinctions between public and private, and between immorality and indecency. Hart favored these distinctions and, approvingly, reported that "the recent English law relating to prostitution attends to this difference. It has not made prostitution a crime but punishes its public manifestation in order to protect the ordinary citizen, who is an unwilling witness of it in the streets, from something offensive" (1963:45; see also Packer 1968:331; Feinberg 1985:43).

Since the early 1980s, however, proponents of regulation have turned to the harm argument and disarmed the progressive position. MacKinnon's writings are partly responsible for this shift (MacKinnon 1989:138). But what also has transformed the debate over prostitution is precisely the broken windows theory. Of special relevance here, the theory highlights the role of prostitution as part of the disorder. Prostitutes are among the disorderly—they are among "the disreputable or obstreperous or unpredictable people: panhandlers, drunks, addicts, rowdy teenagers, *prostitutes*, loiterers, the mentally disturbed" (Wilson and Kelling 1982:30, emphasis added). And prostitution plays a central role in the process whereby disorder causes serious crime:

[A disorderly] area is vulnerable to criminal invasion. Though it is not inevitable, it is more likely that here, rather than in places where people are confident they can regulate public behavior by informal controls, drugs will change hands, *prostitutes will solicit,* and cars will be stripped. That the drunks will be robbed by boys who do it as a lark, and *the prostitutes' customers will be robbed by men who do it purposefully and perhaps violently.* That muggings will occur. (1982:32, emphasis added)

As this passage makes clear, prostitution is central to the causal chain connecting disorder and crime in the broken windows hypothesis.

The conception of harm at the heart of the "Broken Windows" essay—in conjunction with MacKinnon's harm argument—has significantly altered the structure of the debate over the enforcement of laws against prostitution. The proponents of regulation or prohibition have changed the equation of harm, undercut the earlier progressive argument, and neutralized the harm principle: the principle is no longer an effective argument because it is silent once a threshold of harm has been met.

The broken windows theory has had the same effect in debates over disorderly conduct. What the theory accomplished was to transform these quality-of-life offenses from mere nuisances or annoyances into *seriously harmful conduct*—conduct that in fact contributes to serious crimes, such as murder and armed robbery. A good illustration is loitering. In the 1960s and 1970s—prior to the broken windows hypothesis—anti-loitering statutes were most often justified on the grounds of preventing annoyance to the public and idleness among the able-bodied. Many of the anti-loitering ordinances specifically referred to idleness and annoyance in proscribing conduct. The ordinance that the Supreme Court struck down in *Coates v. City of Cincinnati* in 1971, for instance, made it a criminal offense for a group of persons to "conduct themselves in a manner *annoying* to persons passing by" (*Coates* 1971:611). The ordinance that the Court struck down in *Papachristou v. City of Jacksonville* in 1972 criminalized, among other things, "habitual loafers," "persons able to work but habitually living upon the earnings of their wives or minor children," and "persons neglecting all lawful business and habitually spending their time by frequenting houses of ill fame, gaming houses, or places where alcoholic beverages are sold or served" (*Papachristou* 1972:156 n.1). As the comment to the Model Penal Code explains, anti-loitering ordinances most commonly proscribed "living in idleness without employment and having no visible means of support" (MPCC 1985:250.6 cmt. 1). Even the 1960s reforms—new ordinances and shifts in legal doctrine—continued to treat minor quality-of-life offenses as an annoyance. The Model Penal Code revision of the crime of "disorderly conduct," for instance, was specifically drafted to "penalize public nuisance" (MPCC 1985:250.2 cmt 2). The drafters required as the mental state that the offender have the "purpose to cause public inconvenience, annoyance or alarm" (MPCC 1985:250.2 cmt 2).

In fact, the few references to the criminogenic effects of minor offenses were often dismissed summarily. In *Papachristou,* for instance, Justice Douglas rejected the broken windows–type argument out of hand. Douglas remarked, writing for a unanimous Court: "A presumption that people who might walk or loaf or loiter or stroll or frequent houses where liquor is sold, or who are supported by their wives or who look suspicious to the police are to become future criminals is too precarious for a rule of law. The implicit presumption in these generalized vagrancy standards—that crime is being nipped in the bud—*is too extravagant to deserve extended treatment*" (*Papachristou* 1972:171, emphasis added)

Things changed, however, with the "Broken Windows" essay. Increasingly, municipalities are offering evidence of the broken windows argument to support loitering and curfew ordinances. The most telling cases involve litigation arising in New York City, where the city specifically introduced "broken windows" evidence of the harm caused by loitering. In *Loper v. New York City Police Department,* a case involving a First Amendment challenge to a New York State anti-loitering statute, the city introduced the expert testimony of George Kelling to provide evidence of the broken windows theory and the harm that loitering causes (*Loper* 1992:1034–35). Based on Kelling's testimony, the city argued that the loitering ordinance was "justified due to the 'Broken Windows' message beggars convey" (*Loper* 1992:1040). Three years earlier, in *Young v. New York City Transit Authority,* a case challenging the prohibition against begging in the New York City subways, the city had similarly presented expert evidence from Kelling concerning the broken windows theory (*Young* 1990:149–150).

Other municipalities similarly have been presenting evidence of harm. In litigation over the San Diego youth curfew, the city introduced evidence, including national and local statistics, to support the claim that a juvenile curfew would reduce juvenile crime and victimization (*Nunez* 1997:947). In the Supreme Court litigation in *City of Chicago v. Morales*, Dan Kahan and Tracey Meares presented evidence that enforcement of the anti-loitering ordinance would result in significant declines in gang-related violence. Their amicus curiae brief to the Supreme Court contains a long list of harms caused by gang loitering (Kahan and Meares 1999b:21–24). To be sure, these claims do not always prevail. They did not prevail in *Morales, Loper,* or *Nunez*—although they did in *Young.* What matters, though, is that the proponents of regulation have turned increasingly to harm arguments and that these harm arguments have begun to shape the debates in the quality of life context as well.

## The Collapse of the Harm Principle

In a wide range of political debates, proponents of legal intervention have turned to harm to justify their positions. This turn to harm has produced a significant but unintended consequence. The proliferation of harm arguments has effectively collapsed the harm principle. Harm to others is no longer today a *limiting* principle on legal intervention.

More formally, in the writings of John Stuart Mill, H. L. A. Hart, and Joel Feinberg, the harm principle acted as a *necessary but not sufficient* condition for legal enforcement. The harm principle was used to *exclude* certain categories of activities from legal enforcement (necessary condition), but it did not determine what to *include* (but not sufficient condition), insofar as practical, constitutional, or other factors weighed into the ultimate decision whether to regulate conduct. Although the harm principle formally remains a necessary but not sufficient condition, harm is no longer in fact a necessary condition because non-trivial harm arguments are being made about practically all conduct. As a result, we no longer focus on the existence or nonexistence of harm. Instead, we focus on the types of harm, the amounts of harms, and the balance of harms. As to these questions, the harm principle offers no guidance. It does not tell us how to compare harms. It served only as a threshold determination, and that threshold is being satisfied in most categories of conduct, especially traditional categories of moral offense. As a result, the harm principle no longer acts as a *limiting principle* on the legal enforcement of morality. Instead of focusing on whether certain conduct causes harm, the debates center on the types of harm, the amounts of harm, and our willingness, as a society, to bear the harms. And the harm principle is silent on those questions.

The harm principle is silent in the sense that it does not determine whether a non-trivial harm justifies restrictions on liberty, nor does it determine how to compare or weigh competing claims of harms. It was never intended to be a *sufficient* condition. It does not address the comparative importance of harms. Joel Feinberg's thorough discussion of the harm principle recognized this important fact. In discussing the relative importance of harms, Feinberg admitted that "[i]t is impossible to prepare a detailed manual with the exact 'weights' of all human interests, the degree to which they are advanced or thwarted by all possible actions and activities, duly discounted by objective improbabilities mathematically designated" (Feinberg 1984:203). Thus, Feinberg concluded, "in the end, it is the legislator himself, using his own fallible judgment rather than spurious formulas and 'measurements,' who must compare conflicting interests and judge which are the more important" (1984:203).

Feinberg proposed a three-prong test to determine the relative importance of harms:

> Relative importance is a function of three different respects in which opposed interests can be compared:
> a. how 'vital' they are in the interest networks of their possessors;
> b. the degree to which they are reinforced by other interests, private and public;
> c. their inherent moral quality. (1984:217, 204–206)

But what are the inherent moral qualities of interests affected by claims of harm? And how could the harm principle tell us what those inherent moral qualities are? In the end, it cannot. The harm principle itself—the simple notion of harm—does not address the relative importance of harms. Once non-trivial harm arguments have been made, we inevitably must look beyond the harm principle. We must look beyond the traditional structure of the debate over the legal enforcement of morality. We must access larger debates in ethics, law, and politics—debates about power, autonomy, identity, human flourishing, equality, freedom, and other interests and values that give meaning to the claim that an identifiable harm *matters*. In this sense, the proliferation of harm arguments and the collapse of the harm principle has fundamentally altered the structure of the debate over legal and political intervention.

### Some Implications of the Rhetorical Shift

The rhetorical shift and collapse of the harm principle suggests a final weakness in the order-maintenance approach. The approach focuses on the harms of challenged conduct—such as loitering and prostitution—but fails to investigate or explore sufficiently the harms of the proposed policing initiatives. The point is, after the proliferation of harm arguments, the harms associated with quality-of-life offenses are no longer *determinative* of the outcome of the debate. They are no longer the touchstone of the discussion. They are but one set of harms among others that need to be assessed, compared, weighed, and judged.

As I demonstrated in Part I, there is little if any evidence supporting the broken windows theory. That does not mean, of course, that disorder and disorderly conduct cause no harm. It would be misleading to stop the discussion here. Disorderly conduct does cause economic and aesthetic harms. Graffiti spraying is vandalism, and causes some economic harm: graffiti either has to be removed by the property owner, or will reduce the value of the property. The same is true of public urination and littering. Turnstile jumping results in decreased public revenues for mass transportation, and may increase the cost of ridership for other subway riders. Homelessness, loitering, and aggressive panhandling are aesthetically unpleasant, and may have a negative impact on commercial activities in downtown neighborhoods. Many people are bothered by panhandlers, and may in fact change their behaviors in order to avoid homeless street people. Although these phenomena are not evidence of the broken windows theory, they are nevertheless harms, and they must be weighed in the analysis. As Kelling and Coles write:

> Let us suppose that police order-maintenance activities have not reduced crime and have little potential for doing so, in spite of the fact that we do not believe this to be true. Such an outcome would dampen only slightly our enthusiasm for restoring order. Both disorder and the fear it generates are serious problems that warrant attention in and of themselves. Disorder demoralizes communities, undermines commerce, leads to the abandonment of public spaces, and undermines public confidence in the ability of government to solve problems; fear drives citizens further from each other and paralyzes their normal, order-sustaining responses, compounding the impact of disorder. Restoring order is key to revitalizing our cities, and to preventing the downward spiral into urban decay that threatens neighborhoods teetering on the brink of decline, regardless of whether a reduction in crime results. (1996:242)

These effects on communities are serious and need to be weighed in the balance. These are part of the indirect neighborhood effects that many, including Sampson and Raudenbush, attribute to disorder. Recall that Sampson and Raudenbush did not conclude that disorder is theoretically irrelevant. Although they rejected the main thesis of broken windows, they too assign to disorder indirect effects that need to be considered. "Disorder may turn out to be important for understanding migration patterns, investment by businesses, and overall neighborhood viability," Sampson and Raudenbush suggest. "Thus, if disorder operates in a cascading fashion—encouraging people to move (increasing residential instability) or discouraging efforts at building collective responses—it would indirectly have an effect on crime" (1999:637). These are, though indirect, important costs associated with disorder.

Moreover, what must also be weighed as a benefit is the effect of aggressive arrests on gun seizures, outstanding warrants, arrest/offense ratios, and general deterrence. I have argued that the broken windows effect is unlikely to have had much impact on the crime rate in New York City. But I am not suggesting, of course, that the quality-of-life initiative had no effect on crime. The turnstile jumper who is going to commit greater offenses once he is in the subway is certainly deterred when he is arrested and detained. The policy of aggressive misdemeanor arrests provides the police with enhanced powers of surveillance, and these have had significant consequences for the detection and prevention of crime. This has probably contributed to the decline in crime in New York City.

But there are other harms to consider. Order maintenance in New York City has been achieved, in large part, by means of a significant increase in misdemeanor arrests, and these arrests, as we have seen, can be quite an ordeal. Being arrested, handcuffed, transported, and booked, and spending the night in jail, is an experience that many of us have had the good fortune to avoid. The quality-of-life initiative has been accompanied by a significant increase in the number of complaints of police misconduct, and it ends up targeting minorities because misdemeanor arrests have a disproportionate effect on them. It reinforces the stereotype of black criminality, and in many cases delegates the power to define order and disorder to police officers and designated community members in a manner inconsistent with our conception of democratic theory or constitutional principles. It shapes how we understand disorder and judge the disorderly in ways that may facilitate unfair treatment.

These are some of the harms that are associated with order-maintenance policing. They are troubling, some extremely troubling. We might be willing to bear some or all of these costs if the broken windows theory did in fact work—if the evidence suggested that creating order significantly reduces serious crimes such as murder, rape, and armed robbery. Barring that evidence, though, the hard question is whether the indirect benefits of order, the economic and aesthetic harms of disorder, and the potential benefits of increased surveillance outweigh the harms of order maintenance. I think the answer is no, particularly since we can promote order and attack the active ingredients of crime in other ways. As I discuss in Chapter 8, there *are* alternatives to arrest and incarceration—alternatives that avoid the negative implications of broken windows policing, especially the construction of the disorderly.

Many readers may simply respond: "But what about all the people who feel safer in the new, orderly New York? Aren't their feelings entitled to some weight in the analysis?" The simple answer is that people are feeling safer because they *are* safer. Crime rates have tumbled in New York City—and across the country—for a number of reasons. There is every reason to feel safer in New York, in Chicago, and in most major cities in the country. Some readers may nevertheless persist and call attention to the social-scientific studies that suggest people feel safer in more orderly neighborhoods. "New Yorkers are feeling safer not only because of the lower crime rates," they may argue, "but also because of the additional order." The simple answer is that these feelings of safety are most likely explained by the level of crime, not order, in the neighborhood (Skogan 1990:77). The longer answer is that this comeback is really about aesthetic preferences—about an aesthetic preference for order that is not shared by all. That, I argue, is not sufficient to explain or justify increased arrests—especially since there are other ways to increase order, if that is the goal.

# PART IV

# Rethinking Punishment and Criminal Justice

With crime rates plummeting in New York City and across the country, few are foolish enough to take issue with the quality-of-life initiative and, more generally, the order-maintenance approach. Many people praise it, especially elected officials, police commissioners, and policy makers, who, by doing so, can take full credit for the decline in crime. But the order-maintenance approach overestimates the role of disorder in the production of crime. By overestimating disorder, it creates a false choice between the police and the disorderly—a choice that facilitates a policy of aggressive arrests despite a lack of empirical evidence. The tragic consequence is that the approach—touted as an *alternative* to the severe punishments that dominate the criminal law—falls back on aggressive arrests and incarcerations, and in doing so merely *supplements* three-strikes and mandatory minimum sentencing laws.

What is hidden by order-maintenance theory? I think we see it best in the "Broken Windows" essay. The text suggests that reducing crime is simply a question of minor details—of fixing broken windows, sweeping up litter, hiding the street people. Recall the description in the essay about neighborhood decline: "A piece of property is abandoned, weeds grow up, a window is smashed. Adults stop scolding rowdy children; the children, emboldened, become more rowdy. Families move out, unattached adults move in. Teenagers gather in front of the corner store. The merchant asks them to move; they refuse. Fights occur. Litter accumulates" (Wilson and Kelling 1982:32).

This description may tell us a few things about litter and public drinking. But there is also lurking in this description a much more complex story about urban decay, with complicated race, wealth, class, and ethnic dimensions, to name only a few. The more complex story would raise questions about property values, the quality of neighborhood public schools, racial demographics, environmental pollution, public transportation systems, access to business loans and mortgages, and zoning laws. The life cycle of a neighborhood is not as simple as the essay suggests.

We need to look again at the social-scientific data on disorder and reexamine the connection between neighborhood poverty, stability, collective efficacy, and crime. In this sense, both my replication of Skogan's study and, more important, Sampson and Raudenbush's study offer a compelling alternative to the broken windows theory. Rather than our viewing disorder as the cause of crime, certain specific acts that are called "disorder," such as vandalism or illicit drug use, may be better understood as part of crime itself, and both "disorder" and crime may then be seen to have similar origins. In their work, Sampson and Raudenbush focus on weakened collective efficacy and structural disadvantage as the active ingredients of crime and disorder.[1] These may be fruitful avenues to investigate.

My ambition in this part is far more limited, though. I do not propose to develop a general theory of crime, nor even to espouse one at this point. Instead, I propose an alternative *approach* to the study of punishment and criminal justice and an alternative research agenda. My goal is to offer another way to think about criminal laws and policing. This alternative approach and research agenda focuses not only on criminogenic factors, and not only on social meaning, but also, more important, on how the policing and punishment practices that we adopt may shape us as contemporary subjects.

# CHAPTER 8

# An Alternative Vision

Edward Banfield, James Q. Wilson, and the New Progressives have trained our sights on propensities and human nature, on behavioral norms, and on social meaning. They have focused our attention on the norm of orderliness and its influence on behavior. These are important contributions, and it is crucial not to discard what may be of value in them. The problem with order maintenance, I have argued, is not the focus on norms or meaning. Insofar as Banfield, Wilson, and the New Progressives have pushed criminal justice to take the social meaning turn, they are to be applauded. The difficulty with order maintenance, instead, is that the norm and meaning of orderliness have become fixed, natural, and uncontested. As in Durkheim's work, order comes to resemble a work of art—an "art that imitate[s] nature ever more perfectly" (1995:17 n.22). The other problem is that Banfield, Wilson, and the New Progressives do not explore how the central categories—order and disorder, the disorderly, but also thicker propensities and human nature—are shaped by the punitive and policing strategies that surround us.

There is a need to infuse social meaning with critical potential—to take the social meaning turn one step further. The alternative approach I propose begins with social meaning, but rather than focus exclusively on norms and meaning, it goes further and focuses on subject creation. In assessing policing strategies, it is simply not enough to focus on the social meaning of prostitution, gang membership, or juvenile gun possession. We must also ask, first, how our strategies of policing and the mechanisms of punishment transform the subject; second, how this influences our assessment of the policing strategies under consideration; and third, how these effects relate to the goal of reducing crime. Rather than focus exclusively on the immediate interplay between social meaning and short-term behavior and perceptions, we should also concentrate on the relationship between, on the one hand, the norms and meanings of order and, on the other hand, the perceptions, thoughts, feelings, understandings, and relations of the contemporary subject. The social meaning of the proposed police practices does not simply change our behaviors; it may fundamentally alter the way we think about and judge other people, and the way we relate to others. These law enforcement techniques may form us—and it is here that we must begin to rethink punishment and criminal justice.

My alternative approach examines, beyond social norms, subject creation. In part, the different focus raises different questions or hypotheses. Instead of asking only how a policy of rewarding snitching would change the social meaning of gun carrying—which is an important question, no doubt—we might also ask how that policy might shape our children in other ways, and, equally important, how that policy might shape the way we think about propensities to commit crime. Instead of limiting our attention to the effect of order maintenance on gang behavior—again, an important question—we might also ask how it changes the way we think about and thus behave toward the homeless. We might explore whether there is a link between a policy of aggressive misdemeanor arrests and police brutality, and what impact such a policy is likely to have on race relations. What is the relationship between order maintenance and our treatment of the unemployed? Do the norms of order undermine other socioeconomic programs intended to alleviate homelessness? How will curfews and anti-loitering ordinances affect our children's intellectual and cultural development? How does order-maintenance policing affect our conception of human nature? These are the types of questions that are called for by the turn to subject creation.

In relation to social norm theory, this alternative approach entails an additional, marginal movement away from behavioralism, a greater emphasis on the meaning and effect of the public policies themselves, an increased willingness to question the other consequences and implications of purportedly effective policing techniques, and heightened sensitivity to the way affected citizens judge and relate to others. These important differences will influence research design and methods of proof. It is likely, for instance, that in-depth open-ended interviews of neighborhood residents will better identify perceptions of the homeless than a survey or opinion poll. Likewise, an ethnographic analysis of a comparable social situation or historical research into similar social phenomena will probably increase our understanding of how police practices shape the subject, above and beyond interviewing contemporary informants. What is called for is an eclectic approach that is self-conscious and reflexive, but that allows us to acquire as much information as possible to better assess the multiple relations between policing and the modern subject. By better, I mean a deeper and richer understanding of the possible changes to our self-conceptions and ways of judging and relating to others—and the same understanding (based on the same research) of the more immediate behavioral consequences.

Another critical implication for research is the need for heightened critical reflection about the role of the *researcher as subject.* Clifford Geertz had alerted us to this issue in his discussion of the interpretive turn. Geertz emphasized the important role of his own experiences, history, and identity in his understanding of the anthropological enterprise. "It is in the trajectory of *my professional life,*" Geertz writes, "neither regular nor representative, very fitfully planned, very inspecifically aimed, that the anthropologist is to be found" (1995:98, emphasis added). Geertz's insights are, if anything, even more penetrating in the context of this alternative approach.

The researcher (as subject) is also shaped in part by the policing practices that exist today. The conceptions of propensities and inducements that the researcher brings to bear on the empirical evidence are themselves shaped by policing practices. The very intellectual framework that the researcher uses—consciously and subconsciously—when interpreting data is itself formed by the disciplinary practices that surround us. The framework itself is not pre-political, it is not natural, nor fixed, nor uncontestable.

There is, accordingly, an urgent need to imbue research with ongoing examination of the researcher—a need for what Pierre Bourdieu has referred to as "a full sociological objectivation of the object *and* of the subject's relation to the object" or "participant objectivation" (Bourdieu and Wacquant 1992:68). It is crucial to the research enterprise to take a critical reflexive look at the very act of research and at the subject who does the research: to make a full investigation of, in Bourdieu's words, "not only everything he is, his own social conditions of production and thereby the 'limits of his mind,' but also his very work of objectivation, the hidden interests that are invested in it and the profits that it promises" (1992:68 n.9). The researcher must try to understand how his or her own intellectual framework and methods are influenced by prior experience and by his or her web of meaning, including the meaning of police practices.

Bourdieu famously explored this realm through his "epistemological experiment" of researching what were to him familiar environments, namely, the community where he grew up in Béarn, France, and the higher education system of which he was an integral part. In this way, Bourdieu investigated "the effects produced on the observation, on the description of the thing observed, by the situation of the observer" in order to "uncover all the presuppositions inherent in the *theoretical* posture as an external, remote, distant or, quite simply, non-practical, non-committed, non-involved vision" (1990:60; see also Bourdieu and Wacquant 1992:67). And Bourdieu discovered from this that

> there was an entire, basically false social philosophy which stemmed from the fact that the ethnologist has "nothing to do" with the people he studies, with their practices and their representations, except to study them: there is an enormous difference between trying to understand the nature of matrimonial relations between two families so as to get your son or daughter married off, investing the same interest in this as people in our own world invest in their choice of the best school for their son or daughter, and trying to understand these relations so as to construct a theoretical model of them. (1990:60)

As a result, Bourdieu's writings emphasize the strategies and practical sense that agents use to achieve their ends. He takes account of "the real principle behind strategies, namely the practical sense, or, if you prefer, what sports players call a feel for the game, as the practical mastery of the logic or of the immanent necessity of a game—a mastery acquired by experience of the game, and one which works outside conscious control and discourse" (1990:61). Bourdieu drew from his own experience the importance of this self-objectivization—and a radical self-objectivization at that.

Heightened sensitivity to the researcher as subject thus may also entail a different research relationship to social meaning. Instead of approaching social norms as rules that may cause certain behavior or that may be changed in order to shift behavior, we may want to approach social norms and meaning more as the environment within which subjects engage strategically in their daily activity (Taylor 1999:42–43). Instead of approaching social meaning as social scientists trying to construct a theoretical model, we may want to approach social meaning from the perspective of the actor whose conduct we are trying to understand. Instead of approaching social norms mechanically, we may want to approach them more strategically and flexibly.

## Alternatives to Arrest and Detention

The fact is, even if we want to attack "disorder," there are many different ways of proceeding. There are numerous alternatives to policies of aggressive misdemeanor stops and frisks and arrests. Cities such as San Diego have demonstrated this well. Instead of arresting turnstile jumpers, for instance, we can—and New York City has begun to—install turnstiles that cannot be jumped. This is an approach similar to "target-hardening" or "access control," methods of situational crime prevention that are commonly discussed in criminology (Clarke 1995:91). Instead of arresting prostitutes, we could investigate the possibility of licensing prostitution. It turns out, in fact, that prostitution may be related to crime in a more direct way than the broken windows theory immediately suggests. Deborah Rhode has compiled some relevant statistics: "Recent research," she writes, "estimates that two-thirds to three-fourths of streetwalkers are raped or beaten an average of four to 15 times a year" (Rhode 1995; see also Clark 1993:514; Drexler 1996:207–208; Miller, Romenesco, and Wondolkowski 1993:320). Studies suggest that decriminalizing prostitution (in the case of the Netherlands) or legalizing prostitution (in the case of eleven counties in Nevada) has resulted in lower crime rates against prostitutes, as well as lower rates of sexually transmitted diseases (Drexler 1996:228, 230; see also Rio 1991:212–214; Sterk-Elifson and Campbell 1993:200–202;

Stout and Tanana 1994:498). A full exploration of these alternatives is beyond the scope of this book; and, to be sure, decriminalizing or licensing prostitution may not eliminate an underground black market in prostitution. It is, however, an alternative worth investigating. After all, aggressive arrests have not eliminated prostitution in New York City. As the *New York Times* reports, "[W]hile prostitution may be less visible in the city, it is no less prevalent. The Internet, pagers, cellular phones and subterfuges like escort services have enabled more discreet forms of prostitution to thrive beyond the reach of the street-level crackdown, the authorities and prostitutes themselves say" (Roane 1998).

How can we deal with graffiti? Well, in fact, we can take our cue from the New York City subways. The problem with graffiti there was *not* solved by law enforcement techniques; it was solved, instead, by an obstinate effort to keep the cars clean. As Kelling and Coles explain, the New York City Transit Authority under NYCTA president David Gunn "succeeded because the Gunn administration abandoned the use of a law-enforcement strategy in dealing with graffiti" (1996:117). What they did, instead, was to implement a Clean Car Program: under the new policy, any subway car entered into the program would not be used if it had graffiti on it. Any new graffiti had to be removed within two hours, or the car would be pulled out of service. Gunn also had transit police officers assigned to the clean trains, and had them protect the trains in special yards. He poured resources, resolve, and leadership into the problem. And that, apparently, did the trick (1996:116–118).

How can we discourage aggressive panhandling and other forms of street economies? Instead of arrest, perhaps we should explore the possibility of work programs for people living on the street. The programs could target cleaning up abandoned buildings, creating public parks out of vacant lots, creating space for public art projects, or maintaining public spaces. If the programs were flexibly designed to facilitate changing work schedules, they might offer a substitute for panhandling and windshield washing. As for the financing, we could investigate the possibility of fining owners of abandoned property or using proceeds from the sale of such properties, as well as a tax on emissions, or fines for littering.

A possible model for such a program—though not without controversy—is the Doe Fund in New York City, an organization in fact closely tied to the Giuliani administration. The fund, which was started in the mid-1980s, is dedicated to putting homeless people to work. In 1990 the fund implemented its "Ready, Willing & Able" (RWA) program, a residential paid work and training program for the homeless. Homeless people who join the RWA program are hired to clean city streets and are paid a minimum wage. In exchange, they must pay the fund a small rent ($50 per week) and stipend for food (another $15), and must set aside savings of $30 per week. The program lasts eighteen months. RWA trainees have branched out into renovating low-income city-owned apartment buildings (Doe Fund 2000). A study of the RWA program, funded by the Doe Fund, collected data on 150 RWA clients who successfully completed the program between July 1994 and June 1996. According to the study, 62 percent of the clients were employed in jobs either outside the Doe Fund (45 percent) or within it (17 percent); 49 percent found jobs within a year of employment. At the time of follow-up, nearly two-thirds of the clients were living in independent housing, with just 1 percent known to be in shelters (Philliber Research Associates 1998).

The Doe Fund is not without its critics. Some suggest it is forced labor, others "a throwback to the days of Dickens" (Seifman and Dicker 1999:30). But clearly it offers at least an alternative model for thinking about ways to reduce panhandling and street hustling without homeless sweeps. As for keeping the homeless off the streets at night without arresting them, some cities are experimenting with safe sleeping zones for the homeless. The city of Santa Cruz, California, for instance, passed a measure in May 2000 to turn two industrial parks into such safe sleeping zones. The areas allow people to sleep in their vehicles or on the ground, and provide trash bins, portable toilets, and a police officer dedicated to patrolling the area. As of this writing there was no evidence yet of its success (Nieves 2000:A14). It is, however, an alternative to arrests worth investigating.

As an alternative to gun-oriented crackdowns, the police could offer a promise not to prosecute in exchange for permission to search. In St. Louis, for instance, the police department has implemented a policy, called the Firearm Suppression Program, that seeks to reduce the number of guns in the hands of juveniles by means of a voluntary search. When the police have reason to believe that a juvenile possesses a firearm, they go to the juvenile's home and request voluntary consent to search for and seize any guns in the juvenile's possession, in exchange for a promise not to prosecute the parents or the child. In 1994 the program reportedly resulted in the confiscation of 402 firearms, which represented half of all the firearms seized by the police from juveniles. Police officers had a 90 percent rate of compliance with their requests, and half of those searches netted firearms (Rosenfeld and Decker 1996:204–206, 209–210, 214–215).

There are endless ways of resolving problems of "disorder"—should we want to—short of arrest and incarceration. All we need to do is let our imaginations roam within a realistic and practical range. The mayor of Bogotá, Colombia, Antanas Mockus, hired mimes to follow and imitate jaywalkers crossing the street in an effort to curb jaywalking (Tierney 1998:26). Mockus also gave motorists "cards with a thumb-downs sign that they could hold up, like soccer referees, to signal that another driver had committed a foul" (Tierney 1998:26). It is an unusual approach, but the point is, even if we set out to create "order," we should consider how we are going to go about it. We need to examine critically what effect the policies will have on individuals in society, how the policies construct the subject, and how that construction reinforces the very strategies we are justifying.

The example of prostitution again provides a useful illustration. Licensing prostitution might have a very different effect on the subject than aggressively arresting (mostly female) prostitutes. It would likely have less of a marginalizing effect on the women and men who engage in prostitution. Persons engaged in sex work would likely receive more protection from our sexual assault laws. Prosecutors' charging decisions may be affected. Sex workers might acquire a voice in the debate about whether and how to change the social meaning and social practice of prostitution. They likely would gain greater control over their identities. And there might be corresponding effects on the construction of sexuality in society more generally. This is just the beginning of the type of inquiry that subject creation theory calls for. The point here is not to resolve that inquiry in the case of prostitution or any other specific misdemeanor offense, but rather to illustrate the types of questions that we should be asking.

## The Methodological Implications

The critical methodological implications, then, are fourfold. First and foremost, research design and methods should dovetail with the underlying social-theoretic approach. In the case of subject creation theory—a constructivist theory—it is imperative that the research integrate *in practice* qualitative and quantitative analyses. As Michael Gottfredson and Travis Hirschi emphasize, "there must be an intimate connection between the conceptualization of a problem and the design of research focused on that problem" (1990:252). In this case, the research design and methods must focus on *interpreting* social meanings and *assessing* their effect on the modern subject, both of which call for integrated methods. Second, research not only should focus on the social meaning of practices such as juvenile gun possession or gang membership, but also should explore the social meaning of the proposed policing techniques and policies themselves. Policing and criminal law research should continue to deploy the insight of social meaning, but should do so evenhandedly by focusing as well on the social meaning of police practices. Third, research should focus less on the immediate impact of social meaning on short-term behavior and perception, and more on the way in which the social meaning of practices and public policies shapes the contemporary subject. In addition to integrated methods, this approach also suggests the need for further in-depth investigation into analogous past or present social experiments with similar public policies. Finally, the researcher should critically reflect on his or her influence on research design, data collection, methods, findings, and conclusions. Again, in the case of subject creation theory—or any interpretive theory after the "social meaning turn"—it is imperative that the researcher engage in the kind of reflexive sociological examination that is today associated with the complex task of "objectify[ing] the act of objectification and the objectifying subject" (Bourdieu 1990:59). The shift in focus from social meaning to subject creation simply demands increased awareness of the role of the researcher as subject.

What kind of research, then, is specifically called for? Let's take the case of the proposed policy of encouraging snitching among juveniles. This alternative approach would implicate research along three axes. First, the alternative approach would involve qualitative research concerning how juveniles perceive gun possession and snitching, why they would or would not own and carry a firearm, why they would or would not snitch, and whether and how snitching might change their perceptions and thoughts about gun carrying and about themselves. At a minimum it would call for interviewing teenagers, including those who have been convicted of gun possession and those who have snitched on others, but also those who have never carried guns or who would never snitch. It would call for interviewing police officers, school counselors, teachers, and parents of schoolchildren, and observing school routines, neighborhood interactions, extracurricular activities, and teenage practices (such as cruising and hanging out). In addition, it would be important to try to quantify these observations in order to explore whether there are useful correlations between meaning, behavior, context, and self-conception.

Second, this alternative approach would call for historical, comparative, and ethnographic analyses exploring other social systems in which snitching plays or played an important role. These could involve an ethnographic study of the prison system or, more generally, the criminal justice system in the United States, where snitching is encouraged. Such studies would explore the consequences of encouraging snitching on gang activity in prisons or the meaning in prison of snitching. They could involve a historical study of other societies where snitching has been encouraged, such as eighteenth-century France or the Stalinist Soviet Union—if, in fact, snitching was encouraged there. They might involve studying and interpreting the *lettres de cachets* in the Bastille archives (Farge and Foucault 1982). Such studies would investigate how the encouragement of snitching affected those societies, and whether and how it shaped the subjects in those societies. Third, this alternative approach would, of course, also involve quantitative analyses of the jurisdictions that have implemented snitching policies to determine whether they have been accompanied by decreased carrying, and if so, what other factors may have played a role in causing the decrease. This alternative research agenda would attempt to focus on mental processes in addition to behavior, and would integrate several methodological approaches in order to increase the amount of information to bring to bear on the question and enrich our public policy debate.

In all of this research, it would be critically important for the researcher continually to reflect on his or her own feelings and judgments about snitching and about gun possession—as well, of course, as to reflect critically on the larger intellectual framework through which the researcher interprets the data. Snitching and gun possession are two very significant and contentious phenomena, and it would be crucial for the researcher to account for biases with respect to both. Moreover, it would be equally important for the researcher to conceptualize social norms and meaning not as rules that determine behavior, but rather as the environment within which juveniles make strategic choices. The researcher must investigate social meaning not simply from the perspective of the social scientist trying to extract rules, but also from the perspective of the juvenile trying to negotiate strategically his or her own world.

This three-pronged research agenda is the type of project that is called for under this alternative vision of criminal justice. I have described, naturally, an ideal type. I emphasize that it is not intended to be a prerequisite to policy implementation. But it is the type of research that should continually accompany the implementation and rejection of policy initiatives.

## Some Preliminary Objections

This alternative approach is likely to prompt two different types of responses. Many who resist the social meaning turn and norm-focused hypotheses are likely to object to the research methods as too soft. Many may worry that the inquiry into subject creation is not sufficiently objective. At the other end of the theoretical spectrum, social norm theorists and others are likely to object that such a demanding research agenda will insert an inherently conservative bias favoring the status quo in policy analysis. These responses, coming as they do from opposing methodological and political perspectives, place me in a bit of a whipsaw. Nevertheless, I offer here a first reply to each.

### The Problem of Objectivity

A first set of reactions will question the very usefulness of the social meaning turn and criticize this alternative approach and research agenda as overly subjective. The two-step movement away from behavior, represented first by the turn to social meaning and second by the turn to subject creation, is likely to cause resistance from law and economics quarters, rational choice theorists and behavioral psychologists. Stephen Morse, writing in response to my proposal, argues that "the core variables—including social meaning itself—seem immensely soft and there is always serious question about whether qualitative analysis yields reliable and valid data, as opposed to being an undeniably fertile source of hypotheses" (Morse 2000:3). He suggests that my proposed research agenda indicates just "how slippery the social meaning hypothesis can be" (2000:2). Others, in a similar vein, question the usefulness of social meaning. Richard Posner, for instance, writes: "I do not think that the idea of social meaning adds a lot to the economic analysis of symbolic expression or signaling" (1998a:563). From this first perspective, the question is, why take the social meaning turn in the first place? What does it add to more objective analyses of behavior? How is it going to be possible to pin down a social meaning? And isn't it going to undermine the very possibility of agreement over public policy implications?

These are tough questions, but there is an answer. And the answer is that what matters about behavior is not merely the behavior itself or the physical movement but its *significance*—its meaning to others, the way it is interpreted, what it communicates. Physical behavior is mediated through mental processes, and it is these mental processes that matter to us as social scientists, not just the physical movement. Geertz famously illustrated this point with his discussion of winks and sheep raids. A physical movement of the eyelid can be an involuntary twitch, or it can be a wink. It can be a wink that communicates a conspiratorial signal, or a wink that parodies a twitch—or even a rehearsal of a wink parodying a twitch. Each of these eye movements is embedded within a socially established code that conveys a different message. Yet, from the behavioralist perspective, they are identical. As Geertz explains: "[T]he two movements are, as movements, identical; from an I-am-a-camera, 'phenomenalistic' observation of them alone, one could not tell which was twitch and which was wink, or indeed whether both or either was twitch or wink" (1973:6). Anyone interested in understanding that human behavior would need to decipher the cultural code that gives these identical movements their different meaning. The very same is true of the sheep raid—which for some may be a repayment of debt, for others evidence of a conspiracy (1973:8–9).

In order to learn anything from those behaviors, the social scientist must seek to understand their meaning. As Geertz wrote: "The thing to ask about a burlesqued wink or a mock sheep raid is not what their ontological status is. It is the same as that of rocks on the one hand and dreams on the other—they are things of this world. The thing to ask is what their import is: what it is, ridicule or challenge, irony or anger, snobbery or pride, that, in their occurrence and through their agency, is getting said" (1973:10).

This focus on social meaning has important implications on the question of objectivity—some of which I discussed earlier in Chapter 4. In essence, it is no longer possible today to speak of objectivity in social science in the traditional paradigm of the natural sciences. The idea that social meaning is, in Morse's words, "immensely soft" is a trope that stems from a misguided desire to equate the social sciences with the natural sciences—perhaps, from the late development of the social sciences and the resulting inferiority complex that has plagued them. As Bourdieu has remarked, "[T]he social sciences owe a great number of their characteristics and their difficulties to the fact that they . . . only got going a lot later than the others, so that, for example, they can use consciously or unconsciously the model of more advanced sciences in order to simulate scientific rigour" (1990:37).

The conception of objectivity that treats social meaning as "soft" fails to take account of the historical dimension of scientific discovery. It assumes a fixed object of study that is independent of our historical, cultural, personal, and interpersonal webs of meaning. It assumes a correspondence theory of truth that is no longer acceptable, at least in the human sciences. It assumes a notion of "accurate representation" that is, as Richard Rorty suggests, "simply an automatic and empty compliment which we pay to those beliefs which are successful in helping us do what we want to do" (1979:10). This conception of objectivity has to be refitted to modern size. Even the simplest of behaviors are mediated through mental processes that give them meaning. The wink is an example. But so is the homicidal act—whether it is justifiable self-defense or first-degree murder, whether it is legally sanctioned intervention or excusable heat of passion. The *meaning* we give behavior is what matters, not the physical movement. In the gun possession context, for instance, we do not simply care about the number of guns in circulation—although this is an important fact and may affect their meaning. We care more significantly about what those guns mean to people, how they are used, how they change social situations, what they communicate to others.

Meanings are, perhaps, the hardest phenomena to study. Certainly they pose the greatest challenge to traditional notions of objectivity. But these challenges are not insurmountable. When we discuss the *correctness* of an interpretation, we need to acknowledge that our findings may not be absolute, permanent, and universal; they may not be for all time. But they must be the best we can achieve at this historical, political, and cultural moment. When we think about objectivity, we should acknowledge and recognize—and even embrace—a number of different aspects of our own situation, including, chiefly, the fact that we are operating within a specific intellectual framework with distinct epistemological matrices. The most difficult task is to balance the situatedness—cultural, historical, and intellectual—of social research with the notion of objectivity. It is crucial not to become too self-indulgent, subjective, or self-revelatory. But it is equally important to avoid falling back on an anachronistic conception of objectivity or "hard" science. Here, I suggest, we have no alternative but to do the best we can to get at what matters most, namely, the meaning and significance of behavior. This means using the best research methods that exist today, integrating those methods, triangulating research as much as possible, and being as self-critical and reflexive as we can.

### Inserting an Inherently Conservative Bias in Public Policy

Social norm theorists, naturally, do not question the social meaning turn. But they do resist the shift in focus from social meaning to subject creation. The principal problem, they suggest, is that the demand for more research can only lead to complacency at the public policy level. Dan Kahan argues, for instance, that my research project reflects what he playfully describes as a conservative Burkean sensibility. Kahan and Meares suggest an affinity—again, playfully, I assume—between my proposal and the writings of Justice Antonin Scalia. They write:

We don't view the Harcourt-Scalia position as a reason to back off our initial arguments. Their anxiety that admittedly "reasonable" policing techniques—such as curfews, gang-loitering laws, and building searches—might nevertheless erode our society's "virtuous" resentment of state authority is speculative. We can't disprove it. But only someone who is complacent about the status quo would treat such speculation as sufficient grounds to abort experimentation with milder public-order alternatives to the crack-down policies that dominate law enforcement today. (1999a:23)

As a preliminary matter, I would emphasize that, although the proposed order-maintenance policies may be "milder" than three-strikes laws, they are not without consequence. A policy of encouraging juvenile snitching may result in juvenile deaths. During the three years that the Chicago anti-gang loitering ordinance was enforced, the Chicago police arrested more than forty-two thousand persons for violating the ordinance (*Morales* 1999:49). As Dorothy Roberts persuasively demonstrates, these public order alternatives are "connected to lengthy imprisonment in a more practical way" (1999:818). In many cases they may destroy a young person's opportunities. And they may result in increased incidences of police misconduct. In other words, these "milder" policing strategies are not without significant costs.

More important, though, I am not suggesting that we need to complete the full complement of research or achieve 95 percent confidence levels before implementing any public policy. To be sure, in the policy-making context, we will often need to act on less than perfect knowledge. We may not always have the luxury of completing this kind of elaborate research *before* implementing public policies. In the rough-and-tumble of policy making, we may often need to implement a policy based on our considered judgment that the likelihood of success outweighs the possible costs. Public policies often will be implemented—correctly, I believe—on the basis of sketchy evidence or preliminary findings. But that evidence, however sketchy, should at the very least point in the right direction. In other words, if there is any evidence to assess and evaluate, it should support the policy. Moreover, when we consider policies that may have significant adverse effects—such as juvenile snitching, for instance, which may result in harm to the snitches—there should be at least some indicia, some evidence, however slight, that the policy is likely to be effective. Absent any such evidence, we should probably not implement controversial public policies without further research. I do not think that this is really a conservative public policy orientation; rather, it avoids being reckless or negligent. In any event, if it is what Kahan and Meares have in mind as a conservative Burkean tendency, then to that I happily plead guilty.

As I have suggested, there does not appear to be any reliable evidence that anti-gang loitering ordinances are effective in reducing gang-related criminal activity. What evidence there is, in fact, suggests inverse correlations between enforcement of the ordinance and gang-related crime in the context of overall crime trends in Chicago (*Morales* 1999:50 n.7; Roberts 1999:794–795; Schulhofer and Alschuler 2000:7–12). Similarly, there does not appear to be any reliable evidence that juvenile snitching policies are effective in reducing juvenile gun possession. The only indicator here is a statement by the chief of police of Charleston (Blumstein and Cork 1996:17; Butterfield 1996). What is missing, though, is any longitudinal evidence about rates of juvenile gun possession. On these grounds, I argue, it would be foolish to implement these policies without some further research suggesting that they are effective.

In the context of order-maintenance policing, I have argued that there is no reliable evidence that the broken windows hypothesis is valid, although I suggest that there is evidence that order-maintenance policing may have a positive effect on solving crimes and reducing gun carrying. My point is not that we should resist order maintenance because we have not fully researched it. Nor is my point that we should resist order maintenance because there is no evidence of effectiveness. My argument is that we should resist order maintenance because the evidence of harms of the policy outweighs the evidence of benefits, and because there exist alternatives to a policy of aggressive stops, frisks, and arrests.

In all three cases, the problem is not that we have not yet completed the type of comprehensive research that I have described. The problem is that, in some cases, we do not even have the modicum of evidence barely to suggest that the policies will be effective or that changes in social meaning are doing any positive work. In this, at least, Stephen Morse agrees. "At present," he writes, "we have only what Paul Meehl calls fireside inductions concerning how law and legal practices and norms causally interact" (2000:1). In the other case, the problem is that the evidence suggests that the mechanism of crime reduction likely operates through increased surveillance, discrimination, and disciplinary practices that have unacceptable costs and for which there are alternatives. In other words, my resistance to order-maintenance policing techniques is not because of the fact that proper ethnographies have not yet been conducted.

The desirability of complete and comprehensive research should not paralyze policy making. But the converse is equally true: the demands of policy making should not inhibit social-scientific inquiry. We should not limit our research projects simply to satisfy the demands of public policy. While we are implementing or not implementing policies, it is our responsibility as social scientists, legal scholars, policy makers, and public citizens to conduct the rich kind of research that will help us fully to assess or reassess these policies and their important consequences on us as contemporary subjects of society. The type of research project that I propose here certainly should not inhibit policy making, but neither should it be inhibited by the demands of policy making.

### An Illustration: Researching Juvenile Gun Possession

The scope of the ideal research agenda also should not inhibit actual research. To be sure, the agenda I propose is somewhat formidable. It may seem to some daunting. "I wonder," Morse writes, "if the sheer ambition of Bernard [Harcourt]'s proposal isn't an implicit argument that it's not worth doing" (2000:3). I emphasize here: It is not. The kind of rich qualitative and quantitative research that I propose is an ideal type. It is an ideal of the type of research that we should conduct to assess public policies fully. It is an ideal of the research that we as researchers should aspire to, that we should try to achieve, and that we should encourage graduate students to envisage. In all likelihood, though, this type of agenda calls for interdisciplinary teamwork among researchers from different disciplines and different methodological backgrounds. The investigation into social meaning and subject creation requires traditional qualitative approaches, quantitative methods, historical research, and ethnographic study. This is a tall order, and no one researcher may have the competence to conduct all aspects of the research project. But that is not a reason to forgo the project. To the contrary, it is a compelling reason to do the investigation that we feel competent doing, and to team up with other researchers for the rest. After all, we are assessing policing strategies and techniques of punishment. These are crucial practices—practices that fundamentally define the type of society that we live in and that fundamentally shape who we are.

To conclude, I offer, as an illustration of the proposed research agenda, one specific project. It is not the ideal, but it is a manageable project, and one that can be expected from someone interested in exploring and assessing policing techniques and public policies from the perspective of social meaning and subject creation. I will use as an illustration a possible research project on issues of juvenile gun possession and related policing techniques in Tucson, Arizona—a small city, still called by many the "Old Pueblo," located along a major drug-trafficking corridor near the U.S.-Mexico border, a region with a strong southwestern gun culture. The focus of the project is on juvenile gun possession, by which I mean not the tragic high-profile cases of school shootings, but rather the more common juvenile street possession of guns that resulted in a surge in juvenile homicides in the early to mid-1990s.

## Background

Juvenile gun violence increased sharply during the late 1980s and early 1990s in Tucson, as well as in the state of Arizona and nationally. While juvenile non-gun homicides remained steady at the national level from 1976 to 1991, juvenile gun homicides more than doubled from 1985 to 1991 (Blumstein and Cork 1996:8, 20 fig. 4). After studying and discounting the possibility of increased juvenile propensity for violence, Alfred Blumstein and Daniel Cork concluded that "the diffusion of guns played an important part in the growth of youth homicide rates" (1996:12; see also Zimring and Hawkins 1997:109; Blumstein and Rosenfeld 1998:1191–1201).

In the state of Arizona a similar trend occurred with a three-to-four-year delay, resulting in a sharp increase in juvenile homicides that peaked in 1995. At the statewide level, there was a marked increase in both gun and juvenile violence, and the combination of the two trends proved lethal for many youths. Homicides of juveniles fifteen to nineteen years old increased sharply from 1990 to 1995, and firearm homicides accounted almost entirely for the increase in total deaths. This is illustrated in Figure 8.1.

The city of Tucson, including South Tucson, also experienced both a sharp increase in gun homicides and in youth violence, resulting in a significant rise in the number of gun homicides committed by juveniles (fourteen to seventeen) and young adults (eighteen to twenty-four), both in absolute terms and in relation to total homicides, as shown in Figure 8.2. A number of explanations have been offered to account for the apparent increase in juvenile gun violence, the leading hypothesis being Alfred Blumstein's account concerning the crack cocaine epidemic. Blumstein has argued that the rapid expansion of the crack market resulted in the arming of many young people involved in the drug trade, and that increased overall gun possession among juveniles translated into an escalation of violence. Ordinary juvenile disputes, Blumstein suggests, began to escalate into more lethal violence (Blumstein 1995). According to Blumstein, this is true as well in small

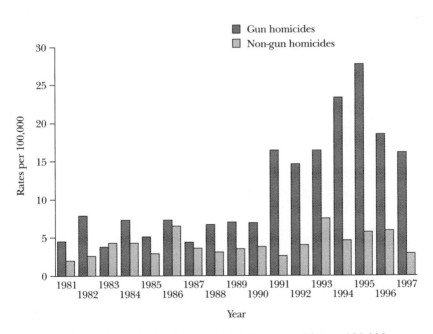

**Figure 8.1** Rates of homicide of juveniles 15–19 years old (per 100,000 persons 15–19 years old) in Arizona, 1981–1997 (derived from Mrela 1993:32 and 1999:28)

cities. "The market recruits kids to sell drugs and provides the guns for protection," Blumstein explains. "This makes for a cycle that has turned fistfights into fatalities among youths, even in smaller cities such as Tucson" (Haussler 1995).

Blumstein's hypothesis may work well in a city like New York, where there was a solid predicate—a wave of crack trade-related homicides (Goldstein et al. 1989)—and evidence of gun dispersion. It is less clear, however, whether the same mechanism operated in a small city such as Tucson. First, Tucson may not have experienced the same type or character of crack epidemic that major urban areas suffered. Because of its proximity to the Mexican border, marijuana has traditionally been the drug of choice in Tucson. Arizona has, to be sure, also become one of the leading importation points and corridors of drug trafficking for cocaine: according to the Drug Enforcement Agency, Colombian cocaine is shipped primarily by land or air to sites in northern Mexico, and then driven across the border by land vehicles (U.S.

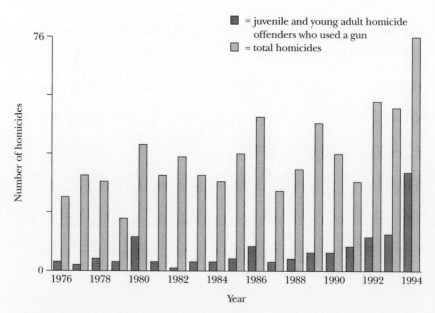

**Figure 8.2** Number of known juvenile (14 to 17) and young adult (18 to 24) homicide offenders who used a gun as compared to total homicides, Tucson, 1976–1994 (derived from Fox 1999)

Department of Justice 1999). But the use of cocaine in Tucson remains at a relatively lower level than in other comparable cities. In 1998, for instance, among male juvenile arrestees aged nine through eighteen, a smaller proportion tested positive for cocaine in Tucson (4.9 percent) than in other cities including Los Angeles (14.6 percent), Denver (12.6 percent), Cleveland (12.1 percent), and Birmingham, Alabama (9.4 percent) (see Riley 1999). There may in fact be a border-town effect, whereby the drugs are being shipped through Tucson but distributed more widely at other points (Walsh 1989).

Second, gun availability in Tucson is much greater than in a city such as New York. This may strike some as bizarre, but not in Tucson, where you can walk down the main street with a loaded handgun strapped to your hip or a loaded rifle over your shoulder. So long as the firearm is not concealed, there are few restrictions on carrying one. You can keep a loaded revolver in your car and can easily buy a nine-millimeter handgun in Tucson for a hundred dollars or less. The point is that guns flow pretty freely in and around Tucson (Kilborn 1992:A10).

Tucson also has its own idiosyncratic mix of policing strategies and public polices. Law enforcement authorities have taken a four-pronged approach to reducing juvenile gun possession. Their approach includes, first, occasional curfew sweeps and order-maintenance crackdowns. During these operations, the police use violations of the youth curfew ordinance or other minor misdemeanor laws (such as traffic violations) to conduct searches of juveniles and their automobiles. These sweeps and crackdowns generally target a high-risk neighborhood at a peak time of potential gun carrying—such as an area of high cruising activity on a Friday or Saturday night. Second, juveniles who violate gun laws may be transferred to federal court for prosecution and sentencing. Federal law provides for enhanced sentences. Third, juveniles who engage in violent offenses with a firearm are automatically transferred to adult court and convicted as adults. They are then sentenced to an adult term, and serve their time in the Department of Corrections—in a special juvenile unit until they are eighteen, when they are transferred to the general population to serve the rest of their sentence. In addition to these three measures, the county attorney's office sponsors an educational diversionary program for youths adjudicated in Juvenile Court for gun violations. The program—Firearm Awareness and Safety Training—is a four-hour class, generally held on Saturday mornings, at which the juveniles, accompanied by a parent, learn about the dangers of firearms and safety issues.

## An Illustrative Research Project

An illustrative research project on juvenile gun possession in Tucson would investigate how teenagers in Tucson perceive and give meaning and significance to guns, as well as how they experience and understand the different policing strategies that have been enforced, in order to assess the role of social meaning, to judge how these policies shape juveniles, and to determine the effectiveness of the policies. In this sense, the research project takes a threefold approach to the problem of juvenile gun possession. First, it attempts to understand the context within which juveniles decide to carry a firearm. It explores the various social meanings of guns and gun possession for juveniles in Tucson. It investigates the mental, emotional, and behavioral situation within which juveniles experience their everyday life, with specific reference to guns. Second, the research attempts to understand how law enforcement policies affect these youths and their environment. It explores whether and how much juveniles know about the different law enforcement policies, what experience they have had with these policies, and what they have heard about them. It investigates how juveniles incorporate knowledge of the policies into their attitudes and behavior, whether and how the policies affect their behavior, and how the policies change their environment and decision-making processes. It probes into the way the different policies affect their sense of self, their relation to authority, to parents, to friends, to other youths, their judgment of others and of the justice system. Third, and building on these two, the research project assesses the potential effectiveness of these various policies in reducing firearm possession and weighs the different impacts of the policies on youths, crime, political participation, families, and society.

Throughout, the research project focuses on understanding and modeling behavior by means of social meaning and subject creation theory. It explores and compares the different theoretical frameworks—rational choice, bounded rationality, reflexive sociology, social interaction, and contextual frameworks—that might shed light on juveniles' actions, and relates these different theoretical frameworks to conceptions of social meaning. And throughout, the researcher is constantly self-reflexive about his or her role in and impact on the research. The researcher is continuously reflecting on how these intellectual frameworks may be shaped by the policing and punitive practices that surround us.

As a first cut, the research project would consist of in-depth structured interviews with a wide range and number of juveniles, including those incarcerated in a juvenile detention center, juveniles in intensive probation, juveniles in both at-risk high schools and lower-risk schools. The focus of the interviews would be dual: on the one hand, to explore the social meaning of guns and the role of guns in their lives, relationships, and identities, and on the other, to explore the social meaning of the law enforcement policies and how they shape these youths and their environment.

Jeff Fagan and Deanna Wilkinson have demonstrated how useful such an approach can be at uncovering the meaning of guns. In their study, interviewing 377 active gun offenders between the ages of sixteen and twenty from two neighborhoods in New York City, they develop what they call violence scripts. They describe these scripts as the "cumulative knowledge gained through participation in and observation of violent interactions" (Fagan and Wilkinson 1998:133). They show how gun possession and use may be central to the formation, maintenance, and communication of social identities among young males in inner-city neighborhoods (1998:145–173; Fagan 1999:26–36; Fagan and Wilkinson 2000:4–1—4–38). Their work focuses on the meaning of guns, which is part of this project. The other important part, of course, is the meaning of the public policies and how they shape youths.

This is, as I have said, a first cut on the issues of social meaning and subject creation. It of course needs to be supplemented with more traditional criminological study of juvenile crime trends, drug usage, and policy implementation in Tucson, with historical research into the gun culture of the Southwest, with ethnographic work on youth culture in the numerous ethnic communities in Tucson—Tohono O'Odham, Pascua Yaqui, Mexican, Mexican-American, Latin American, African-American, and Anglo—and with comparative analysis of the numerous other policing initiatives that have been designed to combat youth gun violence. There is a lot more to do and a lot more that can be done. But this research project is a reasonable and manageable starting place for someone interested in social meaning and subject creation.

The important point is that these different policing practices and public policies have significantly different effects on juveniles, their parents, and us all. As discussed earlier, the St. Louis police department has implemented a policy called the Firearm Suppression Program that seeks to reduce the number of guns in the hands of juveniles by means of a voluntary search (Rosenfeld and Decker 1996:204–206, 209–210, and 214–215). In Boston, authorities have implemented the Boston Gun Project, a strategy aimed at decreasing both the supply of and demand for guns among juveniles by trying to communicate directly with at-risk juveniles that gun possession will not be tolerated (David Kennedy 1997). In Detroit, a judge has launched an educational program—the Handgun Intervention Program—that is intended to foster attitudinal and behavioral changes among young offenders who have been arrested for carrying a concealed weapon (Roth 1998:1). A number of other approaches have been devised, including "weed and seed" programs in, for instance, Baltimore and Indianapolis, the Hope, Education, and Law and Safety program in Minneapolis, gun tracing by the ATF, municipal firearms ordinances in Oakland—in all several hundred programs and strategies that deploy or combine different law enforcement techniques, educational approaches, and community organizing (see generally Reno 2000). Each of these different policies will have radically different effects on youths and on us as contemporary subjects and researchers of policing strategies. A policy of voluntary consent to search with a promise of no prosecutions will have a different effect on us and our society than a policy of adult prosecutions, a policy of firearm safety education, or a policy of juvenile snitching. These effects are real and they need to be investigated. It is a daunting task, but that should not stop us from doing what we can to begin investigating the problem.

Clifford Geertz once remarked that "'the move toward meaning' has proved a proper revolution: sweeping, durable, turbulent, and consequential" (1995:115). This is certainly true in policing and criminal law policy analysis. The turn to social meaning has been turbulent, and in my opinion it has been very consequential. In this book I have explored some of the further consequences and implications of the turn, and in the process have proposed an alternative vision to order maintenance. This alternative builds on the important conceptual contributions of the social meaning turn. To be sure, this alternative vision does not immediately produce easily articulated crime-fighting policies like anti-gang loitering ordinances, youth curfews, or reverse stings. It does not come with a package of policy prescriptions. It does not cater as well to the demands of public policy debate. And it may give rise to policies that are not as politically feasible as those endorsed by the New Progressives. But it may generate compelling alternatives both to the more traditional solution of severe incarceration and to the renewed call for order-maintenance crackdowns.

This alternative vision projects an image of the researcher immersed in the field, knee-deep in archives, interpreting practices and texts, interviewing informants, compiling and comparing historical data, collecting and regressing data, looking for clues as to how practices and institutions shape us as contemporary subjects. How they fundamentally reconfigure our ways of thinking, above and beyond our immediate perception and short-term behavior. How they influence our beliefs about the appropriateness of practices and policies. It is concerned, above all, with the kind of society and citizens these police practices produce.

# CHAPTER 9

# Toward a New Mode of
# Political Analysis

In *Thinking about Crime,* James Q. Wilson wrote that "the demand for causal solutions is, whether intended or not, a way of deferring any action and criticizing any policy. It is a cast of mind that inevitably detracts attention from those few things that governments can do reasonably well and draws attention toward those many things it cannot do at all" (1975:xv). There may well be good reasons to be weary of strong causal reasoning in social policy and, in particular, in criminal law policy analysis (see, e.g., Rein and Winship 1999). The goal of this book, however, has been to emphasize that *regardless* of the types of policies being proposed—whether they be "root cause," rehabilitative, deterrence-minded, or inducement-oriented—we must explore how those proposed policies are going to shape us as contemporary subjects of society. When we assess policing strategies and punitive practices, we need to think about how they will affect our perceptions, desires, thoughts, and judgments—how they will, for instance, influence the way we interpret the propensities of the homeless person, of the unattached adult, of the rowdy teenager, or of the prostitute. We need to explore them critically not only to determine their potential effectiveness, and not only to understand their social meaning, but also, and more important, to examine how they create us as modern subjects. Our intellectual and conceptual frameworks—as citizens and as researchers—are shaped in part by the punitive practices that we experience. Whether we adopt a thicker conception of propensities or of human nature may *itself* be the product of the policing and punitive practices that surround us.

At the end of the day, there is little if any empirical evidence supporting the cardinal proposition of the order-maintenance approach to criminal justice. The claim that "disorder causes crime" is even less plausible at the theoretical level. The term "disorder" is the locus of the problem. What we are referring to when we talk about "disorder" in this context are certain minor acts that we have come to view as "disorderly" mostly because of police and punitive strategies—such as the quality-of-life initiative and, long before it, the disciplinary practices of orderliness—that shape the way we judge others and experience the world. We have come to identify certain things (graffiti, litter, panhandling, turnstile jumping, public urination) and not others (paying workers under the table, minor tax evasion, fraud, and police brutality) as "disorderly" and somehow connected to crime, in large part because of the social practices that surround us. But the concept of "disorder" is not natural. Nor do these various ingredients of "disorder" have a fixed meaning. They do not necessarily, on their own, communicate that a neighborhood has lost control over crime, or does not care about rule violation. The meaning of these various acts is contextual and is itself constructed. Loitering only signals—as one possible meaning among many others—that the community is not in control *if* loitering is perceived by community members as violating certain rules of conduct. But of course loitering is not necessarily perceived that way in all communities. Urinating in the street signals that rules have broken down *only if* the meaning of public urination is associated with rule breaking. Again, that is not always the case.

When we think that the "disorderly" person—the homeless person, the squeegee man, the prostitute, or the panhandler—has certain propensities that cannot easily be changed, this belief itself is in part the product of disciplinary practices that we experience consciously and subconsciously. When we conclude that some acts are "disorderly" and others not, these conclusions are shaped by punitive and policing strategies. They are the product in part of the regimen of order that we have been subjected to.

The order-maintenance approach has gained popularity partly because of the way in which it shapes the category of the "disorderly" and partly because it has capitalized on the rhetoric of harm. In this sense, the order-maintenance approach represents one of a large number of harm arguments that have effectively shifted the ideology of punitive justification and seized the upper hand in a fractured debate where harm has become the touchstone of legal and political intervention. Minor disorderly conduct, which had previously been viewed as a nuisance, is today perceived as an affirmative harm.

A number of other theorists have similarly identified this turn to harm in late modern social and political theory. In *Achieving Our Country,* Richard Rorty associates the new focus on victimization with the "cultural Left" and the influence of Nietzsche, Heidegger, Foucault, and Derrida on young leftist academics. The cultural left, Rorty argues, has redirected leftist concerns from a more materialist pre-1960s focus on issues of labor, welfare, health care, and poverty to a contemporary concern with issues of identity, difference, stigma, and victimization (1998:77). The chief culprit, according to Rorty, is "postmodern" theory, especially the Foucauldian critique of liberal humanism and leftist reformism—the argument that humanist impulses over the past two centuries have veiled disciplinary practices which have oppressed, marginalized, and normalized the "other." This Foucauldian critique, Rorty suggests, has demoralized leftist academics and trained their sights on victimization. It has produced a distrust of the progressive leftist tradition and, more generally, of humanism. It has produced, in his words, a "spirit of detached spectatorship" (1998:11).

Wendy Brown, in *States of Injury,* similarly observes that contemporary political theory is marked by a "codification of injury" with negative consequences for political action and the pursuit of freedom (1995:27). She argues that the turn to injury, though intended to combat gender, racial, and sexual discrimination, inadvertently replicates and perpetuates the very relationships and pathologies that it seeks to displace. She argues that "the inscription of gendered, racial or sexual identity in legal discourse could be shown to have the effect of reaffirming the historical injuries constitutive of those identities, thus installing injury as identity in the ahistorical discourse of the law" (1995:xi). The turn to harm, Brown contends, has created a pervasive sense of despair and political powerlessness, and has demoralized contemporary advocates. It has triggered a loss of utopian faith in politics, and has reinforced a form of bitterness similar to what Nietzsche described as *ressentiment* (1995:27). The result, Brown argues, is a turn to the state—for instance, to state regulation of pornography and hate speech—as the only possible avenue of relief.

Still other theorists discuss the trend toward harm in terms of a new "politics of recognition," in contrast to an older "politics of redistribution." The politics of recognition, they argue, entails a focus on cultural domination and acts of disrespect (Honneth 1995; Fraser 1997:14). These theorists draw our attention to larger issues in political and social thought. Their perspectives are provocative and, in some respects more than others, convincing. The idea that we are experiencing late modern anxiety and a sense of powerlessness reflects, to some extent, the *Zeitgeist* of the late twentieth and early twenty-first centuries. This is, after all, a time in which the term "postmodernism" has flourished—a term that captures, as Seyla Benhabib suggests, "the widespread sentiment of the exhaustion of the project of modernity, of being at the end of certain cultural, theoretical, and social-political paradigms" (1995:107). It is a period that has been described as suffering from "the exhaustion of utopian energies" (Habermas 1984). A period in which, Nancy Fraser suggests, "progressive struggles are no longer anchored in any credible vision of an alternative to the present order" (1997:2). A time of disenchantment and disenfranchisement. A Generation X.

In contrast to Rorty, who associates the turn to harm with "postmodernism," I argue that claims of harm have proliferated across the full political spectrum. On the left, the emergence of identity politics certainly has focused attention on the discrimination and oppression experienced by women, persons of color, and gay men and lesbians. Claims to identity often are grounded, today, on claims of injury. The growth of cultural studies, and its fragmentation into ethnic group and gender studies—Afro-American studies, critical race theory, Latino studies, and women's studies—highlights the construction and marginalization of whole groups of people. Strands of feminist theory emphasize the constitutive harms of pornography and prostitution to women and women's sexuality. But leftists are not the only ones to focus on victimization. The right has done the same thing, having abandoned the rhetoric of legal moralism and turned instead to harm arguments. On the right, theorists and activists focus on the injuries to children, to the traditional nuclear family, and to social solidarity caused by homosexuality and heterosexual promiscuity. Proponents of anti-drug measures highlight the multiple harms associated with the use of drugs and the illicit drug trade. There has been, as I document in Chapter 7, a veritable proliferation of harm arguments in most of the important political debates of the day. The order-maintenance approach is just one manifestation.

And, in sharp contrast to Rorty, Brown, and others, I draw drastically different implications from this trend in social and political theory. Far from decrying this rhetorical shift, I applaud it. The proliferation of harm arguments—conservative or neoconservative, progressive or New Progressive, "postmodern" or poststructuralist—is ultimately a positive development for political debate. It augurs a new and improved mode of political analysis—a mode of analysis that confronts, head-on, the difficult task of assessing, comparing, and weighing harms. It forces the participants in the debate to address and balance harms in a manner that had previously been obfuscated by the harm principle.

In contrast to an earlier period when the debate was between arguments of harmlessness and legal moralism, the collapse of the harm principle forces us today to face the hard task of assessing harms and making explicit choices among them. In the debate over commercial sex, for instance, progressive thinkers in the 1960s argued that prostitution caused no harm, and their opponents argued that prostitution was immoral. Both of these arguments, however, obscured the real debate. The fact is, prostitution *does* cause harm. At the very least—even if it does not cause serious crime such as murder and robbery—it causes harm to the HIV-infected, drug-addicted, sexually and emotionally abused streetwalker who is dependent on an exploitative pimp. And, of course, prostitution violates most moral codes. But that is not the real issue. The issue is not whether prostitution is harmless or immoral. The real issue is how the harms of prostitution compare to the harms of the proposed legal or political intervention, and how to design policies—legal, political, or extralegal—to reduce the harms associated with commercial sex. The very same is true in the debate over "disorder." Graffiti writing, aggressive panhandling, and public urination may well cause some harm. The evidence, as I have demonstrated, does not establish that they cause serious crime, but they nevertheless may cause financial and other economic harms, as well as aesthetic harms to some. These harms, as well as the benefits of order-maintenance policing, have to be weighed. I argue, ultimately, that they are outweighed, but not that they should not be considered.

The increased awareness of harms has highlighted the injuries associated with political and legal intervention. Again, in the context of commercial sex, the focus on harm has not only revealed the injury to women, sexuality, and city neighborhoods caused by pornography and prostitution. It has also focused attention on the harms associated with legal and political responses. The crackdown on prostitution in New York City beginning under Mayor Giuliani's administration, for example, has by no means been a costless political and legal intervention. Order-maintenance policing has its own meaning—often reinforcing the stereotype of black criminality—and that meaning has significant costs. In addition, the focus on victimization has highlighted hidden harms embedded within certain harm arguments themselves. Wendy Brown demonstrates, for example, how Catharine MacKinnon's work mirrors, perpetuates, and solidifies women's identity as object of pornography, and undermines radical opposition (1997:90–95). This is, after all, a potential harm caused by MacKinnon's theory. In a similar vein, the treatment of prostitutes as "disorderly" constructs a category of disorderly persons that ultimately legitimizes costly but entirely speculative crime prevention policies.

The proliferation of harm arguments in political debate, including poststructuralist claims of injury, *is* a positive development because, among other things, it forces us to address the hidden normative dimensions lurking beneath conceptions of harm. It helps us realize that there is probably harm in most human activities and, in most cases, on both sides of the equation—on the side of the persons harmed by the purported offense, but also on the side of the actor whose conduct is restricted by legal intervention. By highlighting the harms on both sides of the equation, the shift in harm rhetoric may help us make more informed arguments and reach more informed decisions. It may alert us to the possible harms of political and legal intervention, as well as the hidden harms in harm arguments. It may force us to analyze carefully the harm to others, as well as the harm to the purportedly immoral actor, remembering that the punishment itself may affect, positively or negatively, the subject of punishment, our assessment of harm, and society as a whole.

In this sense, the rhetorical shift to harm in social and political debate creates the opportunity to deploy interpretive and poststructuralist insights in contemporary political decision making. To borrow from Iris Marion Young, it allows us "to close the gap and use Foucauldian insights to interpret and criticize policies and programs in specific social contexts" (1997:9). I would only add that it also allows us to use Foucauldian insights to *assess, propose, and adopt* policies and programs in specific social contexts. It is a positive development in criminal law policy analysis because it makes possible a more informed mode of decision making: political analysis that takes advantage of the insights of the linguistic turn and of poststructuralist theory. Political analysis that no longer hides behind formalism and ignores the multiple hidden normative dimensions of harm. Political analysis that asks hard questions and forces us to make hard choices.

NOTES

BIBLIOGRAPHY

INDEX

# Notes

## 2. The Order-Maintenance Approach

1. This account is somewhat simplified. In fact, there *was* a ban on panhandling in the subways. The federal courts upheld that ban, and it continued in effect throughout the period ("Supreme Court Refuses to Hear Challenge to Anti-Begging Law" 1990:1). Lessig does recognize this in a footnote (see Lessig 1995:1040 n.329). What it suggests, though, is that a full account of the change in social meaning would have to take into consideration whether it was the prohibition or the education campaign that affected the amount of panhandling. This fuller account would have to look at arrest rates for panhandling in the subways, deployment of police force in the subways, and the effect of that deployment on the behavior of subway riders.

2. This interpretation of social norm theory emphasizes the role of social meaning. Tracey Meares has suggested that, in fact, it overemphasizes the role of social meaning at the expense of another important category, namely, "social organization." Meares argues that she and Dan Kahan have offered a taxonomy of at least three mechanisms by which social norms operate in society, including social organization, social influence, and social meaning. I am not entirely persuaded, however, that these are three distinct mechanisms. In the first place, the concept of social influence is derivative of the notion of social meaning: social meaning has its effect through its influence on social action. Second, social organization, though slightly more conceptually independent than social influence, also operates in important ways through social meaning and influence. The loss of social organization in a neighbor-

252 · Notes to Pages 44–51

hood is a phenomenon that feeds into the web of meanings that make up a community and socially influences neighborhood residents to act in ways that aggravate crime. In discussing social organization theory, Meares emphasizes that "socially organized or cohesive communities are better able to engage in informal social control . . . because such communities are able to *realize common values,* which can be continually reinforced in daily community life through *conduct and discourse* that centers on law abidingness" (Meares 1998a:197, emphasis added; see also Meares 1998b:675). This seems to suggest that social organization is not purely behavioral, but operates in large part through the meaning of social norms. In this sense, I would argue, social meaning *is* at the heart of the social norm project. It is the expressive dimension that, like Banfield's notion of class or Wilson's idea of human nature, thickens our notion of human preferences. It is the linchpin of the New Chicago School approach, and it is what generates so many highly controversial and provocative policy proposals.

3. Significant battle lines have been drawn around these terms. Jeffrey Rosen, for instance, has suggested that the policing strategy fundamentally changed—in his words, "morphed"—from a broken windows approach to a policy of zero tolerance once the Giuliani administration realized that aggressive misdemeanor arrests were resulting in the arrests of serious criminals (Rosen 2000:26). This, however, is not entirely correct. Bratton's approach was, from its inception, a zero-tolerance approach. Bratton himself described his first experiment in the New York subways as a "fare evasion mini-sweep." He explained: "I put a sergeant and five, eight, sometimes ten cops in plain clothes at these problematic stations day and night, and they arrested the people who were streaming in for nothing. The cops nabbed ten or twenty jumpers at a time. They pulled these men and women in one by one, cuffed them, lined them up on the platform, and waited for the next wave" (Bratton 1998:153). This is not an exercise in police discretion. It is an exercise in zero tolerance. Similarly, Bratton's strategy with squeegee people— the first wave of the quality-of-life strategy—was not about discretion. It was about sweeps—about constantly checking and rechecking the squeegee corners and arresting all violators (Bratton 1998:213–214). Bratton and Giuliani understood from the beginning the close relationship between order maintenance, sweeps, and catching criminals (Bratton 1998:154).

4. Interestingly, in personal conversation in January 1999, James Q. Wilson in fact told me that New York City's ongoing experiment with aggressive misdemeanor arrests was the best example of the kind of policing he had had in mind in the "Broken Windows" essay.

5. In addition, across the country, courts and other authorities have begun to impose shaming penalties—and the media are having a field day reporting bizarre shaming rituals (Alter and Wingert 1996; El Nasser 1996; Hoffman 1997). The *Cleveland Plain Dealer* reports that a group of young adults convicted of throwing rocks at cars were ordered to stand at the side of the road for five hours and hold a sign reading, "We threw rocks from the A Rt. 2 bridge. We're Sorry!!" (Morris 1999). A Tacoma newspaper reports that a person convicted of car theft was ordered by a superior court judge to wear a sign reading, "I am a car thief," and that an Ohio man convicted of harassing his ex-wife was ordered to let her spit in his face ("Public Humiliation Makes a Comeback" 2000; see also Deardorff 2000a and 2000b). On signs, bumper stickers, posters, and cable television shows such as *John TV*, the new shaming penalties abound, and they have generated heated debate (*Letterlough* 1995; Walsh 1997; Garvey 1998). My colleague Toni Massaro first challenged the practice in 1990, and has since been joined in her opposition to shaming penalties by Yale law professor James Whitman (1990, 1997, and 1999; Whitman 1998). Dan Kahan, however, continues to affirmatively advocate shaming sanctions (1996 and 1998:615–617).

### 3. The Broken Windows Theory

1. Skogan acknowledges, however, that fear of crime is more strongly correlated with crime than with disorder, and that when levels of crime are controlled for, "the relationship between disorder and fear no longer is significant" (1990:77).

2. Skogan also argues that this correlation "document[s] that disorder and crime problems go together in a substantial way" (Skogan 1990:74). The reliability of this finding and the validity of the conclusion are somewhat questionable given that the data for both variables were obtained by asking the same people if there was disorder in their neighborhood and if they perceived that there was a crime problem in their neighborhood. It seems that residents who believe there is a crime problem in their neighborhood will also perceive their neighborhood as disorderly. Perception of crime problems and perception of disorder would seem to go hand in hand. The fact that there is a strong correlation may thus be due to the fact that the data were collected from the same individuals.

3. There are only two differences: first, I have labeled the *y*-axis "*Proportion* victims of robbery" rather than "*Percent* victims of robbery," as Skogan does in his figure 4–2. "Proportion" seems more accurate since the robbery victimization variable in the data is measured by the proportion of

respondents who answered yes (Skogan 1988:13). Thus, in the data, the values of robbery victimization range from 0 to 0.07 (or 0 to 7 percent) for the neighborhoods surveyed, not from 0 to 0.07 of 1 percent, as Skogan's figure 4–2 might suggest. Second, I use letters in the graph for abbreviations of the neighborhood locations by city (A for Atlanta, C for Chicago, H for Houston, and N for Newark).

4. It is important to get a sense of these findings. All of the values for Skogan's index of neighborhood disorder were located between 1.20 and 2.20 on a scale of 1 to 3—where a score of 1 meant that respondents indicated disorder was "no problem," a score of 2 meant that respondents indicated disorder was "some problem," and a score of 3 meant that respondents indicated disorder was "a big problem" (Skogan:1987:106; 1988:6). In other words, the entire spectrum of observations of neighborhood disorder was located between something slightly more than "no problem" and something slightly more than "some problem"—a one-unit increase in level of disorder. Therefore, what the analysis suggests is that, from the lowest observed level of disorder in thirty neighborhoods all the way to the highest observed level of disorder in those thirty neighborhoods—which incidentally were chosen to reflect both disorderly and orderly neighborhoods, both high-crime and low-crime neighborhoods—the expected increase in the proportion of robbery victimization is on average 5 percent: "All of the areas were in the nation's largest cities. They were selected for a variety of reasons—among them, because they were high or low-crime areas, because programs were about to be started in them, and because they were stable or undergoing racial transition." (Skogan 1990:188).

5. Skogan 1988:7. Skogan's treatment of these variables is inconsistent. Compare Skogan 1987:16 (gangs and insults variables not listed as part of index) with Skogan 1987:107 (gangs and insults variables included in the index). I believe that the ICPSR *Codebook* (Skogan 1988) and the *Final Report* (Skogan 1987:107) are correct.

6. What Skogan found was that there is an independent commercial sex factor distinct from social and physical disorder: that these measures of disorder do not hang together. Using the data, I find that the correlation between prostitution and robbery victimization is $-0.10$ and that there is no statistically significant relationship (p-value of 0.712). Smut and robbery victimization are correlated at $-0.27$, and the regression produces a p-value of 0.304. This is a fascinating challenge to the broken windows theory and puts into serious question the essay's emphasis on prostitutes.

7. Skogan's 1981 article "On Attitudes and Behaviors" does not address the cross-jurisdictional reliability of victimization surveys either.

8. "During the past year, *in the neighborhood where you live now,* has anyone picked your pocket or taken a bag or package directly from you without using force or threatening you?" (Skogan 1988:13; see also Skogan 1987:115).

9. "During the past year, *in the neighborhood where you live now,* has anyone physically attacked you or has anyone threatened or tried to hurt you even though they did not actually hurt you?" (Skogan:1987:115; see also Skogan 1988:13).

10. "Since the first of this year, has anyone stolen something directly from you by force or after threatening you with harm? PLUS: Other than that, has anyone tried to take something from you by force even though they did not get it?" (Skogan 1988:13; see also Skogan 1987:115).

11. "Has anyone sexually attacked you, or tried to, since the first of this year?" (Skogan 1988:13; see also Skogan 1987:115).

12. Skogan recognizes this and writes, in his methodological appendix, that "[t]he small size of the neighborhood and project-level samples examined here raises the spectre that a few cases exerted excessive influence on the statistical findings" (Skogan 1990:191; see also Skogan 1987:117). Skogan ran a number of tests to defend against this problem (see Skogan 1987:117–118), but may have focused excessively on single observations rather than citywide clusters as with Newark.

13. The five Newark neighborhoods have the highest levels of disorder of the thirty observed. Excluding those five neighborhoods could be interpreted as selecting on the explanatory variable. That, however, should cause no inference problems. See King, Keohane, and Verba (1994:137): "By limiting the range of our key causal variable, we may limit the generality of our conclusion or the certainty with which we can legitimately hold it, but we do not introduce bias." Since the five neighborhoods do not have the highest levels of robbery victimization, their exclusion does not amount to selecting on the dependent variable, which in contrast would be problematic (King, Keohane, and Verba 1994:129).

14. I have one final reservation—though it could be tested by going back to the data tapes. The study relies on self-reporting by the same people for the variables of disorder *and* crime victimization. In other words, the same people were asked to give their impression of the level of disorder in their neighborhood and to indicate whether they had been victimized by crime. The question I have is whether this might bias the study. After all, there is good reason to believe that persons who have been

the victims of crime in their neighborhood are likely to perceive their neighborhood as disorderly. In fact, this is something that Skogan himself recognizes in another context (Skogan 1981:20–23). It is possible that the correlation Skogan identifies is due in some part to the fact that an individual's assessment of neighborhood disorder will be affected by that person's experience as a victim of crime—even though non-victimized respondents constituted more than 90 percent of the interviewees. Again, this is something that could be tested and controlled for.

15. I am following Skogan's lead in weighing equally physical and social disorder (see Skogan 1988:8; see also Skogan 1987:19).

16. In order to standardize the values for each variable, I calculate the mean of the variable and then conduct the following calculation: standardized value = (value − mean)/mean.

17. The authors acknowledge that other studies have found no relationship between indices of aggressive policing (number of traffic citations issued) and robbery rates (see Sampson and Cohen 1988:167, referring to Jacob and Rich 1981:109, 113), although Sampson and Cohen join Wilson and Boland in criticizing these findings.

18. The authors explain how a model can be unidentified by defining the alternative: "The crime function in such a model is 'identified' when an instrumental variable is selected (e.g., police aggressiveness) that is both highly correlated with the sanction variable (e.g., arrest certainty) and at the same time does not have a direct effect on crime" (Sampson and Cohen 1988:165 n.1). In their case study the model is unidentified because the instrumental variable, police aggressiveness, apparently has a direct effect on crime (see 1988:175–176).

19. In addition to providing a permanent, replicable record, SSO also alleviates any concern about using a survey instrument to measure both disorder and victimization (see note 14). As Sampson and Raudenbush explain: "The perception of disorder seems also to reflect a psychological construct—perhaps fear itself. Residents fearful of crime report more disorder than do residents who experience less fear, even though both sets of observers are reporting on the *same* neighborhood. In this scenario, the fear (or vulnerability) of residents might be said to induce perceptions of disorder" (1999:606). Through the use of SSO, this problem disappears.

20. Sampson and Raudenbush conducted a number of other tests on these data to double-check the robustness of their results. In addition to the weighted least squares regression, discussed here, they also ran, for instance, logistic regression with neighborhoods that experienced no vic-

timization, coded as "0," and those with one or more incidents of victimization, coded as "1" (1999:628).

21. Robert Sampson has indicated to me that he is trying to develop ways to engage in reliable nighttime observation. My only final reservation is that it would have been preferable to replicate Models 1 and 2 identically with regard to survey-reported and police-recorded victimization. In Model 1, regarding police-recorded crime incidents (see 1999: table 5), Sampson and Raudenbush did not include the prior 1993 crime variable, whereas they did in Model 1 regarding survey-reported victimization (see 1999: table 4). They did include the 1993 crime variable in Model 3 for police-recorded crime, and the correlation between 1995 and 1993 crime is so strong that it rendered the estimated coefficients very conservative. That is, in fact, why they decided not to hold the prior crime variable constant in the second Model 1. As Sampson explained to me, "Because the correlation in official crime over time was so high (unlike for survey outcome) we wanted to give disorder a chance before controlling for prior crime" (communication with Sampson, May 30, 2000). I understand the reasoning, but would nevertheless prefer identical models.

### 4. Policing Strategies and Methodology

1. These statistics regarding the drop in the crime rate in New York City are from the FBI's Uniform Crime Reports, compiled from local police data (see generally Gove, Hughes and Geerken 1985). Police statistics are more susceptible to human manipulation than are victimization surveys. It is important to keep this in mind, particularly during periods of intensive policing initiatives. See, e.g., "For One NYC Captain, Crime Reductions Are a Numbers Racket" 1996, reporting that the commander of a high-crime precinct in the South Bronx is under investigation for falsifying reports to show huge reductions in crime; and Butterfield 1998b, reporting that, "[s]o far this year, there have been charges of falsely reporting crime statistics [in Philadelphia], in New York, Atlanta and Boca Raton, Fla." As Kelling and Coles observe, "the difference between reported and recorded crimes can be trivial, but examples abound in policing of 'cooking the books' to keep crime statistics low" (1996:27). Unfortunately, victimization survey data from the National Crime Victimization Survey are not available at the city level, according to Ann Pastore (1998), editor of the *Sourcebook of Criminal Justice Statistics,* published by the Hindelang Criminal Justice Research Center at the State University of New York in Albany.

2. The number of police officers is derived from the Uniform Crime Reports (UCR) for each respective year. See UCR—1960 (table 36); UCR—1970 (table 57); UCR—1980 (table 71); and UCR—1990 (table 72). The population numbers are derived from U.S. Census Bureau, *Annual Time Series of Population Estimates, 1991 to 1998, and 1990 Census Population for Places,* rev. December 14, 1999, <http://www.census.gov/ftp/pub/population/www/estimates/cityplace.html> (hereinafter *Annual Time Series*), for the population figure for 1990; and U.S. Department of Commerce, Bureau of the Census, for 1960, 1970, and 1980.

3. See UCR—1993 (table 78); UCR—1994 (table 78); UCR—1995 (table 78); UCR—1996 (table 78); UCR—1997 (table 78); and UCR—1998 (table 78) for the number of police department employees. See *Annual Time Series* for the population estimates for 1993–1998.

4. See the study by Andrew Golub and Bruce Johnson of the National Development and Research Institutes in New York (showing steep decrease in crack use among people being sent to jail in Manhattan), discussed in Butterfield 1997 (documenting these trends in other cities) and Witkin 1998:36; see also generally Katyal 1997 (citing studies). But see Fagan, Zimring, and Kim 1998 (suggesting that the incidence of drug-positive arrestees has been stable and is unrelated to homicide trends).

5. See Newcombe 1997; see also Dodenhoff 1996; and Silverman 1996 ("Perhaps the most significant aspect of the department's organizational changes within the past few years has been the process known as Compstat").

6. Schulhofer and Alschuler discuss the possibility of a multiyear delay in the operation of social influence, and cast serious doubt on it (Schulhofer and Alschuler 2000:13–14). I would only emphasize, though, that the very possibility of a delay of two or more years is *precisely* what creates the urgent need for in-depth qualitative analyses regarding the social meaning and influence of the ordinance. Without this kind of research, there is no way to assess whether the speculation about a time delay has any basis in reality. And the same would be true even if there *were* a simultaneous temporal correlation between enforcement and reductions in gang-related crime. Such a correlation might simply reflect the operation of *earlier* social norms and practices. In the absence of qualitative research, the quantitative data are essentially uninterpretable.

7. I conducted the interview with Huber in preparation for a large research project on juvenile gun possession. The discussion here is, accordingly, preliminary and sketchy. I do not intend to convey hard evi-

dence about the social meaning of juvenile gun possession, so much as to sketch different possible meanings and to illuminate the kind of research that is required after the social meaning turn.

8. While I draw here specifically on the work of anthropologist Clifford Geertz, naturally similar themes can be drawn from the writings, among others, of Charles Taylor in political theory or Herbert Blumer in sociology (Taylor 1985:15–90; Blumer 1969:1–60).

## 5. On Disorderly, Disreputable, or Unpredictable People

1. Whenever possible in citing Foucault, I will try to give the corresponding citation to the French text in case the reader would like to return to the original writings. For this reason, the chronology of the citations will be reversed.

2. The extent to which Foucault's work on punishment is a reaction against Durkheim's is underestimated in the secondary literature. Even David Garland, who provides perhaps the most insightful and comprehensive review of Foucault's theory of punishment in *Punishment and Modern Society*, does not give adequate emphasis to this reading of Foucault. He suggests, for instance, that "Foucault's analysis of punishment is quite distinct from Durkheim's, appearing to contradict it at a number of points, and, for the most part, dealing with phenomena which hardly appear in Durkheim's work" (Garland 1990:132). I would suggest a slightly different interpretation: Foucault, instead, reinterprets the *same* phenomena. He writes directly against Durkheim, turning Durkheim's analysis on its head. He revisits the same history of punitive enlightenment. Most readings of Foucault, I argue, overestimate the place of power in his analysis and underestimate the role of subject creation.

3. See also Foucault 1979:23: "Instead of treating the history of penal law and the history of the human sciences as two separate series . . . see whether there is not some common matrix or whether they do not both derive from a single process of 'epistemologico-*juridical*' formation."

4. Foucault 1975:214. Alan Sheridan translates this as "state-control" (1979:213), but that does not capture well the active sense of encroachment in Foucault's term.

## 6. The Implications of Subject Creation

1. The relationship and important differences between labeling theory in criminology and subject creation theory are complex and clearly be-

yond the scope of this book. For present purposes, it is enough to note that subject creation theory, in contrast to labeling theory, does not necessarily suggest that the category of the disorderly creates more disorderly behavior on the part of the disorderly persons. (Cf. Becker 1963:34: "Treating a person as though he were generally rather than specifically deviant produces a self-fulfilling prophecy. It sets in motion several mechanisms which conspire to shape the person in the image people have of him.") The focus of my deployment of subject creation theory here is instead on the apparatuses of punishment and discipline that naturally flow from the category of the disorderly. For a classic expression of labeling theory, see Becker 1963:31–35 and the essays in Becker 1964.

2. More than one allegation of misconduct may be contained in any one complaint filed with the CCRB. Therefore, both numbers are generally reported and analyzed. The CCRB, however, has expressed concern that the allegation figure may not be reliable and may change from one year to another as different definitions of allegations and ways of counting them are employed (CCRB 2000:21).

3. The CCRB contends that it is "difficult to draw valid conclusions from [these] data" because in each of the previous five years, anywhere from 19 to 32 percent of the complainants were categorized as "ethnicity unknown" (CCRB 2000:24).

4. The 1999 figure for police officers was obtained from CCRB 2000:21. The 1999 figure is an average for the year. The rest of the police officer figures were obtained from the yearly Uniform Crime Reports. Those figures represent the total number of police officers on October 31 of each respective year. See Uniform Crime Reports 1993–1998. The complaint and allegation numbers were obtained from Jackson 1998; CCRB 2000.

5. The arrest data for 1999 are preliminary. All arrest data are from Criminal Justice Indicators, New York City.

6. The arrest data are from U.S. Department of Justice 1996:386, table 4.12 (listing racial breakdown of arrests in all cities, including cities with fewer than 10,000 inhabitants; *see* appendix 3 at 595). I used the more conservative numbers of total arrests rather than the numbers for arrests of persons eighteen and older. It appears that adult misdemeanor arrests are even more skewed against blacks. The racial breakdown of the population for large cities is from the 1990 Census (U.S. Department of Commerce 1990:7, table 5, listing racial breakdown inside metropolitan areas, defined as including urbanized areas with a minimum population of 50,000; see A–8).

7. NYPD officers are required to fill out a UF-250 if they stop a person and (1) they use force, (2) they frisk the person, (3) they arrest the person, or (4) the person who was stopped refused to identify himself. UF-250s filled out in these situations are called "mandated reports." Police officers may also fill out a UF-250 form for any other stop. Of the 175,000 UF-250s in the data set, about three-quarters were mandated reports. Although Spitzer discovered that police officers do not fill out UF-250s in all mandated stops, the data were tested and were determined to represent a statistically reliable picture of the occurrence and type of stops conducted in New York City (Spitzer 1999:89–92). More recently a preliminary report by the CCRB determined that police officers routinely fail to fill out mandated UF-250s. In about half the cases investigated, the CCRB staff found that officers had not filed the written report (Rashbaum 2000:B1). This fact may affect the reliability of Spitzer's findings.

8. As a result of civil rights litigation against New York City, persons arrested for misdemeanor offenses are no longer being strip-searched (Flynn 1999).

### 7. The Turn to Harm as Justification

1. The harm principle, of course, traces back to early liberal thought. Thomas Hobbes, for instance, defined civil laws as "hedges" intended to protect citizens from the harmful consequences of the actions of others. As Hobbes explained, "the use of Lawes, (which are but Rules Authorised) is not to bind the People from all Voluntary actions; but to direct and keep them in such a motion, as not to hurt themselves by their own impetuous desires, rashnesse, or indiscretion; as Hedges are set, not to stop Travellers, but to keep them in the way" (Hobbes 1996:239–240). And John Locke borrowed the same image of hedges to describe laws (Locke 1988:305: law "hedges us in . . . from Bogs and Precipices"). Locke too defined liberty in terms of freedom from harm: "For *Liberty* is to be free from restraint and violence from others which cannot be, where there is no Law" (1996:306; Laslett 1996:112). These early definitions reflected "the simple liberal principle that people should be able to live their lives as they choose without interference from others so long as they are not preventing others from doing the same" (Young 1997:9). For present purposes, though, it makes sense to start with Mill.

2. Hart qualified his endorsement insofar as he supplemented the harm principle with an offense principle. It is not clear, however, that Mill

would have disagreed with Hart, since the Millian notion of other-regarding conduct seems to embrace both the harm principle and the offense principle.

3. Feinberg also supplemented the harm principle with an offense principle. See Feinberg 1975:297; see also Feinberg 1985:49.

4. The Model Penal Code was a proposed model of legislation drafted by the American Law Institute. It significantly influenced state legislation insofar as it was implemented or significantly influenced the enactment of new criminal codes in approximately thirty-four states during the 1960s, 1970s, and 1980s. See Model Penal Code, Official Draft and Explanatory Notes 1985:xi.

5. See Ala. Code §13A–1–3(1) (1994); Alaska Stat. §11.81.100(1) (1998); Del. Code Ann. tit. 11, §201(1) (1995); Fla. Stat. Ann. §775.012(1) (West 1992); Ga. Code Ann. §26–102(1) (1998); Neb. Rev. Stat. §28–102(1) (1998); N.J. Stat. Ann. §2C:1–2(a)(1) (West 1998); N.Y. Penal Law §1.05(1) (McKinney 1998); Or. Rev. Stat. §161.025(1)(b) (1992); 18 Pa. Cons. Stat. Ann. §104(1) (West 1998); Tenn. Code Ann. §39–11–101(1) (1997); Tex. Penal Code Ann. §1.02 (West 1994); Wash. Rev. Code Ann. §9A.04.020(1)(a) (West 1998).

6. *Hudnut,* 771 F.2d at 329 (citing Indianapolis, Ind., Code §16–1[a][2] [1984]). To be sure, in the margin Easterbrook couched these observations as a judicial acceptance of legislative findings: "In saying that we accept the finding that pornography as the ordinance defines it leads to unhappy consequences, we mean only that there is evidence to this effect, that this evidence is consistent with much human experience, and that as judges we must accept the legislative resolution of such disputed empirical questions" (*Hudnut* n.2). Nevertheless, his very comment ("that this evidence is consistent with much human experience"), as well as his lengthy discussion, in which he equates pornography with Nazism, communism, and sedition, reflect his acceptance of MacKinnon's harm argument.

7. "Illocutionary" describes speech acts that, in the very expression, produce effects. The conventional examples are the judge saying "I sentence you" or the groom saying "I do." In each case, the speech is simultaneously an act, a doing. "Perlocutionary" describes speech acts that may trigger consequences, but do not do so at the very moment of speaking. In perlocutionary acts there is a temporal space between the saying and the consequences.

8. To be sure, legal moralist arguments have not always trumped harm principle arguments. In several important cases the harm principle has been used to protect the interests of gay men and lesbians (*Baehr*

1997:18; *Powell* 1988:26). More important, in the decision of *Romer v. Evans*, 517 U.S. 620 (1996), the United States Supreme Court took a different approach than it had in *Hardwick*. In *Evans*, the Court can be interpreted as having relied on a harm principle; and it is possible—in fact, probable—that the logic of *Evans* will eventually prevail over the reasoning of *Hardwick* (Massaro 2000). But the legal moralism argument had been accepted in *Hardwick*, and thus, within the framework here, it is fair to say that legal moralism still appeared to be a viable argument in the late 1980s. In contrast to the other categories of conduct discussed previously, the legal moralism argument had not been disabled by the harm principle in the debate over the legal regulation of homosexual conduct.

## IV. Rethinking Punishment and Criminal Justice

1. At this general level, Sampson and Raudenbush's study resonates well with Tracey Meares's emphasis on social disorganization as a mechanism of social norms (Meares 1998a and 1998b). Sampson and Raudenbush nevertheless distinguish their theoretical structure from the social disorganization theory of Clifford Shaw and Henry McKay, which Meares relies on. As Sampson and Raudenbush explain, their theory "diverges from a concern with the production of offenders" in the classic model. "In the modern urban system, residents traverse the boundaries of multiple neighborhoods during the course of a day, a problematic scenario for neighborhood theories seeking to explain contextual effects on individual differences in offending." Their approach, in contrast, is focused more on "how neighborhoods fare as units of control or guardianship over their own public spaces—regardless of where offenders may reside." In their work, "the unit of analysis is thus the neighborhood, and our phenomenon of interest is the physical and social disorder within its purview" (1999:613–614). Despite the theoretical differences, though, Sampson and Raudenbush's findings do support Meares's emphasis on social organization, which suggests that Meares's work may be the more fruitful avenue within the order-maintenance approach.

# Bibliography

**Books, Reports, Journals, and Communications**

Alschuler, Albert W., and Stephen J. Schulhofer. 1998. "Antiquated Procedures or Bedrock Rights? A Response to Professors Meares and Kahan." *University of Chicago Legal Forum*, 1998: 215–244.

Amnesty International. 1996. "United States of America: Police Brutality and Excessive Force in the New York City Police Department." AI Index AMR 51/36/96 June.

Balkin, J. M. 1991. "The Promise of Legal Semiotics." *Texas Law Review*, 69: 1831–52.

——— 1993. "Ideological Drift and the Struggle over Meaning." *Connecticut Law Review*, 25: 869–891.

Balsdon, Sam. 1996. "Improving the Management of Juvenile Informants." Policing and Reducing Crime, Home Office, Research, Development and Statistics Directorate. Unpublished manuscript.

Banfield, Edward C. 1958. *The Moral Basis of a Backward Society*. New York: Free Press.

——— 1974. *The Unheavenly City Revisited*. Boston: Little, Brown.

——— 1991. *Here the People Rule: Selected Essays*, 2d ed. Washington, D.C.: American Enterprise Institute.

Banfield, Edward C., and James Q. Wilson. 1963. *City Politics*. Cambridge, Mass.: Harvard University Press.

Baxter, Hugh. 1996. "Bringing Foucault into Law and Law into Foucault." *Stanford Law Review*, 48: 449–479.

Beaumont, Jeff A. 1998. "Nunez and Beyond: An Examination of Nunez v.

City of San Diego and the Future of Nocturnal Juvenile Curfew Ordinances." *Journal of Juvenile Law,* 19: 84–122.

Becker, Howard S. 1963. *Outsiders: Studies in the Sociology of Deviance.* New York: Free Press.

———, ed. 1964. *The Other Side.* New York: Free Press.

Becker, Lawrence. 1999. "Crimes against Autonomy: Gerald Dworkin on the Enforcement of Morality." *William and Mary Law Review,* 40: 959–973.

Beckett, Katherine. 1997. *Making Crime Pay: Law and Order in Contemporary American Politics.* New York: Oxford University Press.

Benhabib, Seyla. 1995. "Feminism and Postmodernism: An Uneasy Alliance." In *Feminist Contentions: A Philosophical Exchange,* ed. Seyla Benhabib et al., 17–34. New York: Routledge.

Berger, Fred R. 1984. *Happiness, Justice, and Freedom: The Moral and Political Philosophy of John Stuart Mill.* Berkeley: University of California Press.

Blumer, Herbert. 1969. *Symbolic Interactionism: Perspective and Method.* Berkeley: University of California Press.

Blumstein, Alfred. 1995. "Youth Violence, Guns, and the Illicit-Drug Industry." *Journal of Criminal Law and Criminology,* 86: 10–36.

Blumstein, Alfred, and Daniel Cork. 1996. "Linking Gun Availability to Youth Gun Violence." *Law and Contemporary Problems,* 59: 5–19.

Blumstein, Alfred, and Richard Rosenfeld. 1998. "Explaining Recent Trends in U.S. Homicide Rates." *Journal of Criminal Law and Criminology,* 88: 1175–1216.

*Boston Review.* 1999. "Do Rights Handcuff Democracy?" 24(2): 4–23.

Bourdieu, Pierre. 1977. *Outline of a Theory of Practice.* Cambridge: Cambridge University Press.

——— 1990. *In Other Words: Essays Towards a Reflexive Sociology.* Stanford: Stanford University Press.

Bourdieu, Pierre, and Loïc J. D. Wacquant. 1992. *An Invitation to Reflexive Sociology.* Chicago: University of Chicago Press.

Boydstun, John E. 1975. *San Diego Field Interrogation Evaluation: Final Report.* Washington, D.C.: Police Foundation.

Braithwaite, John. 1989. *Crime, Shame, and Reintegration.* Cambridge: Cambridge University Press.

Bratton, William J. 1995. "The New York City Police Department's Civil Enforcement of Quality-of-Life Crimes." *Journal of Law and Policy,* 3: 447–464.

——— 1996. "New Strategies for Combating Crime in New York City." *Fordham Urban Law Journal,* 23: 781–795.

——— (with Peter Knobler) 1998. *Turnaround: How America's Top Cop Reversed the Crime Epidemic.* New York: Random House.

Brown, Wendy. 1995. *States of Injury: Power and Freedom in Late Modernity.* Princeton, N.J.: Princeton University Press.

Buchanan, Allen E. 1989. "Assessing the Communitarian Critique of Liberalism." *Ethics,* 99: 852–882.

Burchell, Graham, Colin Gordon, and Peter Miller, eds. 1991. *The Foucault Effect: Studies in Governmentality.* Hemel Hempstead: Harvester Wheatsheaf.

Burnham, Margaret A. 1999. "Twice Victimized," *Boston Review,* 24(2): 16–17.

Butler, Judith. 1995. "Contingent Foundations: Feminism and the Question of 'Postmodernism.'" In *Feminist Contentions: A Philosophical Exchange,* ed. Seyla Benhabib et al., 35–57. New York: Routledge.

———— 1997. *Excitable Speech: A Politics of the Performative.* New York: Routledge.

Caplow, Theodore, and Jonathan Simon. 1998. "The Incarceration Mania: A Preliminary Diagnosis." Paper presented at the 1998 New England Political Science Association Annual Meeting, Worcester, Mass., May 2.

Civilian Complaint Review Board (CCRB). 2000. *Semiannual Status Report: January–December 1999,* vol. 7, no. 2 (March).

Clark, Charles. 1993. "Prostitution," *CQ Researcher,* June 11: 514.

Clarke, Ronald. 1995. "Situational Crime Prevention." In *Building a Safer Society: Strategic Approaches to Crime Prevention,* ed. Michael H. Tonry and David P. Farrington, 91–150. Chicago: University of Chicago Press.

Cole, David. 1999. "Foreword: Discretion and Discrimination Reconsidered: A Response to the New Criminal Justice Scholarship." *Georgetown Law Journal,* 87: 1059–93.

Community Policing Consortium. 2000. "Understanding Community Policing: A Framework for Action." In *Community Policing: Classical Readings,* ed. Willard M. Oliver. Upper Saddle River, N.J.: Prentice Hall.

"Could California Reduce AIDS by Making Nevada Prostitution Law?" 1994. *San Diego Justice Journal,* 2: 491–506.

Curtis, Richard. 1998. "The Improbable Transformation of Inner City Neighborhoods: Crime, Violence, Drugs, and Use in the 1990s." *Journal of Criminal Law and Criminology,* 88: 1233–70.

Decker, Scott, and Carol Kohfeld. 1985. "Crimes, Crime Rates, Arrests, and Arrest Ratios: Implications for Deterrence Theory," *Criminology,* 23: 437–450.

Dershowitz, Alan M. 1999. "Rights and Interests." *Boston Review,* 24(2): 10.

Devlin, Patrick. 1977. "Morals and the Criminal Law." In *The Enforcement of Morals.* London: Oxford University Press.

Dixon, David. 1999. "Beyond Zero Tolerance." Paper presented at Third Annual Outlook Symposium on Crime in Australia, March, 22–23.

Dodenhoff, Peter. 1996. "Law Enforcement News Salutes Its 1996 People of the Year, the NYPD and Its Compstat Process," *Law Enforcement News*, December 31: 1, 4.

Doe Fund. 2000. "The Doe Fund, Inc." <http://www.doe.org>.

Dolinko, David. 1999. "The Future of Punishment." *UCLA Law Review*, 46: 1719–26.

Donner, Wendy. 1991. *The Liberal Self: John Stuart Mill's Moral and Political Philosophy*. Ithaca, N.Y.: Cornell University Press.

Dressler, Joshua. 1995. "When 'Heterosexual' Men Kill 'Homosexual' Men: Reflections on Provocation Law, Sexual Advances, and the 'Reasonable Man' Standard." *Journal of Criminal Law and Criminology*, 85: 725–763.

Drexler, Jessica N. 1996. "Government's Role in Turning Tricks: The World's Oldest Profession in the Netherlands and the United States." *Dickinson Journal of International Law*, 15: 201–236.

Durkheim, Emile. 1901. "Deux lois de l'évolution pénale," *L'Année Sociologique* 1899–1900.

—— 1984. *On the Division of Labor in Society*. New York: Free Press.

—— 1995. *The Elementary Forms of Religious Life*. New York: Free Press.

—— 1996. *De la division du travail social*, 4th ed. Paris: Presses Universitaires de France.

Dworkin, Gerald. 1999. "Devlin Was Right: Law and the Enforcement of Morality." *William and Mary Law Review*, 40: 927–946.

Dworkin, Ronald. 1966. "Lord Devlin and the Enforcement of Morals." *Yale Law Journal*, 75: 986–504.

—— 1989. "Liberal Community." *California Law Review*, 77: 479–504.

Eig, Jonathan. 1996. "Eyes on the Street: Community Policing in Chicago." *American Prospect*, 29 (November–December): 60–68.

Ellickson, Robert C. 1991. *Order without Law: How Neighbors Settle Disputes*. Cambridge, Mass.: Harvard University Press.

—— 1996. "Controlling Chronic Misconduct in City Spaces: Of Panhandlers, Skid Rows, and Public-Space Zoning." *Yale Law Journal*, 105: 1165–1248.

—— 1998. "Law and Economics Discovers Social Norms." *Journal of Legal Studies*, 27: 537–552.

Elshtain, Jean Bethke. 1999. "Getting It Right." *Boston Review*, 24(2): 11

Elster, Jon. 1989. *The Cement of Society: A Study of Social Order*. Cambridge: Cambridge University Press.

Eskridge, Jr., William N. 1999. *Gaylaw: Challenging the Apartheid of the Closet*. Cambridge, Mass.: Harvard University Press.

Fagan, Jeffrey. 1999. "Social Contagion of Violence." Paper presented at the Fortunoff Colloquium Series, Center for Research on Crime and Justice, New York University Law School, New York, April 19.

Fagan, Jeffrey, and Deanna Wilkinson. 1998. "Guns, Youth Violence, and Social Identity in Inner Cities." In *Crime and Justice: A Review of Research,* no. 24, ed. Michael Tonry et al., 105–188. Chicago: University of Chicago Press.

——— 2000. *Situational Contexts of Gun Use by Young Males: Final Report, January 2000.* Report submitted to National Science Foundation, National Institute of Justice, and U.S. Department of Health and Human Services.

Fagan, Jeffrey, Franklin Zimring, and June Kim. 1998. "Declining Homicide in New York City: A Tale of Two Trends." *Journal of Criminal Law and Criminology,* 88: 1277–1323.

Farge, Arlette, and Michel Foucault. 1982. *Le désordre des familles: lettres de cachet des Archives de la Bastille au XVIIIe siècle.* Paris: Gallimard.

Farrell, Michael J. 1998a. Personal correspondence, April 10.

——— 1998b. Letter to Jenna Karabdil, April 13.

Feinberg, Joel. 1975. "Moral Enforcement and the Harm Principle." In *Ethics and Public Policy,* ed. Tom L. Beauchamp, 283–296. Englewood Cliffs, N.J.: Prentice-Hall.

——— 1984. *The Moral Limits of the Criminal Law: Harm to Others.* New York: Oxford University Press.

——— 1985. *The Moral Limits of the Criminal Law: Offense to Others.* New York: Oxford University Press.

——— 1988. *The Moral Limits of the Criminal Law: Harmless Wrongdoing.* New York: Oxford University Press.

Fielding, Nigel. 1995. *Community Policing.* Oxford: Clarendon Press.

"For One NYC Captain, Crime Reductions Are a Numbers Racket." 1996. *Law Enforcement News,* December 15:9.

Foucault, Michel. 1966. *Les mots et les choses.* Paris: Gallimard.

——— 1970. *The Order of Things.* Trans. R. D. Laing. New York: Vintage Books

——— 1975. *Surveiller et punir.* Paris: Gallimard.

——— 1979. *Discipline and Punish.* Trans. Alan Sheridan. New York: Vintage Books.

——— 1980. "Two Lectures." In *Power/Knowledge: Selected Interviews and Other Writings, 1972–1977,* ed. Colin Gordon. Brighton, Sussex: Harvester Press.

——— 1983. "The Subject and Power." In *Michel Foucault: Beyond Structuralism and Hermeneutics,* ed. Herbert L. Dreyfus and Paul Rabinow. Chicago: University of Chicago Press.

Fox, James Alan. 1999. *Uniform Crime Reports [United States]: Supplementary Homicide Reports,* 1976–1994 (ICPSR 6754).

Fraser, Nancy. 1997. *Justice Interruptus: Critical Reflections on the "Postsocialist" Condition.* New York: Routledge.

Galanter, Marc, and Mark Alan Edwards. 1997. "Introduction: The Path of the Law *Ands.*" *Wisconsin Law Review,* 1997: 375–387.

Garland, David. 1983. "Durkeim's Theory of Punishment: A Critique." In *The Power to Punish,* ed. David Garland and Peter Young, 37–61. London: Heinemann Educational Books.

———— 1990. *Punishment and Modern Society.* Chicago: University of Chicago Press.

———— 1996. "The Limits of the Sovereign State: Strategies of Crime Control in Contemporary Society." *British Journal of Criminology,* 36(4): 445–471.

————. 2001. *The Culture of Control: Crime and Social Order in Contemporary Society.* Chicago: University of Chicago Press.

Garvey, Stephen P. 1998. "Can Shaming Punishments Educate?" *University of Chicago Law Review,* 65: 733–794.

Gaubatz, Kathlyn Taylor. 1995. *Crime in the Public Mind.* Ann Arbor: University of Michigan Press.

Geertz, Clifford. 1972. "Deep Play: Notes on the Balinese Cockfight." *Daedalus,* 101: 1–37.

———— 1973. *The Interpretation of Cultures: Selected Essays.* New York: Basic Books.

———— 1995. *After the Fact: Two Countries, Four Decades, One Anthropologist.* Cambridge, Mass.: Harvard University Press.

George, Robert P. 1990. "Social Cohesion and the Legal Enforcement of Morals: A Reconsideration of the Hart-Devlin Debate." *American Journal of Jurisprudence,* 35: 15–46.

———— 1993. *Making Men Moral.* Oxford: Oxford University Press.

Giuliani, Rudolph W. 1998. "The Next Phase of Quality of Life: Creating a More Civil City." <http://www.ci.nyc.ny.us/html/om/html/98a/quality.html>.

———— 1999. "An Agenda to Prepare for the Next Century: 1999 State of the City Address." <http://www.ci.nyc.ny.us/html/om/html/99a/stcitytext.html>.

Giuliani, Rudolph W., and William J. Bratton. 1994a. *Police Strategy No. 1: Getting Guns off the Streets of New York.* New York: City of New York Police Department.

———— 1994b. *Police Strategy No. 2: Curbing Youth Violence In the Schools and on the Streets.* New York: City of New York Police Department.

———— 1994c. *Police Strategy No. 3: Driving Drug Dealers out of New York.* New York: City of New York Police Department.

———— 1994d. *Police Strategy No. 4: Breaking the Cycle of Domestic Violence.* New York: City of New York Police Department.

———— 1994e. *Police Strategy No. 5: Reclaiming the Public Spaces of New York.* New York: City of New York Police Department.

———— 1994f. *Police Strategy No. 6: Reducing Auto-Related Crime in New York.* New York: City of New York Police Department.

Goldstein, Paul J., Henry H. Brownstein, Patrick J. Ryan, and Patricia A. Bellucci. 1989. "Crack and Homicide in New York City, 1988: A Conceptually Based Event Analysis." *Contemporary Drug Problems,* 16 (Winter): 651–687.

Golstein, Anne B. 1988. "History, Homosexuality, and Political Values: Searching for the Hidden Determinants of *Bowers v. Hardwick.*" *Yale Law Journal,* 97: 1073–1103.

Gottfredson, Michael R., and Travis Hirschi. 1990. *A General Theory of Crime.* Stanford: Stanford University Press.

Gove, Walter R., Michael Hughes, and Michael Geerken. 1985. "Are Uniform Crime Reports a Valid Indicator of the Index Crimes? An Affirmative Answer with Minor Qualifications." *Criminology,* 23(3): 451–501.

Greene, Judith A. 1999. "Zero-Tolerance: A Case Study of Police Policies and Practices in New York City." *Crime and Delinquency,* 45(2): 171–187.

Greenawalt, Kent. 1995. "Legal Enforcement of Morality." *Journal of Criminal Law and Criminology* 85: 710–725.

Grey, Thomas C. 1983. *The Legal Enforcement of Morality.* New York: Knopf.

Habermas, Jürgen. 1984. "The New Obscurity and the Exhaustion of Utopian Energies." In *Observations on the Spiritual Situation of the Age,* ed. Jürgen Habermas, 1–30. Cambridge, Mass.: MIT Press.

Hacking, Ian. 1999. *The Social Construction of What?* Cambridge, Mass.: Harvard University Press.

Harcourt, Bernard E. 1998. "Reflecting on the Subject: A Critique of the Social Influence Conception of Deterrence, the Broken Windows Theory, and Order-Maintenance Policing New York Style." *Michigan Law Review,* 97: 291–389.

———— 1999a. "Matrioshka Dolls." *Boston Review,* 24(2): 19–20.

———— 1999b. "The Collapse of the Harm Principle." *Journal of Criminal Law and Criminology,* 90: 109–194.

———— 2000. "After the 'Social Meaning Turn': Implications for Research Design and Methods of Proof in Contemporary Criminal Law Policy Analysis." *Law and Society Review* 34(1):179–211.

Hart, H. L. A. 1959. "Immorality and Treason" *Listener,* 62: 162–163.

——— 1963. *Law, Liberty, and Morality.* Stanford: Stanford University Press.

Henkin, Louis. 1963. "Morals and the Constitution: The Sin of Obscenity." *Columbia Law Review,* 63: 391–414.

Hittinger, Russell. 1990. "The Hart-Devlin Debate Revisited." *American Journal of Jurisprudence,* 35: 47–53.

Hobbes, Thomas. 1996. *Leviathan.* Ed. Richard Tuck. Cambridge: Cambridge University Press.

Honig, Bonnie. 1993. *Political Theory and Displacement of Politics.* Ithaca, N.Y.: Cornell University Press.

Honneth, Axel. 1995. *The Struggle for Recognition: The Moral Grammar of Social Conflicts.* Trans. Joel Anderson. Cambridge: Polity Press.

Huber, Steve. 1999. Interview, November 16.

Human Rights Watch. 1998. *Shielded from Justice: Police Brutality and Accountability in the United States.* New York: Human Rights Watch.

Hunt, Alan, and Gary Wickham. 1994. *Foucault and Law: Towards a Sociology of Law as Governance.* London: Pluto Press.

Jackson, Sherman. 1998. Personal communication, June 17.

Jacob, Herbert, and Michael J. Rich. 1981. "The Effects of the Police on Crime: A Second Look." *Law and Society Review,* 15: 109–122.

Joanes, Ana. 1999. "Does the New York City Police Department Deserve Credit for the Decline in New York City's Homicide Rates? A Cross-City Comparison of Policing Strategies and Homicide Rates." *Columbia Journal of Law and Social Problems,* 33: 265–318.

Kadish, Sanford H., and Stephen J. Schulhofer. 1995. *Criminal Law and Its Processes,* 6th ed. Boston: Little, Brown.

Kahan, Dan M. 1996. "What Do Alternative Sanctions Mean?" *University of Chicago Law Review,* 63: 591–653.

——— 1997a. "Social Influence, Social Meaning, and Deterrence," *Virginia Law Review,* 83: 349–395.

——— 1997b. "Between Economics and Sociology: The New Path of Deterrence." *Michigan Law Review,* 95: 2477–97.

——— 1998. "Social Meaning and the Economic Analysis of Crime." *Journal of Legal Studies,* 27: 609–622.

——— 1999a. "Privatizing Criminal Law: Strategies for Private Norm Enforcement in the Inner City." *UCLA Law Review,* 46: 1859–72.

——— 1999b. "The Secret Ambition of Deterrence." *Harvard Law Review,* 113: 413–500.

Kahan, Dan M., and Tracey L. Meares. 1998a. "Foreword: The Coming Crisis of Criminal Procedure." *Georgetown Law Journal,* 86: 1153–84.

———— 1998b. "Law and (Norms of) Order in the Inner City." *Law and Society Review,* 32: 805–838.

———— 1999a. "When Rights Are Wrong." *Boston Review,* 24(2): 4–8, and "Meares and Kahan Respond," *Boston Review,* 24(2): 22–23.

Kahan, Dan M., and Martha C. Nussbaum. 1996. "Two Conceptions of Emotion in Criminal Law." *Columbia Law Review,* 96: 269–374.

Kaplan, John. 1970. *Marijuana: The New Prohibition.* New York: World Publishing.

Katyal, Neal Kumar. 1997. "Deterrence's Difficulty." *University of Michigan Law Review,* 95:2385–2476.

Kelling, George, and Catherine M. Coles. 1996. *Fixing Broken Windows: Restoring Order and Reducing Crime in Our Communities.* New York: Free Press.

Kennedy, David M. 1997. "Juvenile Gun Violence and Gun Markets in Boston." NIJ Research Preview, March.

———— 1998. "Pulling Levers: Getting Deterrence Right." *National Institute of Justice Journal,* 236 (July): 2–8.

Kennedy, Duncan. 1989. "A Semiotics of Legal Argument." In *Law and Semiotics,* vol. 3, ed. Roberta Kevelson, 167–192. New York: Plenum Press.

———— 1991. "A Semiotics of Legal Argument." *Syracuse Law Review,* 42: 75–116.

———— 1993. "Sexual Abuse, Sexy Dressing, and the Eroticization of Domination." In Duncan Kennedy, *Sexy Dressing Etc.* Cambridge, Mass.: Harvard University Press.

———— 1997. *A Critique of Adjudication.* Cambridge, Mass.: Harvard University Press.

King, Gary, Robert O. Keohane, and Sidney Verba. 1994. *Designing Social Inquiry: Scientific Inference in Qualitative Research.* Princeton, N.J.: Princeton University Press.

———— 1995. "The Importance of Research Design in Political Science." *American Political Science Review,* 89(2): 475–481.

Kuhn, Thomas S. 1996. *The Structure of Scientific Revolutions,* 3d ed. Chicago: University of Chicago Press.

LaFree, Gary, and Christopher Birkbeck. 1998. "Working Paper No. 27: Controlling New Mexico Juveniles' Possession of Firearms." New Mexico Criminal Justice Statistical Analysis Center, University of New Mexico Institute for Social Research. Unpublished manuscript.

Laslett, Peter. 1996. Introduction to *Two Treatises of Government,* ed. Peter Laslett, 3–152. Cambridge: Cambridge University Press.

Lessig, Lawerence. 1995. "The Regulation of Social Meaning." *University of Chicago Law Review,* 62: 943–1045.

—— 1996. "Social Meaning and Social Norms." *University of Pennsylvania Law Review,* 144: 2181–89.

—— 1998. "The New Chicago School." *Journal of Legal Studies,* 27: 661–691.

Livingston, Debra. 1997. "Police Discretion and Quality of Life in Public Places: Courts, Communities, and the New Policing." *Columbia Law Review,* 97: 551–672.

Locke, John. 1988. *Two Treatises of Government.* Ed. Peter Laslett. Cambridge: Cambridge University Press.

Lukes, Steven, and Andrew Scull. 1983. Introduction to *Durkeim and the Law,* ed. Steven Lukes and Andrew Scull, 1–27. New York: St. Martin's Press.

MacKinnon, Catharine A. 1985. "Pornography, Civil Rights, and Speech." *Harvard Civil Rights–Civil Liberties Review,* 20: 1–70.

—— 1989. *Toward a Feminist Theory of the State.* Cambridge, Mass.: Harvard University Press.

—— 1993. *Only Words.* Cambridge, Mass.: Harvard University Press.

Massaro, Toni M. 1990. "Shame, Culture, and American Criminal Law." *Michigan Law Review,* 89: 1880–1944.

—— 1996. "Gay Rights, Thick and Thin." *Stanford Law Review,* 49: 45–110.

—— 1997. "The Meanings of Shame: Implications for Legal Reform." *Psychology, Public Policy, and Law,* 3(4): 645–704.

—— 1998. "The Gang's Not Here." *The Green Bag,* 2: 25–34.

—— 1999. "Show (Some) Emotions." In *The Passions of Law,* ed. Susan Bandes, 80–120. New York: New York University Press.

—— 2000. "History Unbecoming, Becoming History." *Michigan Law Review,* 98: 1564–89.

McCaffrey, Barry R. 1999. "The Drug Legalization Movement in America." Hearings before the Subcommittee on Criminal Justice, Drug Policy, and Human Resources of the Government Reform and Oversight Committee, U.S. House of Representatives.

McEwen, Todd. 1995. "National Assessment Program: 1994 Survey Results." *Research in Brief,* National Institute of Justice (May).

Meares, Tracey L. 1997. "It's a Question of Connections." *Valparaiso University Law Review,* 31: 579–596.

—— 1998a. "Social Organization and Drug Law Enforcement." *American Criminal Law Review,* 35: 191–227.

—— 1998b. "Place and Crime." *Chicago-Kent Law Review,* 73: 669–705.

Mill, John Stuart. 1978. *On Liberty.* Ed. Elizabeth Rapaport. Indianapolis: Hackett Publishing Co.

Miller, Eleanor M., Kim Romenesko, and Lisa Wondolkowski. 1993. "United States." In *Prostitution: An International Handbook on Trends, Problems, and Policies,* ed. Nanette J. Davis. Westport Conn.: Greenwood Press.

Mison, Robert B. 1992. "Homophobia in Manslaughter: The Homosexual Advance as Insufficient Provocation." *California Law Review,* 80: 133–178.

Model Penal Code, Official Draft and Explanatory Notes (MPCOD). 1985. Complete text of Model Penal Code as adopted at the 1962 Annual Meeting of the American Law Institute, Washington, D.C., May 24, 1962.

Model Penal Code and Commentaries (MPCC). 1985. Pt. 1, vol. 1.

Moore, Mark H., Robert C. Trojanowicz, and George Kelling. 2000. "Crime and Policing." In *Community Policing: Classical Readings,* ed. W. M. Oliver. Upper Saddle River, N.J.: Prentice Hall.

Morse, Stephen J. 2000. "Comment on Harcourt, 'Beyond the "Social Meaning Turn."'" Paper presented at the Stanford/Yale Junior Faculty Forum, Yale Law School, New Haven, May 12.

Mrela, Christopher K. 1993. *Firearm-Related Fatalities, Arizona, 1991.* Phoenix: Office of Planning, Evaluation and Public Health Statistics, Arizona Department of Health Services.

———— 1999. *Firearm-Related Fatalities, Arizona, 1987–97.* Phoenix: Office of Planning, Evaluation and Public Health Statistics, Arizona Department of Health Services.

Murphy, Jeffrie G. 1995. "Legal Moralism and Liberalism." *Arizona Law Review,* 37: 73–93.

———— 1999. "Moral Reasons and the Limitation of Liberty." *William and Mary Law Review,* 40: 947–957.

Nadelmann, Ethan A. 1988. "The Case for Legalization." *Public Interest,* 92: 3–31.

———— 1992. "Thinking Seriously about Alternatives to Drug Prohibition." *Daedalus,* 121(3): 85–132.

National Crime Prevention Council. 1998. *Annual 1998 Report.* <http://www.ncpc.org.boston.html>.

Nelson, William E. 1993. "Criminality and Sexual Morality in New York, 1920–1980." *Yale Journal of Law and the Humanities,* 5: 265–341.

New York State, Division of Criminal Justice Services. 2000. *Criminal Justice Indicators.* <http://criminaljustice.state.ny.us/cgi/internet/areastat.cgi>.

Note. 1989. "Deadly and Dangerous Weapons and AIDS: The Moore Analysis Is Likely to Be Dangerous." *Iowa Law Review,* 74: 951–967.

NYCLU Report. 1997. "NYCLU Report: A Fourth Anniversary Overview of the Civilian Complaint Review Board, July 5, 1993–July 5, 1997." Sept. 14.

NYPD Response. 2000. "NYPD Response to the Draft Report of the United States Commission on Civil Rights—Police Practices and Civil Rights in New York City." <http://www.ci.nyc.ny.us/html/nypd/html/dclm/exsumm.html>.

Packer, Herbert. 1968. *The Limits of the Criminal Sanction*. Stanford: Stanford University Press.

Pastore, Ann. 1998. Telephone interview, June 15.

Pattillo, Mary E., and Reuben A. B. May. 1994. "Gun Talk: Culture and Social Control in an African-American Community." Center for the Study of Urban Inequality, Irving B. Harris Graduate School of Public Policy Studies, University of Chicago.

Paul, Jeremy. 1991. "The Politics of Legal Semiotics." *Texas Law Review,* 69: 1779–1829.

Paulsen, Monrad G., and Sanford H. Kadish. 1962. *Criminal Law and Its Processes,* 1st ed. Boston: Little, Brown.

Perkins, Rollin, and Ronald Boyce. 1982. *Criminal Law.* New York: Foundation Press.

Philliber Research Associates. 1998. "The Doe Fund, Inc.'s Ready, Willing, and Able Program Client Profile and Outcomes." *The Philliber Report,* September. <http://www.doe.org/phillib/html>.

Pildes, Richard. 1999. "The New Progressives." *Boston Review,* 24(2): 21–22.

Posner, Richard A. 1998a. "Social Norms, Social Meaning, and Economic Analysis of Law: A Comment." *Journal of Legal Studies,* 27: 553–565.

——— 1998b. "Emotion versus Emotionalism in Law." Paper delivered at the Conference on Emotions and the Law, University of Chicago, May 23.

Postema, Gerald J. 1987. "Collective Evils, Harms, and the Law." *Ethics,* 97: 414–440.

"Preliminary Annual Uniform Crime Report, 1999." 1999. <www.fbi.gov/ucr>.

Privor, Brian. 1999. "Dusk 'til Dawn: Children's Rights and the Effectiveness of Juvenile Curfew Ordinances." *Boston University Law Review,* 79: 415–492.

Rabinowitz, Clarice B. 1995. "Proposals for Progress: Sodomy Laws and the European Convention on Human Rights." *Brooklyn Journal of International Law,* 21: 425–469.

Reichardt, Charles S., and Sharon F. Rallis. 1994. "The Relationship between the Qualitative and Quantitative Research Traditions." In *The Qualitative-Quantitative Debate: New Perspectives,* ed. Charles S. Reichardt and Sharon F. Rallis, 5–11. New Directions for Program Evaluation, no. 61. San Francisco: Josey-Bass.

Rein, Martin, and Christopher Winship. 1999. "The Dangers of 'Strong' Causal Reasoning in Social Policy." *Society*, July–August: 38–46.

Reno, Janet. 2000. "Promising Strategies to Reduce Gun Violence." Publication of the Office of Juvenile Justice and Delinquency Prevention, U.S. Department of Justice. <http://www.ojjdp.ncjrs.org/pubs/gun_violence/contents.html>.

Richards, David A. J. 1979. "Commercial Sex and the Rights of the Person: A Moral Argument for the Decriminalization of Prostitution." *University of Pennsylvania Law Review*, 125: 1195–1287.

Riley, Jack. 1999. "1998 Annual Report on Drug Use Among Adult and Juvenile Arrestees." National Institute of Justice Arrestee Drug Abuse Monitoring Program.

Rio, Linda M. 1991. "Psychological and Sociological Research and the Decriminalization or Legalization of Prostitution." *Archives of Sexual Behavior*, 20: 205–218.

Roberts, Dorothy E. 1993. "Crime, Race, and Reproduction." *Tulane Law Review*, 67: 1945–77.

———— 1999. "Foreword: Race, Vagueness, and the Social Meaning of Order-Maintenance Policing." *Journal of Criminal Law and Criminology*, 89: 775–836.

Robinson, Paul. 1997. *Criminal Law*. New York: Aspen Publishers.

Rorty, Richard. 1979. *Philosophy and the Mirror of Nature*. Princeton, N.J.: Princeton University Press.

———— 1998. *Achieving Our Country*. Cambridge, Mass.: Harvard University Press.

Rose, Nikolas, and Peter Miller. 1992. "Political Power beyond the State: Problematics of Government." *British Journal of Sociology*, 43(2): 173–205.

Rosenfeld, Richard, and Scott H. Decker. 1996. "Consent to Search and Seize: Evaluating an Innovative Youth Firearm Suppression Program." *Law and Contemporary Problems*, 59: 197–220.

Roth, Jeffrey. 1998. "The Detroit Handgun Intervention Program: A Court-Based Program for Youthful Handgun Offenders," *NIJ Research Preview*, November.

Ryan, Alan. 1988. *The Philosophy of John Stuart Mill*, 2d ed. London: Macmillan.

Sampson, Robert J., and Jacqueline Cohen. 1988. "Deterrent Effect of the Police on Crime: A Replication and Theoretical Extension." *Law and Society Review*, 22: 163–189.

Sampson, Robert J., and Stephen W. Raudenbush. 1999. "Systematic Social Observation of Public Spaces: A New Look at Disorder in Urban Neighborhoods." *American Journal of Sociology*, 105(3): 603–651.

Sanchez, Lisa. 1997. "Boundaries of Legitimacy: Sex, Violence, Citizenship, and Community in Local Sexual Economy." *Law and Social Inquiry*, 22: 543–580 .

Sandel, Michael. 1989. "Moral Argument and Liberal Toleration: Abortion and Homosexuality." *California Law Review*, 77: 521–538.

Sartorius, Rolf E. 1972. "The Enforcement of Morality," *Yale Law Journal*, 81: 891–910.

Schechter, Marvin E. 1988. "AIDS: How the Disease Is Being Criminalized." *Criminal Justice*, 3 (Fall): 6–42.

Scheff, Thomas. 1990. "Review Essay: A New Durkheim." *American Journal of Sociology*, 96: 741–746.

Schneyer, Theodore J. 1971. "Problems in the Cost-Benefit Analysis of Marijuana Legislation." *Stanford Law Review*, 24: 200–216.

——— 1993. "Policymaking and the Perils of Professionalism: The ABA's Ancillary Business Debate as a Case Study." *Arizona Law Review*, 35: 363–396.

Schulhofer, Stephen J. 1984. "Is Plea Bargaining Inevitable?" *Harvard Law Review*, 97: 1037–1107.

——— 1986. "No Job Too Small: Justice without Bargaining in the Lower Criminal Courts." *American Bar Foundation Research Journal*, 1985: 519–598.

Schulhofer, Stephen J., and Albert W. Alschuler. 2000. "Getting the Facts Straight: Crime Trends, Community Support, and the Police Enforcement of 'Social Norms.'" *Law and Society Review* (in press).

Schwartz, Louis B. 1963. "Morals Offenses and the Model Penal Code." *Columbia Law Review*, 63: 669–686.

Seale, Clive. 1998. Introduction to *Researching Society and Culture*, ed. Clive Seale. London: Sage Publications.

Sherman, Jeffrey G. 1995. "Love Speech: The Social Utility of Pornography." *Stanford Law Review*, 47: 661–705.

Shusterman, Richard. 1999. *Bourdieu: A Critical Reader*. Oxford: Blackwell.

Silverman, Eli. 1996. "Mapping Change: How the New York City Police Department Re-engineered Itself to Drive Down Crime." *Law Enforcement News*, December 15: 10–12.

Skogan, Wesley G. 1981. "On Attitudes and Behaviors." In *Reactions to Crime*, ed. Dan A. Lewis, 19–46. Beverly Hills, Calif.: Sage Publishing.

——— 1987. *Disorder and Community Decline: Final Report to the National Institute of Justice*. Center for Urban Affairs and Policy Research, Northwestern University.

——— 1988. *Disorder and Community Decline in Forty Neighborhoods of the United States, 1977–1983*, Data and Codebook. Inter-University Consortium for

Political and Social Research (ICPSR no. 8944). Ann Arbor: University of Michigan.

———. 1990. *Disorder and Decline: Crime and the Spiral of Decay in American Neighborhoods.* New York: Oxford University Press.

———. 1994. "The Impact of Community Policing on Neighborhood Residents." In *The Challenge of Community Policing,* ed. Dennis P. Rosenbaun, 167–181. Thousand Oaks, Calif.: Sage Publications.

———. 1999. "Everybody's Business." *Boston Review,* 24(2): 15–16.

Skogan, Wesley, and Susan M. Hartnett. 1997. *Community Policing, Chicago Style.* New York: Oxford University Press.

Skogan, Wesley, and Michael Maxfield. 1981. *Coping with Crime: Individual and Neighborhood Reactions.* Beverly Hills, Calif.: Sage Publishing.

Spitzer, Eliot. 1999. *The New York City Police Department's "Stop and Frisk" Practices: A Report to the People of the State of New York from the Office of the Attorney General.* New York: Office of the Attorney General of the State of New York, Civil Rights Bureau. <http://www.oag.state.ny.us/press/reports/stop_frisk/stop_frisk.html>.

*Statistical Abstract of the United States, 1988.* 1988. 108th ed. United States Department of Commerce, Bureau of the Census, Washington, D.C.: Government Printing Office.

Steiker, Carol. 1997. "Punishment and Procedure: Punishment Theory and the Criminal-Civil Procedural Divide." *Georgetown Law Journal,* 85: 775–819.

———. 1999. "More Wrong than Rights." *Boston Review,* 24(2): 13–14.

Steiker, Carol, and Jordan Steiker. 1995. "Sober Second Thoughts: Reflection on Two Decades of Constitutional Regulation of Capital Punishment." *Harvard Law Review,* 109: 355–438.

Stephen, James Fitzjames. 1973. *Liberty, Equality, Fraternity.* Cambridge: Cambridge University Press.

Sterk-Elifson, Claire, and Carole A. Campbell. 1993. "The Netherlands." In *International Perspectives on Female Prostitution,* ed. Nanette J. Davis, Westport, Conn.: Greenwood Press.

Stewart, Gary. 1998. Note: "Black Codes and Broken Windows: The Legacy of Racial Hegemony in Anti-Gang Civil Injunctions." *Yale Law Journal,* 107: 2249–79.

Stout, James R., and Thomas S. Tanana. 1994. Note: "Could California Reduce AIDS by Modeling Nevada Prostitution Law?" *San Diego Justice Journal,* 2: 491–506.

Sullivan, Kathleen, and Martha Field. 1988. "AIDS and the Coercive Power of the State." *Harvard Civil Rights–Civil Liberty Law Review,* 23: 139–197.

Taqi-Eddin, Khaled, and Dan Macallair. 1999. "Shattering 'Broken Windows': An Analysis of San Francisco's Alternative Crime Policies." Justice Policy Institute. <http://www.cjcj.org>.

Taylor, Charles. 1985. *Philosophy and the Human Sciences: Philosophical Papers 2*. Cambridge: Cambridge University Press.

—— 1999. "To Follow a Rule . . ." In *Bourdieu: A Critical Reader*, ed. Richard Shusterman, 29–44. Oxford: Blackwell Publishers.

Tonry, Michael. 1996. *Sentencing Matters*. New York: Oxford University Press.

—— 1999. "Why Are U.S. Incarceration Rates So High?" *Crime and Delinquency*, 45: 419–437.

Trainor, Elizabeth. 1999. "Custodial Parent's Homosexual or Lesbian Relationship with Third Person as Justifying Modification of Child Custody Order," *American Law Reports 5th: Annotations and Cases*, 65: 591–621.

Tushnet, Mark. 1998. "'Everything Old Is New Again': Early Reflections on the 'New Chicago School.'" *Wisconsin Law Review*, 1998: 579–590.

Uniform Crime Reports. Annual. Federal Bureau of Investigation, U.S. Department of Justice, Washington, D.C.

U.S. Department of Commerce. Bureau of the Census. 1990. *1990 Census of Population: General Population Characteristics*. Washington, D.C.: United States Printing Office

U.S. Department of Justice. Bureau of Justice Statistics. 1996. *Sourcebook of Criminal Justice Statistics: 1996*. Washington, D.C.

U.S. Department of Justice. Drug Enforcement Administration. 1999. *Drugs of Concern*. <http://www/usdoj.gov/dea/concern>.

United States Conference of Mayors. 1997. "A Status Report on Youth Curfews in America's Cities: A 347-City Survey." <www.usmayors.org/uscm/news/publications/curfew.html>.

Valverde, Mariana. 1998. "Liquor Licencing and the Governance of Consumption." Paper delivered at the Law and Society Association meeting in Aspen, June 4.

Wacquant, Loïc. 1998. "L'ascension de l'état pénal en Amérique." *Actes de la Recherche en Sciences Sociales*, 124: 7–26.

—— 1999. *Les prisons de la misère*. Paris: Raisons d'Agir.

Wechsler, Herbert. 1955. "American Law Institute: A Thoughtful Code of Substantive Law." *Journal of Criminal Law, Criminology and Police Science*, 45: 524–530.

—— 1968. "Codification of Criminal Law in the United States: The Model Penal Code." *Columbia Law Review*, 68: 1425–56.

Welch, D. Don. 1993. "Legitimate Government Purposes and State Enforcement of Morality." *University of Illinois Law Review*, 1993: 67–103.

Whitman, James Q. 1998. "What Is Wrong with Inflicting Shame Sanctions?" *Yale Law Journal*, 107: 1055–92.

Whittaker, David, Charles Phillips, Peter Haas, and Robert Worden. 1985. "Aggressive Policing and the Deterrence of Crime," *Law and Policy*, 7: 395–416.

Wilson, James Q. 1968. *Varieties of Police Behavior.* Cambridge, Mass.: Harvard University Press.

———— 1975. *Thinking about Crime.* New York: Basic Books.

———— 1993. *The Moral Sense.* New York: Free Press.

Wilson, James Q., and Barbara Boland. 1978. "The Effect of the Police on Crime." *Law and Society Review*, 12: 367–390.

———— 1981. "The Effects of the Police on Crime: A Response to Jacob and Rich." *Law and Society Review*, 16: 163–169.

Wilson, James Q., and Richard J. Herrnstein. 1985. *Crime and Human Nature.* New York: Simon and Schuster.

Wilson, James Q., and George L. Kelling. 1982. "Broken Windows." *Atlantic Monthly*, March: 29–38.

Wolfenden Report. 1957. "Report of the Committee on Homosexual Offences and Prostitution." *Cmd.* 247.

Young, Iris Marion. 1997. *Intersecting Voices: Dilemmas of Gender, Political Philosophy, and Policy.* Princeton, N.J.: Princeton University Press.

Zimring, Franklin E. 1999. "Mystery Terms." *Boston Review*, 24(2): 17–18.

Zimring, Franklin E., and Gordon Hawkins. 1995. *Incapacitation: Penal Confinement and the Restraint of Crime.* New York: Oxford University Press.

———— 1997. *Crime Is Not the Problem: Lethal Violence in America.* New York: Oxford University Press.


### Newspaper and Magazine Articles

Alter, Jonathan, and Pat Wingert. 1996. "The Return of Shame." *Newsweek*, February 6: 21–26.

Annin, Peter. 1998. "Prohibition Revisited." *Newsweek*, December 7: 38.

"AMA Wants Smoking Banned in Planes, Hospitals, Schools." 1986. *Atlanta Journal*, June 19: A34.

Barabak, Mark Z. 1985. "Lax Enforcement of Ban; Risky Bathhouse Sex Goes On." *San Francisco Chronicle*, November 18.

Barnes, Patricia G. 1998. "Safer Streets at What Cost? Critics Say the Homeless and Substance Abusers Are Most Likely to Suffer when Police Crack Down on Petty Offenses," *American Bar Association Journal*, June: 24.

Barstow, David. 2000. "In Fatal Shooting, 2 Sides Clash in Portraying Victim and Officer." *New York Times*, March 19: A1.

"The Bathhouse War: San Francisco's Move to Fight AIDS Creates Rift among Gays." 1984. *Washington Post*, April 19: D1.

Beiser, Vince. 1995. "Why the Big Apple Feels Safer," *Maclean's*, September 11: 39–40.

Belluck, Pam. 2000. "Chicago Makes Another Effort to Disrupt Gangs." *New York Times*, August 31: A22.

Bernstein, Nina. 1999. "Labeling the Homeless, in Compassion and Contempt." *New York Times*, December 5: sec. 1, 53.

Bernstein, Richard. 1998. "A Thinker Attuned to Thinking; James Q. Wilson Has Insights, Like Those on Cutting Crime, That Tend to Prove Out." *New York Times*, August 22: B7.

Birnbaum, Gregg, and Robert Hardt, Jr. 1999. "Hill Rips Rudy for Siccing Cops on Homeless." *New York Post*, December 1: 6.

Blair, Jayson. 1999. "Police Scour Shelters for Man Who Hit Woman with Brick." *New York Times*, November 18: B5.

——— 2000. "As Homicides Rise, New York Faces Return to Fear." *New York Times*, May 29: A12.

"Booze and Ballots." 1998. *Indianapolis Star*, December 4: A22.

Boxall, Bettina. 1997. "A Look Ahead." *Los Angeles Times*, October 27: B1.

Bratton, William J. 1997. "New York's Police Should Not Retreat." *New York Times*, August 19: A27.

Butterfield, Fox. 1996. "Police Chief's Success in Charleston, S.C., Is What's Raising Eyebrows Now." *New York Times*, April 28: 16.

——— 1997. "Drop in Homicide Rate Linked to Crack's Decline." *New York Times*, October 27: A12.

——— 1998a. "Reason for Dramatic Drop in Crime Puzzles the Experts." *New York Times*, March 29: A14.

——— 1998b. "As Crime Falls, Pressure Rises to Alter Data." *New York Times*, August 3: A1.

——— 2000a. "Cities Reduce Crime and Conflict without New York–Style Hardball." *New York Times*, March 4: A1.

——— 2000b. "Rising Urban Homicides Raise Officials' Concerns." *New York Times*, June 18: A12.

——— 2000c. "Crime Rates Fall Again, but Decline May Slow." *New York Times*, October 15: A28.

Calderone, Joe. 1985. "Mayoral Candidates Field Questions." *Newsday*, October 5: 10.

Campbell, Geoffrey A. 1997. "Putting a Crimp in Crime: Experts Differ over Reasons for Falling Rates of Serious Offenses." *American Bar Association Journal*, May: 24.

Chiu, Alexis. 1997. "Crime Rate at 29-Year Low in City." *Boston Globe*, August 28: A1.

"City Plan: Get Homeless off Streets." 1999. *Newsday*, November 20: A21.

Cohen, Patricia. 2000. "Oops, Sorry: Seems That My Pie Chart Is Half-Baked." *New York Times,* April 8: A15, 17.

"Complaints against Police Rise." 1998. *New York Times,* June 11: A25.

Cooper, Michael. 1996. "You're Under Arrest." *New York Times,* December 1: sec. 13, 1.

——— 1999. "Safir May Use Data on Frisks to Back Unit." *New York Times,* April 19: B1.

Crawford, Jan. 1994. "Lane Says He Could Back Voluntary CHA Searches." *Chicago Tribune,* April 20: 1.

"Crime in America, Violent and Irrational and That's Just the Policy." 1996. *The Economist,* June 8: 25–26.

Cullen, Kevin. 1997. "The Comish." *Boston Globe Sunday Magazine,* May 25: 12.

Deardorff, Julie. 2000a. "Shame Returns as Punishment Judges Turn to Public for Humiliation for Some Criminals, but Critics Contend Such Sentences Can Be Psychologically Damaging." *Chicago Tribune,* April 15: 18.

——— 2000b. "For Shame: Courts Using Humiliation as Punishment." *Salt Lake Tribune,* April 23: A11.

DiIulio, John J., Jr. 1996. "'Windows' Puts New Light on Crime-Fighting Efforts, Ideas." *Washington Times,* November 10: B8.

Dionnne Jr., E. J. 1996. "A Broken-Window Approach to Crime." *Washington Post,* December 29: C07.

El Nasser, Haya. 1996. "Judges Say 'Scarlet Letter' Angle Works." *USA Today,* June 25: 1A.

Fingeret, Lisa. 2000. "City Approves New Anti-Loitering Law." *Chicago Tribune,* February 16: 1.

Finkelstein, Katherine E. 2000. "Brick-Attack Trial Ends in Conviction, but Not on Most Serious Count." *New York Times,* November 30: A27.

Flynn, Kevin. 1999. "Drawing the Line on the Strip Search." *New York Times,* July 25: sec. 4, 3.

Friedman, Saul. 1985. "AIDS Panel: Regulate Bathhouses." *Newsday,* October 10: 19.

Gibson, Ray. 1999. "New Anti-Liquor Votes Face Legal Challenge." *Chicago Tribune,* February 25: 2C.

Gootman, Elissa. 2000. "A Police Department's Growing Allure: Crime Fighters from Around World Visit for Tips." *New York Times,* October 24: B1.

Haberman, Clyde. 1998. "Better Quality of Life Found behind Wheel." *New York Times,* January 16: B1.

——— 2000. "Attica: Exorcising the Demons, Redeeming the Deaths." *New York Times,* January 9: D3.

Harrington-Lueker, Donna. 1992. "Metal Detectors: Schools Turn to Devices Once Aimed Only at Airport Terrorists," *American School Board Journal,* May: 26–27.

Haussler, Alexa. 1995. "Guns, Gangs, Drugs Raise Toll of Dead Teens." *Arizona Daily Star,* July 23: 1B.

Henican, Ellis. 1986. "AIDS Scare Hasn't Closed Bathhouses." *Newsday,* November 30: 7.

Herbert, Bob. 1997. "Connect the Dots." *New York Times,* August 24: sec. 4, 13.

Hoffman, Jan. 1997. "Crime and Punishment: Shame Gains Popularity." *New York Times,* January 16: A1.

"House Measure Won't Stop Sex, Officials Say." 1985. *Houston Chronicle,* October 4.

"House Passes Tough Bill to Fight AIDS." 1985. *Chicago Tribune,* October 4.

"Injunction Forbids Sweeps by CHA." 1995. *Chicago Tribune,* August 17: 3.

Janofsky, Michael. 1998. "Some Midsize Cities Defy Trend as Drug Deals and Killings Soar." *New York Times.* January 15: A1.

Johnson, Dirk. 2000. "Chicago Council Tries Anew with Anti-Gang Ordinance." *New York Times,* February 22: A14.

Jones, Robert. 1997. "The Puzzle Waiting for the New Chief." *Los Angeles Times,* August 10: B1.

"Justices OK X-Rated Shops Crackdown." 1999. *New York Times,* January 11.

Kaplan, Fred. 1997. "Looks Count." *Boston Globe,* January 19: E1.

Karmen, Andrew, 1996. "What's Driving New York's Crime Rate Down?" *Law Enforcement News,* November 30. <http://www.lib.jjay.cuny.edu/len/96/30nov/html/feature.html>.

Kilborn, Peter T. 1992. "The Gun Culture: Fun as Well as Life and Death." *New York Times,* March 9: A1.

Kirby, Joseph H. 1994. "Judge Reaffirms Order Limiting CHA's Use of Building Sweeps." *Chicago Tribune,* March 31: 12.

Kocieniewski, David, and Michael Cooper. 1998. "New York Tightens Scrutiny of All Suspects under Arrest." *New York Times,* May 28: A1.

Lacayo, Richard. 1989. "Our Bulging Prisons," *Time,* May 29: 28–31.

Langan, Patrick A. 1991. "America's Soaring Prison Population." *Science,* March 29: 1568–73.

Lardner, James. 1995. "The C.E.O. Cop." *New Yorker,* February 6: 45–57.

Lipsyte, Robert. 1997. "Coping: From Sidewalk Skirmish to Main Event." *New York Times,* November 16: sec. 14, 1.

Massing, Michael. 1998. "The Blue Revolution." *New York Review of Books,* November 19: 32–36.

McCaffrey, Barry R. 1999a. "Legalization Would Be the Wrong Direction." *Los Angeles Times,* July 27: A11.

——— 1999b. "Don't Legalize Those Drugs." *Washington Post,* June 29: A15.

Mitchell, Alison. 1999. "Hyde Cites His War Past, Too." *New York Times*, January 22: A17.

Morris, Phillip. 1999. "For Some, Shame Brings the Only True Pain." *Cleveland Plain Dealer*, December 28: 9B.

Moses, Paul. 1985. "Bathhouse Fights Close." *Newsday*, December 28: 11.

Murphy, Sean P. 1992. "Community Policing Gaining Popularity." *Boston Globe*, December 29: 17.

Nadelmann, Ethan A. 1999a. "Learning to Live with Drugs." *Washington Post*, November 2: A21.

——— 1999b. "Perspective of Legalizing Drugs." *Los Angeles Times*, September 19: M5.

Newcombe, Tod. 1997. "Crime Drops 38 Percent in New York City." *Government Technology*, March.

Newman, Andy. 1999. "Woman on Midtown Street Is Hit by Man with a Brick." *New York Times*, November 17: B5.

Nieves, Evelyn. 2000. "Furious Debate Rages on Sleeping in Public." *New York Times*, May 28: A14.

Nifong, Christina. 1997. "One Man's Theory Is Cutting Crime in Urban Streets." *Christian Science Monitor*, February 18: 1.

"N.Y. AIDS Law Padlocks First Gay Bar." 1985. *San Diego Union-Tribune*, November 8: A16.

"N.Y. Health Chief Resigns in Dispute over AIDS." 1985. *San Francisco Chronicle*, December 5: 31.

"NYPD, Inc." 1995. *The Economist*, July 29: 50.

O'Connor, Matt. 1994. "Judge Blocks CHA Sweeps for Weapons." *Chicago Tribune*, February 15: 1.

Onishi, Norimitsu. 1998. "Giuliani Crows as Theft Suspect Is Caught on Jaywalking Charge." *New York Times*, February 21: B1.

Polner, Robert. 1999. "Advocate for Homeless Disputes City Numbers Say 'No Evidence' Nearly 600 Taken to Shelters." *Newsday*, December 21: A4.

"Public Humiliation Makes a Comeback." 2000. *Morning News Tribune*, March 21: B8.

Purdy, Matthew. 1997. "In New York, the Handcuffs Are One-Size-Fits-All." *New York Times*, August 24: A1.

Rashbaum, William K. 2000. "Review Board Staff Faults Police on Stop-and-Frisk Reports." *New York Times*, April 28: B1.

Rhode, Deborah L. 1995. "Who Is the Criminal?" *National Law Journal*, September 25: A22.

Roane, Kit R. 1998 "Prostitutes on Wane in New York Streets but Take to Internet." *New York Times*, February 23: A1.

Rocawich, Linda. 1987. "Lock 'Em Up: America's All Purpose Cure for Crime." *The Progressive*, 51: 16–19.

Roderick, Kevin. 1985. "L.A. Gay Panel Favors Closure of Bathhouses." *Los Angeles Times,* November 11: A1.

Rohde, David. 1999. "Supreme Court Refuses to Hear Appeal by Sex Shops on Zoning." *New York Times,* January 12: A19.

Rosen, Jeffrey. 1997. "The Social Police: Following the Law, Because You'd Be Too Embarrassed Not To." *New Yorker,* October 20: 170–181.

——— 2000. "Excessive Force." *New Republic,* April 10: 24–27.

Saul, Stephanie. 1985. "NY May Shut Some Bathhouses; Targets Acts That Risk AIDS." *Newsday,* October 25: 4.

Schwartz, Jerry. 1985. "Council Authorizes Closure of Bathhouses." Associated Press, October 25.

"Second Bathhouse Closed over AIDS." 1986. *Newsday,* March 7.

Seifman, David, and Fredric U. Dicker. 1999. "Homeless Plan Spurs War of Words." *New York Post,* October 27: 30.

"Sex Clubs Must Close." 1984. *Washington Post,* October 10.

Siegel, Stephen J. 1998. "A Vote for Quality of Life in Chicago; Linking Alcohol and Blight, Neighborhoods Use '30s Law to Oust Purveyors." *Boston Globe,* November 11: A3.

Smolowe, Jill. 1994. "Lock 'em up . . . and throw away the key." *Time,* February 7: 54–56.

Sontag, Deborah, and Dan Barry. 1997. "Challenge to Authority: Disrespect as Catalyst for Brutality." *New York Times,* November 19: A1.

Specter, Michael. 1985. "One of D.C.'s 2 Gay Bathhouses Closes as in Other Cities, Fear of AIDS and Controversy Hurt Business." *Washington Post,* August 17: B1.

Stein, Sharman. 1985. "St. Mark's Baths Shut as AIDS Threat." *Newsday,* December 7: 10.

"Supreme Court Refuses to Hear Challenge to Anti-Begging Law." 1990. *New York Law Journal,* November 27: 1.

Tierney, John. 1998. "Civil Obedience." *New York Times Magazine,* April 19: 26.

Topousis, Tom. 1999. "Number of Homeless in Shelters Declining." *New York Post,* December 21: 18.

Vollmer, Ted, and Cathleen Decker. 1985. "L.A. County to Draft Guide for Gay Bathhouses." *Los Angeles Times,* November 13: 6, sec. 2.

"Vote Dry Referenda." 1999. *NPR Morning Edition,* January 11.

Walsh, Edward. 1997. "Kansas City Tunes In as New Program Aims at Sex Trade: 'John TV.'" *Washington Post,* July 8: A3.

Walsh, Jim. 1989. "'Crack' Attack from Cocaine to 'Crank.' Drugs Span Valley Price Plunge Whips." *Arizona Republic,* October 15: A1.

Witkin, Gordon. 1998. "The Crime Bust." *U.S. News and World Report,* May 25: 28.

Wray, Herbert. 1998. "Behind Bars. We've Built the Largest Prison System in
the World. Here's a Look Inside." *U.S. News and World Report,* March 23:
30–38.

## Cases

*American Booksellers Association, Inc. v. Hudnut,* 771 F. 2d 323, 329 (7th Cir.
1985).
*Baehr v. Miike,* no. 91–1394, 1996 WL 694235 (Haw. Cir. Ct. Dec. 11, 1996),
*aff'd,* 950 P. 2d 1234 (Haw. 1997), *subsequently rev'd,* no. 20371, 1999 Haw.
LEXIS 391 (Haw. Dec. 9, 1999).
*Bowers v. Hardwick,* 478 U.S. 186 (1986).
*City of Chicago v. Morales,* 527 U.S. 41 (1999).
*City of Chicago v. Morales,* 687 N.E. 2d 53 (Ill. 1997).
*City of Chicago v. Youkhana,* 660 N.E. 2d 34 (Ill. App. 1 Dist. 1995).
*City of New York v. New St. Mark's Baths,* 168 A.D. 2d 311, 562 N.Y.S. 2d 642
(1990).
*Coates v. City of Cincinnati,* 402 U.S. 611 (1971).
*John Doe et al. v. City of Minneapolis,* 693 F. Supp. 774 (D. Minn. 1988), *aff'd,*
898 F. 2d 612 (8th Cir. 1990).
Kahan, Dan M., and Tracey L. Meares. 1999b. *Brief Amicus Curiae of the Chicago Neighborhood Organizations in Support of Petitioner,* Chicago v. Morales,
119 S. Ct. 1849 (no. 97–1121), LEXIS, Supreme Court Cases and Materials Library, U.S. Supreme Court Briefs File.
*Loper v. New York City Police Dep't.,* 802 F. Supp. 1029 (S.D.N.Y. 1992), *aff'd,*
999 F. 2d 699 (2d Cir. 1993).
*Nunez v. City of San Diego,* 114 F. 3d 935 (9th Cir. 1997).
*Papachristou v. City of Jacksonville,* 405 U.S. 156 (1972).
*People v. Letterlough,* 655 N.E. 2d 146 (N.Y. 1995).
*Powell v. State,* 510 S.E. 2d 18 (Ga. 1998).
*Weeks v. State,* 834 S.W. 2d 559 (Tex. Ct. App. 1992).
*Young v. New York City Transit Auth.,* 903 F. 2d 146 (2d Cir. 1990).

## Statutes

Chicago Municipal Code §8–4–015 (added June 17, 1992).
Chicago Municipal Code §8–4–015 (added February 16, 2000).
Chicago Municipal Code §8–4–017 (added February 16, 2000).

# INDEX